# HIP HOP MATTERS

# HIP HOP MATTERS

*Politics, Pop Culture, and the*
*Struggle for the Soul of a Movement*

**S. Craig Watkins**

*Beacon Press, Boston*

*Beacon Press*
25 Beacon Street
Boston, Massachusetts 02108-2892
www.beacon.org

Beacon Press books
are published under the auspices of
the Unitarian Universalist Association of Congregations.

08 07 06 05 8 7 6 5 4 3 2

This book is printed on acid-free paper that meets the uncoated paper
ANSI/NISO specifications for permanence as revised in 1992.

Text design by Patricia Duque Campos
Composition by Wilsted & Taylor Publishing Services

Library of Congress Cataloging-in-Publication Data

Watkins, S. Craig (Samuel Craig)
  Hip hop matters : politics, pop culture, and the struggle for the soul of a
movement / S. Craig Watkins.
      p. cm.
  Includes bibliographical references (p.   ) and index.
  ISBN 0-8070-0982-2 (cloth : alk. paper)
  1.  Rap (Music)—History and criticism.  2. Hip-hop.  I. Title.

ML3531.W38 2005
782.421649—dc22
2004024187

FOR ANGELA HALL WATKINS, MY WIFE AND BEST FRIEND

# CONTENTS

# Hip Hop Matters

*Stakes is high.*
—DE LA SOUL

Throughout its career hip hop has produced its share of unusual moments, walking the fine line between the theater of the absurd and the genuinely profound. One such moment occurred on the night of October 29, 2003, when Minister Louis Farrakhan sat down to conduct an interview with well-known rapper Ja Rule. Like most celebrity interviews this one was staged by the rapper's record label, Murder Inc., to promote a forthcoming project, his album *Blood in My Eye*. But there was also a more sobering reality that prompted Ja's sit-down with the Minister. Significantly, the event was arranged because there was genuine fear that the already violent feud between Ja Rule and his chief nemesis, superstar rapper 50 Cent, was spiraling toward another hip-hop tragedy. The elements of their unfolding drama, two talented MCs trapped in a potentially deadly game of ghetto one-upmanship, was painfully familiar to hip hop.

Ja Rule had made a name and niche for himself by combining a rugged hip-hop exterior with less edgy R&B-styled crossover hit singles that appealed to an all but forgotten market in hip hop's soaring economy—girls and young women. The "sensitive thug" moniker he earned was an oxymoron in the coarse world of corporate rap music. But while the kinder and gentler thug-life persona Ja Rule concocted had increased his record sales, it also opened him up to charges that he was not "street" enough. That is exactly what happened when 50 Cent burst on the scene in 2003, unleashing a torrent of taunts that questioned Ja Rule's masculinity and place in hip hop. Though his record label, Interscope Records, packaged him as a new style pop figure 50's image harkened back to a darker and more cynical era in hip hop, a period when ruthless gangstas defined the movement's pop persona and made its move on the nation's pop music charts. Many blamed the celebration of all things gangsta for the senseless murders of two of hip hop's most talented figures, 2Pac (Tupac Shakur) and the Notorious B.I.G. (Christopher Wallace). The marketing of 50 Cent came straight from the script that guided 2Pac's meteoric rise and tragic fall.

While his music was a stirring mix of party anthems, hypercapitalism, gangsta swagger, and pop posturing, it was really the selling of 50's background that upped the ante. His life as a petty drug dealer, the death of his crack-addicted mother, and his miraculous survival of nine bullets formed a classic ghetto tale that put him on the pop map. That biography earned him the most important credential in corporate hip hop, street credibility. Hip hop's claim to fame is the claim of authenticity in its undaunted portrayals of ghetto reality. Cloaked in the armor of authenticity 50 boasted that his rhymes about ghetto life, struggle, and survival were real and not commercially premeditated.

Equally important, the bid for street credibility is also part of the marketing and selling of hip hop, how the movement's entrepreneurial elite manage to generate that all-important buzz and hip presence in a cluttered and competitive pop culture economy. It was, in essence, hip hop's own Faustian bargain. In exchange for global celebrity, pop prestige, and cultural influence hip hop's top performers had to immerse themselves into a world of urban villainy that by the new millennium had lost sight of the line between pop life and real life.

It was, without question, one of the cruelest ironies in the rise and transformation of hip hop: the fact that its livelihood—indeed its very survival as a pop culture juggernaut—rested almost entirely on its ability to sell black death. The embrace of guns, gangsterism, and ghetto authenticity brought an aura of celebrity and glamour to the grim yet fabulously hyped portraits of ghetto life. From the gangsta-inflected anthems of the nineties to the thugged-out caricatures of the new millennium, hip hop or, more precisely, corporate hip hop, played its role with chilling precision. But there was nothing glamorous about the problems that characterized America's decades-old urban crisis. Both Ja and 50 had experienced the harsh realities of ghetto poverty. Like so many in rap music's star-studded world, every decision they made—from movie appearances to product endorsements—was a calculated maneuver designed to insure they never returned to the ghettoscapes valorized in their lyrics, music videos, and carefully orchestrated image.

The meeting between Ja and the Minister was charged with meaning and added yet another intriguing dimension to hip hop's unbelievable career. The fact that it was broadcast by MTV, BET, and on Clear Channel–owned urban radio stations across the nation highlighted hip hop's aura and relevance in the pop media spotlight. For most of its public life hip hop has poignantly reflected the steadily shifting currents in American social, political, and pop cultural life. So much of what hip hop adored and abhorred about itself surfaced during the interview. Over the years the financial stakes in hip hop had grown to once unimaginable heights. But the stakes that brought Ja and the Minister together were considerably higher than the number of radio spins or units sold an artist could count. In the end, the meeting was not only about the life and potential death of two artists, it was, quite simply about the rise and demise of hip hop.

Ja confessed to Farrakhan that he responded to 50's lyrical attacks because hip hop's swelling legion of fans and code of the streets ethos insisted that he do so or run the risk of appearing soft, the ultimate slur in the hard-edged world fashioned by the chieftains of corporate rap. But there was something in Ja's bright eyes, unusually tamed grin, and equally apologetic and apocalyptic demeanor that hinted even he knew a line had been crossed in the vitriolic rhymes that pulsated throughout his latest album. By reaching out to Farrakhan, Ja and his label, Murder Inc., were acknowledging what many of hip hop's most devoted followers had maintained for years: Something had been lost in hip hop's journey from the feisty subcultures of ghetto America to the lavish corridors of media conglomeration.

During the broadcast Ja Rule told Farrakhan, "They [the hip hop audience] want you to stay 'hood.' " But the pressure to stay hood had severe costs; namely, the devotion to the thug life that ran counter to hip hop's claim that it represents the voices and experiences of a generation of marginal youths. It was yet another indication of how market forces rather than commitment to some essential truth drove corporate hip hop. Talking to both Ja and the wider hip-hop world, Farrakhan, playing the role of ghetto oracle with his usual flair and intensity, got real, "See, if you let the public dictate and you continue to follow that, the end result will be death, destruction." That Farrakhan was called in to try to mediate the potentially calamitous clash between Ja and 50 revealed the telling links between America's racial and political past and a pop culture phenomenon that, at its core, has always embodied the nation's historic racial struggle.

Drawing a connection between his own past with the Nation of Islam, the 1960s struggle for civil rights, and the state of hip hop, Farrakhan explained, "When Malcolm [X] went down, Elijah Mohammed was the one that they really wanted so they killed two birds with one stone and darn near destroyed the nation." Farrakhan knew firsthand how violent speech, racial infighting, jealousy, and bitterness could lead to true tragedy and real bloodshed. Now, here he was, blemishes and all, perhaps the only figure from black America's old guard who held any real "juice," that is to say, influence in the new world hip hop was creating. He praised Ja and his contemporaries: "God has given you a gift, the opportunity to touch so many young people when others can't." But he also reprimanded them for wasting that gift and offered what amounted to a spiritual caution and cultural challenge, "May God bless hip-hop to rise to its full potential, to take the youth of the world and instead of making them instruments of death, make them instruments of peace."

• • •

The story of hip hop, like the story of millennial America, is infinitely more intriguing than typical accounts acknowledge. Most assessments of the hip hop "generation" or "nation" present a culture that is monolithic in its worldview or definable simply by age. But if the thirty-plus-year career of the movement suggests anything it is that hip hop belies the established definitions and caricatures that tend to celebrate or condemn the culture. Simply put, hip hop is unlike anything the world has ever seen. It is a vital source of creativity and industry for youth. Hip hop is consumed with pop celebrity and street credibility—and capable, many believe, of transforming young lives. As I prepared to write this book I set out to address a straightforward question: Why does hip hop matter? To address the question I sought to understand what hip hop means to those who identify so passionately with the movement. While I certainly had my own ideas about the significance of hip hop, I also wanted to survey the communities, characters, and currents that make up the movement.

Over the course of its career hip hop has developed a notorious and even self-perpetuating reputation as a spectacular cultural movement committed to defying the cultural and political mainstream. But as the borders of the hip-hop nation continue to expand, its biggest and most important battle is shaping up to be the one it is having with itself. Behind the explosive record sales, trendsetting cachet, and burgeoning economy is an intense struggle for the soul of the hip-hop movement. There has never been a consensus within hip hop about its purpose, identity, or destiny. In fact, the most robust debates about hip hop have always taken place within the movement. Hip hop has and continues to be its most potent critic and courageous champion.

Assessing the social and political state of hip hop is, admittedly, a treacherous enterprise. But as comedian and cultural critic Chris Rock notes about hip hop's more troubling trends, "It's getting hard to defend some of this shit." While writing this book, I took stock of what is really at stake in the struggle for hip hop. At its core the tensions percolating within the movement are a startling recognition that for all of its pop culture allure and economic success hip hop has failed to realize what many believe is its greatest calling: the chance to have a meaningful and enduring effect in the lives of ordinary youths.

The impending struggle for hip hop comes at a time when the movement has never been more commercially successful. And yet, it also comes at a time when the movement has never been more internally divided. Both hip hop's young and old sense that the movement has reached that all-important crossroad—a moment that beckons for greater calm, introspection, and vision. Hip hop never asked to change the world. But in its own noisy and stylish way it has done just that. Imagine pop music today without the inventions inspired by hip hop. Imagine the demeanor of youth without the irreverent spirit of hip hop.

In addition to being a pop culture force, hip hop's widening sphere of influence has shouldered it with the burden of being a genuine political force. Gone are the discussions about *whether* hip hop matters; they have been replaced instead by the key issues of who and what kinds of values will define *how* hip hop matters. The struggle for hip hop is real, and it is being played out across a remarkably rich and varied terrain—in pop culture, old and new media, colleges and universities, in prisons, through the conduit of community activism, in suburbia, among youth, and throughout the political minefields of race and gender.

In its own bizarre and lamentable way, the beef between Ja and 50, the call to Farrakhan to calm the unsteady waters in hip hop, and the commercial impulses that drive the movement to unprecedented heights while also plunging it toward potentially deadly depths demonstrate how many of the issues percolating throughout the world of hip hop—race, politics, history, violence, generational cleavages and the growing power of corporations in everyday life and in the lives of young people—are, in the end, bigger than hip hop. It is the spectacular convergence of these and other issues in the movement that makes hip hop so urgent. For all of the problems and passions it arouses, hip hop connects with its young constituency like nothing else can or will. When virtually nothing else could, hip hop created a voice and a vehicle for the young and the dispossessed, giving them both hope and inspiration. But even as hip hop has been buoyed by a heroic sense of hope it has also been bewildered by its own disturbing and hell-raising antics. These are the contradictions that are woven into the very essence of hip hop and make the struggle for the movement one of the more compelling stories of our time.

# Back in the Day

*Let's keep it underground. Nobody outside*
*the Bronx would like this stuff anyway.*
—GRANDMASTER FLASH

The story of the origins of the hip-hop movement is, by now, a relatively well-traveled one. Most historians and cultural critics trace it back to the early and middle 1970s, back to a time and place affectionately known as the "Boogie Down Bronx." As terms like *innercity* and *underclass* were reinventing America's racial vocabulary, a thriving cultural underworld began to bustle with energy and innovation. It was at once the worst and the best of times for those who pioneered and peopled the hip-hop movement. When the historic aftershocks of urban renewal, resegregation, and capital flight settled, a new social and economic order had emerged in America. In the wake of the massive shifts the gulf between America's cities, populated increasingly by black and brown bodies, and the suburbs, whiter and more affluent, grew wider and more severe. But in the midst of the volatile surge of social and economic change an exuberant youth culture started to take shape. What began in basements, on street corners, in public parks, and throughout the still of the night would furnish young people fertile spaces for crafting new identities, explosive art forms, and later, whole industries.

Not surprisingly as the hip-hop movement evolves into a vibrant cultural industry, nostalgia for the presumably more innocent days grows. This particular narrative imagines a time when hip hop was unsullied, unburdened, and unchained by the commercial forces and

political divisions that generate so much anxiety within the movement today. From this perspective hip hop was real, organic, and
deeply connected to its grass roots. It was, in short, a simpler time in
the movement's history. As understandable as it is, this view belies
the realities that have always made hip hop so irrepressible and impossible to define or contain. Hence, even as the longing for hip hop's
allegedly more innocent days gains momentum, among many in the
hip-hop nation, some of the big issues that generate great division
within the movement—namely the pull between hip hop's commercial vitality and its strivings to be a meaningful source of youth empowerment and social change—were more than apparent back in the
day. No year reflects that more than 1979, the year that hip hop
emerged from the underground world that nourished its soul and
sparked its creative fire.

•••

In a strange way, 1979 represents both the beginning and the end of
the hip-hop movement. The events that unfolded that year ushered
in a new era in hip hop while essentially closing the door on a previous one. Hip hop, once invisible, became visible to the wider public.
Hip hop, once largely recreational, became increasingly commercial.
Throughout the year hip hop, unbeknownst to most, was embarking
on a journey that would make it a cultural and economic juggernaut.

According to hip-hop legend it was the summer of 1979 when
Sylvia Robinson's son, Joey Jr., persuaded her to accompany him on a
talent hunt in, of all places, a New Jersey pizzeria. Under the direction of his mother, Joey had been actively mining his street networks,
determined to find someone who could rap on a recording Sylvia was
eager to produce. Before securing a rapper to record in the beige
stucco and brick building that housed their recording studio, Sylvia
had already laid the musical track for the song. The making of rap
music's first commercial hit is as improbable as the genre's rise to
global prominence twenty years later. It is even more improbable

that in an industry dominated by young men the genre's commercial breakthrough can be attributed, in large measure, to a forty-three-year-old woman.

Their first attempt to secure a rapper failed after he was scared off by a pending litigation battle between the Robinsons' All-Platinum Records and industry heavyweight Polygram Records. On this summer day they made their way to the pizzeria located on 96 West Street in suburban New Jersey to lure Henry "Big Bank Hank" Jackson, a local rapper Joey had heard about, into the studio. Remembering that day as if it were yesterday, Hank says, "I'm making pizza, and Joey and his mother walk in . . . I don't know these people at all, right? It's like somebody walking up to you and saying, 'I want you to make a record for me.'" He thought it was a joke, but Sylvia and Joey soon convinced him that they were serious. Sylvia recalled that Hank "was the manager of the store, but he left the parlor with his apron on. There was flour all over the floor."

They settled in the back of Joey's Oldsmobile, parked outside the pizzeria, where Hank auditioned on the spot. As the Jersey pizzeria employee did his best to impress, a small crowd began to gather around the car. Soon, a friend of Joey's walked by and noted that while Hank's style was entertaining, the Robinsons should listen to his friend Guy O'Brien, who went by the stage name Master Gee. Incredibly, Guy climbed in the car and he and Hank started battling, feeding off of each other's energy and skills. "I did my thing, not thinking of the immensity of what could happen. I mean who could have even dreamed of something like that?" Hank wondered out loud years later. As if the story is not bizarre enough, Michael Wright (also known as Wonder Mike) was playing a guitar across the street when he noticed the commotion around the Oldsmobile. Michael walked over and then made his pitch to the Robinsons: "I can rap, too."

Excited about the chemistry between the three men, they all moved on to Sylvia's house that same evening. After listening to them rhyme and perform more, Sylvia proposed a name for a new record company, Sugar Hill Records. She then told Hank, Guy, and Michael that they would be the label's first act and that the name of the group would be the Sugarhill Gang. That was a Friday. The following Monday they came together in the studio and cut rap's first commercial hit in one day. The record cost Sylvia $750.

•••

Born Sylvia Vanderpool, on March 6, 1936, in New York, Sylvia Robinson was a veteran in the world of R&B music when she stumbled across the still nascent rap music scene. Prior to discovering the Sugarhill Gang she had enjoyed a modestly successful career as an R&B singer, songwriter, producer, and co-owner of several independent record labels. Singing professionally by the age of fourteen she scored her first hit in 1957 as part of the duet Mickey & Sylvia. The corny pop tune "Love Is Strange" reached number one on the R&B charts and peaked at number eleven on the pop charts. Sixteen years later Sylvia recorded another hit, the sensuous R&B single "Pillow Talk," which peaked at number one on the R&B Hot Singles chart and reached as high as number three on the pop charts. After that Robinson spent most of her time writing and producing hits for others and enjoyed some success with songs like "Love on a Two Way Street" and "Sending Out an S.O.S." In a career that spanned four decades, history will likely remember her most for the role she played in the production of "Rapper's Delight," the novelty song that introduced rap to the world.

Though her day in the spotlight as a performer had long passed by the summer of 1979 she and her husband, Joe Robinson, stayed active in the music business. Sugar Hill Records, which was named after the famed Harlem neighborhood, was not the Robinsons first attempt at running an independent recording company. Over the course of the previous eight years they launched a series of labels including Stang, All-Platinum, and Turbo. The Robinsons' label, like many small and independently owned black music labels, found itself struggling in a period of sweeping changes that saw many of the major record labels muscling in on the world of R&B music. The Sugar Hill start-up was a chance for a new beginning and an opportunity to establish an early stake in a musical subculture the majors knew nothing about. According to Love Bug Starski, a popular New York DJ in the 1970s, Sylvia discovered the burgeoning rap music scene while he was spinning records for a birthday bash in her honor. Love Bug's agility in rhyming over records fascinated Sylvia and convinced her that what he was doing was exciting and different enough to record.

Rap music, or what was then recognized as MCing (MC is short for master of ceremonies), had been around a few years prior to the 1979 recording. But in those early days it was essentially a live performance-art form that complemented hip hop's main attraction, the DJ. Ironically, some DJs began to rhyme or add MCs as a way to keep rivals from stealing their two most prized possessions: their records and their technique. In just a few short years, though, the roles reversed, with MCs becoming the main attraction and DJs serving in many instances as background accompaniment. Back then it was all about battling to earn your rep as one of the fiercest DJs or MCs on the block. In the ramshackle black and brown boroughs of a recession-weary New York City, one's rep was no small matter. In many cases it may have been all a poor youth had. Many of hip hop's pioneers—DJ Kool Herc, Kurtis Blow, and Melle Mel among others—earned their battle scars and now legendary status in this environment.

At some point DJs, MCs and even the spectators that attended the shows began recording the performances. The act of recording the live shows served several purposes, both intended and unintended. The DJs realized early on that mix tapes could be an effective source of self-promotion. For many DJs mix tapes became a way to build a loyal legion of underground fans that could enhance the credibility of a DJ or MC in the culture and attract even bigger audiences for future performances. Mix tapes continue to be an important vehicle for aspiring rappers to earn a rep, circulate their music, and build recognition in hip hop's underground milieus. It was through the mix tapes circuit that a young, unknown MC named Curtis Jackson was able to build his reputation and a loyal following as he shopped around for a record deal. When he burst in on the scene in 2003 as 50 Cent, he owed at least part of his meteoric success to the fan base and street cred made possible by mix tapes. In other instances, however, mix tapes were a source of income. While many of the early tapes often lacked the refined qualities of more formal recordings they, nevertheless, marked the beginnings of an alternative economy that has endured in hip hop.

Mix tapes also produced some unintended consequences. Fab Five Freddy, who was both a B-Boy, a break dancer and an aspiring visual artist in hip hop's early days, remembers that some of hip hop's most legendary DJs recorded some of their performances. "Those tapes would then become circulated," Fab Five explains. "They were spreading all through the city." Queens native Darryl McDaniels of Run-D.M.C. asserts, "It was all about tapes back then. In my neighborhood, tapes used to filter in from all the shows that were happening in the Bronx and all the Harlem World tapes." According to McDaniels, "People would go tape these shows, come back to Queens and sell them." He remembers paying fifteen dollars for his first mix tape.

While the circulation of recorded hip-hop music generated wider exposure, it also made it much more difficult to police the culture's boundaries. The music's ability to travel would not only expose it to more people; it also made it easier to learn, imitate, and even modify the genuinely creative flourishes that flowed throughout the movement. Later, the wider circulation of hip hop in the form of albums, radio, music video, and even fashion transformed the culture by subjecting it to a variety of regional, economic, and political interests that have simultaneously broadened and baffled the culture's identity, its sense of community and purpose.

It was inevitable that a more formal effort to record and package the new style of music emerging from hip hop's cultural trenches would occur. Though "Rapper's Delight" was not the first studio-recorded rap song, there is no doubt that it was the first to gain attention beyond what was still a relatively small hip-hop community. The first studio recording was "King Tim III" by the Fatback Band. Distributed by Spring Records, it came and went with little notice.

"Rapper's Delight" was a hit for two immediate reasons. First, there was the timely use of Chic's classic disco recording, "Good Times," which was one of the year's most popular recordings. But rather than use an electronic sample of the song Sugar Hill Records' house band played their own version with Sylvia providing the bass line herself. Second, the art of talking rhythmically or rapping exclusively over a danceable track offered something quite rare in the world of pop culture, an original idea. But what separated Sugar Hill Records most from the other would-be rap labels like West End Records and Enjoy Records was the experience of the Robinsons in the music business. They knew that in order to survive they would need to get a favorable distribution arrangement and labor endlessly to use their contacts from years in "the life" to promote their records.

Once a dub of "Rapper's Delight" was complete and cut it was Sylvia's job to make sure that radio stations around the country received a copy. Armed with more than twenty years of experience in the music business Sylvia was not intimidated by the hard work it would take to make the record a success. In fact, she relished the challenge.

•••

On the verge of making music history the Robinsons had what at the time was a radical, some thought even crazy, idea—cut a 12-inch single of the recording rather than the standard 7-inch single. The longer format allowed the label to take full advantage of the song by letting each MC fully develop his character's narrative and personality. Though mostly lighthearted and fun, the lyrics display much of the male swagger and self-boasting that continue to be steadfast qualities in hip hop. Today, the ability to cite the fifteen-minute extended version of "Rapper's Delight" has become a kind of rite of passage in hip-hop culture. But the fear, of course, from the perspective of the music industry was that 12-inch singles were too long for radio airplay thus there was no incentive to produce them. Recalling the choice to release a 12-inch cut of the recording, Robinson says, "At first it was challenging for us to market 12-inch singles because they were whole-selling [*sic*] for $2.25 vs. the traditional 7-inch singles that were whole-selling for only sixty cents."

The length of the single, however, was just the beginning of the Robinsons' problems. An equally formidable challenge was getting the song on radio. It was still a few years before music video would become a prominent promotional tool thus radio, despite its localness, was still the primary way to gain widespread exposure. The Robinsons had been in the music business long enough to know that their effort to turn hip hop's party anthems and street rhymes into successful records would either be rewarded or thwarted based on their access to the nation's radio airwaves. So Robinson went to work. She did a lot of handholding and maneuvered deftly to persuade DJs around the country to play the record. WESL-AM St. Louis and WBLS-FM New York were the first two radio stations to receive "Rapper's Delight."

What happened that fall in St. Louis typified the march of "Rapper's Delight" into pop music history. After sending the record to Jim Gates, the programmer of WESL St. Louis, Sylvia followed up with a series of phone calls. After she persuaded him to give the record a try, listener response took care of the rest. Recalling that magical moment, Robinson says, "That night, a local distributor phoned in with an order for thirty thousand records. It was so bizarre that the next day I called retailers in the market, who confirmed that the record was that much in demand." Station managers at WESL reported, "Everybody wanted to know immediately after it was aired where the record could be bought." Like many other stations around the country, WESL could not play the song enough to satisfy demand and soon had to play the fifteen-minute record twice every hour just to keep the phone lines from jamming.

But not everyone responded enthusiastically to the record. When WBLS's Frankie Crocker first received a copy he was not impressed. A source from the station was quoted as saying, "He [Crocker] wouldn't play the record because it's too black for his station." Two days after allegedly making that comment Crocker relented and WBLS jumped on the "Rapper's Delight" bandwagon. To the surprise of nearly everyone involved the song was an instant hit.

Though the term was not a common part of the pop culture vocabulary in those days, the song created what industry observers would now call a "buzz." That is, a groundswell of energy and excitement that generated the most effective kind of advertising available, word of mouth. WKTU-FM New York's musical director, Michael Ellis, claimed the record was "the biggest selling 12-inch single in New York. We receive between 100 to 150 calls each day, which is ten times as many calls as we have received on any other record." Calling the record a "word-of-mouth hit" one Los Angeles record store owner told *Billboard*, "This record is something. I received five-hundred at 4 pm on Friday and sold out by Sunday evening. I can't remember when anything like this ever happened."

In retrospect, the arrival of rap music could not have been timelier. Though no one knew it then, the beginning of rap was also the beginning of the end for the radio and music industries, as they existed in 1979. It was a period when an unknown, untested, and unproven style of music could still get access to commercial radio airwaves, the lifeline of the pop music industry. Some twenty years after rap's breakthrough commercial radio was a different kind of business—an entertainment medium reshaped by a variety of factors—consolidation, corporate-controlled play lists, new monitoring technologies, and MTV to name a few. Given the realities of the commercial music industry by the close of the twentieth century a genre as novel as rap was in 1979 would never gain the spins necessary in today's radio industry to establish a viable presence in the world of pop music.

Within three months of those first spins the song became a huge hit and eventually moved more than two million units. The feat would have been remarkable in any case, but it was especially so for a genre widely viewed in 1979 as an urban fad. Even in their wildest dreams the Robinsons never imagined the type of success the record and, subsequently, the label would enjoy. During its extraordinary run "Rapper's Delight" charted number four on the R&B Singles Charts and even peaked at number thirty-six on the pop charts. The song actually reached the top of the charts in Canada and fared extremely well in countries as far as Europe, Israel, and South Africa. Though "Rapper's Delight" was wildly successful there was no real reason to believe that what was still derisively labeled "street music" had any staying power. Still, Sugar Hill Records established rap music as a bankable genre. It was a contribution that would create enormous possibilities and perils for the hip-hop movement.

• • •

Despite their success the Sugarhill Gang was never embraced by those who considered themselves the true guardians of hip hop. The Jersey-based trio was dismissed by many in the up-and-coming world of hip hop as a watered-down knock-off that had neither the style nor the tenacity of the real thing that was emerging across the Hudson River. Many among the hip-hop faithful regarded the Sugarhill Gang as outsiders who were exploiting the culture. There were even charges that Big Hank lifted portions of his rhymes from the Mighty Force Emcees, a Bronx-based crew.

The tension that swirled around The Sugarhill Gang's newfound status presaged some of the enduring tensions in the movement regarding who and what is hip hop. Years later, when Raymond "Benzino" Scott accused Eminem and by extension white and corporate

America of stealing hip hop, it was neither a new nor an unprecedented charge. Protecting the integrity and borders of hip hop has been a constant source of conflict, producing palpable anxiety within a movement that has consistently defied all efforts to restrict or control its influence. The Sugarhill Gang's success, like the success of the movement years later, produced a gripping paradox: At the same time that commercial success established hip hop as a legitimate cultural force it also made it much more difficult to control who participated in the movement.

Even the emergence of the Robinsons as hip hop's first recording moguls reflects some of the contentious claims about ownership and influence that have a long presence in the movement. The Robinsons had no organic connection or entitlement to hip hop. They, like virtually every one else who came after them, saw hip hop as an opportunity to make money. Their reign as hip hop's premier recording label came to a sudden end, in part, because they never understood the need to develop a connection to the culture's grass roots.

As hip hop and the stakes involved in the recording of rap music intensified so did the battle to control the music and the movement. Between 1979 and 1983 Sugar Hill Records outmaneuvered their short list of rival labels in the budding rap music industry. But by 1983 a combination of factors—the rise of hungrier labels with closer ties to hip hop's pulse, squabbles with artists over royalties, lawsuits, and slowly building competition from the majors—turned rap music into a full-fledged, intensely competitive industry that eventually upended Sugar Hill's status as the top label in rap music.

Within a few short years Sugar Hill Records went from being the only label that mattered to a label that no longer mattered as a new generation of record labels and would-be moguls used their street-savvy ways and connections to chart a new era in the production of rap music. That new era would dramatically alter the character and trajectory of the movement raising, eventually, not only the financial stakes but the political stakes, too.

• • •

One of the earliest and most fervent charges made against Sugar Hill Records was that "Rapper's Delight" diluted the raw rhymes and street cadences that captured so much of hip hop's vitality. Over the years Sylvia has been both reviled and revered for her role in establishing rap music's commercial identity. But even as Sylvia established "pop" rap as a commercially viable genre, she was also instrumental in making the recording that established rap music's legacy as a politically viable form of music. Most hip-hop aficionados identify Grandmaster Flash and the Furious Five's "The Message" as rap's initial foray into social and political commentary. The song crafted a revealing window into the conditions of urban blight that were ravaging many of America's biggest cities in the early 1980s. Though the song is attributed to Grandmaster Flash and the Furious Five, the group had little or nothing to do with its creation. Thus, while many recognize Melle Mel's heartfelt performance and biting critique of American apartheid-like conditions, few recognize that Sylvia, the forty-something music producer, was the pivotal mastermind behind the groundbreaking recording.

Members from Sugar Hill Records' house band were taking a break in between recording sessions one day when Duke Bootee, a well-known jazz and pop-funk percussionist, began tapping out an intriguing rhythm on an empty water bottle. "That sounds funny," Sylvia said. Always on the lookout for something new, she asked Duke to come up with a hook and then suggested recording the tune on a catchier, more commercial track. Later that evening they recorded the track, but it sat on the shelf for over a year. Eventually, Duke penned some lyrics that vividly portrayed the grim realities of everyday life in Ghetto USA. Describing his lyrical explorations on the song, Duke says, "I had come up with 'It's like a jungle sometimes it makes me wonder how I keep from going under' cause it gave it that feverish, jungle feel. So I took that verse and that hook that she liked and put it over a new track, which was more commercial." Sylvia then approached Grandmaster Flash and the Furious Five, her label's hottest act, with the idea of recording the song. But they showed no interest in recording what they perceived as a "preachy" rap song. According to Duke, the group was unwilling to think beyond their own style of rap. Bootee remembers them declaring, "This record ain't gonna sell, don't nobody want to bring their problems to the disco. We're a party group, we about being nasty and having parties." Through sheer persistence Sylvia was finally able to persuade Melle Mel to give the song a try. A few days later Melle excitedly approached Bootee, "[M]an, I got a verse that seems like it just go right with that record." All ears, Bootee replied, "Well, what is it?" Melle unleashed parts of his now classic flow about a child's state of mind and the American apartheid-like conditions that characterized vast parts of black ghetto life.

They ran the rhyme by Sylvia, who approved immediately, and off to the studio they went. "The Message" was released in 1982 and went on to reach as high as number four on the R&B charts and sixty-two on the pop chart. Whereas Sylvia had proven that a pop song like "Rapper's Delight" could sell, "The Message" indicated that a place for socially conscious rap music also existed in the marketplace. Between 1987 and 1994 what some labeled "message" or "political" rap emerged and broadened the definition of popular music. Though the popularity of message rap ebbs and flows, it established an expectation for some in the movement that rap should be used as a forum for socially conscious discourse.

Although the making of "The Message" may have been unplanned, there was always something seemingly inevitable about hip hop's political promise. The most enduring images of Old School hip hop suggest a vibrant and pleasure-seeking atmosphere that included, among other things, the now legendary block parties and graffiti-scrawled trains that circled the boroughs of New York. And while the hip-hop nation's first wave of pioneering artists, producers, and consumers were most interested in turning a blighted urban landscape into their very own play-station there was something incredibly insurgent about their elaborate pursuit of pleasure.

Afrika Bambaataa, recognized by many as one of the central figures in the rise of hip hop, has consistently maintained over the years that the culture's political potency can be traced back to the early days of the movement. As a pioneering DJ, Bambaataa experimented with a wide palette of musical styles and genres including German techno, calypso, as well as disco, rock, and soul. Likewise, he experimented with the notion that in addition to being a source of amusement hip hop could also be a force for social change. As much as anyone, he understood why hip hop mattered in the lives of ordinary youths. Hip hop's real power and true significance, Bambaataa professes, resides in its capacity to empower young people to want to change their lives. Before many others did he believed there was something notably serious about the pleasure-seeking ambitions that characterized hip hop back in the day. Perhaps it was his own experience that colored his unique vision of what hip hop could be.

Born Kevin Donovan, Bambaataa came of age at a time when New York's roughest and poorest boroughs spawned a number of street gangs in the early seventies that battled over everything from territory to reputation. The most notorious gangs included the Savage Skulls, a predominantly Puerto Rican clique, and the Black Spades, a rival group made up of mostly African Americans. When they were not at war with each other, many of the gangs spent their time intimidating their neighborhoods. It was not uncommon for gang members to steal from local stores, harass young women, or start trouble at local events. It was as if all of the pain and pessimism that came with being young, poor and black or Latino was channeled inside and often against the very people who shared a similar deprivation.

Bambaataa was no stranger to the gang wars that wreaked havoc throughout the streets of New York. He was an active member of the Black Spades. But like a number of his peers he was drawn to the magnetic powers of hip hop. At some point he started to believe that the energy, loyalty, and passion that defined gang life could be guided toward more socially productive activities. As Bambaataa began to develop a reputation and a following as a DJ, he saw an opportunity to combine his love of music and B-boying with his desire to enhance community life. Though his parties were designed, first and foremost, to rock the crowd he acknowledged that "you [also] had people who were coming together to kick the drug dealers out of the area— we used violence against a lot of the drug pushers and all that." Former members of the Black Spades usually served as a homemade security force. Bambaataa maintains that with the parties and the effort to drive away violent offenders "we went from a negative thing to a positive thing."

As a youngster Bambaataa came up with the idea of starting a group called the Zulu Nation. The name was inspired by a movie he saw as a kid in the early sixties called *Zulu*. "Just to see these black people fighting for what was theirs against the British, that always stuck in my mind," Bambaataa explained. The young Bronx native was also inspired by the ferment of social and political struggle that partially characterized the sixties and seventies. So, when he was old enough, Bambaataa took his vision of unity, anti-violence, and self-help to the streets in an effort to recruit what he called "warriors for the community."

Among its other activities the Zulu Nation held weekly meetings. For some the meetings offered a home, for others a source of discipline. Most important, the meetings provided an open forum to develop ways of eradicating the rising presence of drugs and violence that unleashed terror in some of New York's most disadvantaged housing projects. Behind the outer galaxy outfits, flamboyant hair styles, and the sometimes quirky philosophical views Bambaataa was a man ahead of his time. He was one of hip hop's first street philosophers.

His work with the Zulu Nation was one of the earliest attempts to mobilize hip hop's energy toward effecting change in the lives of those who lived and breathed the culture. Still, his vision for the Zulu Nation exceeded what the group was actually capable of accomplishing back then. The difficulties he faced in realizing hip hop's political potential, in retrospect, are not surprising. While most observers doubted hip hop had an enduring commercial life, virtually no one was prepared to even consider what, if any, political life it had. Because of his previous affiliation with the Black Spades, many dismissed the Zulu Nation as a rogue outfit rather than the community-based initiative Bambaataa wanted to build.

In 1995 New York City officials held a ceremony in the Bronx River projects to celebrate Operation Commitment, the city's official crackdown on crime and graffiti in area housing projects. Mayor Rudolph Giuliani was on hand to help plant a ceremonial tree. During the celebration Bambaataa and his group were conspicuously absent. Those same officials had removed the Zulu Nation from their Bronx River project's headquarters. It was a place, ironically, where many believed the group had made its biggest impact.

Some of the older residents in the housing project expressed concern that the members of the organization were aggressive and even occasionally violent. Though no one, city officials or Bronx River residents, could recall the involvement of any Zulu Nation members in any recent criminal activity, the city still maintained that the group constituted a threat. Ruben Franco, chairman of the city's housing authority, declared, "It was my decision they had to go. There was a general climate of disorder and hopelessness, and they were part of it." A memo produced by the housing authority claimed that, "In the five months since the graffiti and the Zulu Nation are gone, crime is down fifty-two percent and there seems to be a more upbeat feel to the development."

But residents below the age of forty held a very different view of the Zulu Nation. They regarded the Zulus as an important cultural institution and Bambaataa a signature figure in hip-hop history. Part of their outrage was based on the fact that they knew the Zulu Nation was one of the few grassroots organizations that tried to seriously mobilize disaffected young people. Despite the dispute about the legacy of the Zulu Nation, Bambaataa's ultimate message that hip hop could and should play a more activist role in society would not be lost.

According to DJ Spooky, a body-grooving experimental DJ and mind-grooving intellectual, Bambaataa was future-oriented in terms of his approach to hip-hop music and politics. Calling Bambaataa "actionary rather than reactionary," Spooky claims, "he gave the notion of channeling the anger and bitterness of being outside the American mainstream into a constructive thing." Bambaataa understood that the misery associated with poverty bred contempt that was often channeled inward. Though he did not have the formal training of a social worker or youth psychologist, Bambaataa knew that the troubles facing ghetto youths required dramatic intervention. He argued that the solution was to empower people to confront head-on the problems facing their community. When nearly no one else did, Bambaataa believed hip hop could lead the way to a brighter day.

•••

While Bambaataa and others contemplated hip hop's political future, the movement was about to succumb to a more immediate reality, commercialism. The concerns about credibility and authenticity—notwithstanding the growing sensation known as "Rapper's Delight"—confirmed that hip hop's commercial potential was real. Still, the idea that hip hop could have an enduring commercial life seemed farfetched. Back in the day, hip hop's performing elite consisted of DJs, MCs, break dancers, and aerosol artists. This emergent cadre of artists—and that is what they were—had never rejected the idea of making money, they just seldom stopped to think that the art they were creating could command money-paying patrons of any significance beyond their immediate environment.

One such artist was Joseph Saddler. Born in Barbados, Joseph came of age in the Bronx just as hip hop was coming to the world's attention. From an early age Joseph had developed a love for vinyl records. His father maintained a prized collection of LPs that he barred his young son from meddling with. But Joseph could not resist the pull of the records. Whenever his father left the house, he grabbed a handful of LPs and played them on the family's record player even though doing so could lead to a severe beating. His fascination with spinning records, it turns out, would be a lifelong passion.

By the middle 1970s Joseph was emerging as a local celebrity and one of hip hop's most important creative forces. A lot of the fame and prominence accorded to DJs around the world today can be traced directly to the crew of DJs that came together in the early days of hip hop. Saddler's peers and admirers nicknamed him Flash because his hands moved so quickly while handling the records and turntables he used to help revolutionize the skills and image of the DJ in global pop culture. It was the competition between Flash, Bambaataa, Kool Herc, Grand Wizard Theodore, and others that sparked the development of several of the techniques that define the art and science of modern DJing. Their unique approach and magician-like skills turned a seemingly passive exercise—spinning records—into a dynamic display of personal expression and musical performance.

Like many Bronx-based youth in the seventies Flash found himself immersed in a culture that was bubbling over with a creative energy that no sociological theory could ever explain or predict. He tried break dancing but found himself mesmerized by Kool Herc, a Jamaican-born DJ credited with introducing some of the earliest and most raucous block parties that define part of hip hop's lore. Herc's contributions to hip hop are legendary. Born Clive Campbell, Herc and his family came to New York from Jamaica in 1967 when he was a young kid. But he carried with him the memories of his youth in Trenchtown, including the sound system culture that defined part of Jamaica's social world.

Sound systems gave the people mobile discotheques made up of turntables, massive speakers, and charismatic DJs. With little means

to afford the country's live bands, poor and working-class con
nities gravitated toward DJs who built the powerful sound systems.
These homemade sound systems amplified the already bottom-
heavy bass rhythms that provided the essential architecture in
Jamaican music. The most popular DJs earned an even greater following by featuring black American soul music, which U.S. military
personnel based in the Caribbean exposed them to. When he was old
enough, Herc wove elements of that world into his performance as a
DJ in hip hop's burgeoning scene. The cultural flows that connected
North America to the Caribbean suggest that hip hop was global long
before being global was cool.

But as much as Flash admired Herc he noticed a few flaws, too.
According to Flash, "[Herc] might play something that was down-
tempo and then right behind that would play something that was uptempo, and it wasn't on time. In between record A and record B, you
could see how off time it was in the way the audience would go into
disarray." Flash later termed what he observed as the *disarray unison
factor*.

At a time when most young boys his age would have dreamed of
sports stardom or girls, Flash developed a passion for mastering the
fine art and science of DJing. With passion and persistence he pursued the ideas that were revolving in his head as fast as the discs he
became famous for spinning. By his estimation he spent about three
years of his life locked away in his bedroom mastering what, in
essence, would become his craft and a new form of musicianship. "I
sacrificed most of my kid years to—to try to just take this thing that
was just running around in my head and make it a reality."

Flash and his DJ friends believed that in every great record there is
an even greater part, what they called "the get down part." That part
of the song is more formally referred to as the break. Flash wanted to
capture and extend the break beat because it was usually only a few
seconds long. What he really wanted was to take sections of songs from
vinyl and reinvent them by producing newer, longer, and funkier versions: essentially, making new musical soundscapes from previously

recorded materials. Some characterized his efforts as innovative while others dismissed them as thievery and lacking creativity.

As he began to figure out how to manipulate the technology—turntables, amplifiers, mixers, and speakers—he developed a new vocabulary to capture his creative genius. According to Flash, "That's when I had to come up with terms like 'the torque factor'—how I judge the turntable from the state of inertia to when it is up to speed." His close study of turntables revealed the subtle yet important distinctions between different types of needles and how they might affect his efforts to create songs out of previously recorded materials. He even coined the term *clock theory* to describe his decision to re-repeat particular sections of a record by spinning the disc back a few rotations to constantly play the break beat.

What makes the accomplishments of Flash and his contemporaries so impressive is how they imposed their creative will on what was, in reality, a hardscrabble landscape that provided few resources or opportunities for young people who lived on society's margins. "Today," Flash says, "you can buy turntables, needles and mixers that are equipped to do whatever. But at that particular time, I had to build it. I had to take microphone mixers and turn them into turntable mixers. I was taking speakers out of abandoned cars and using people's thrown-away stereos." How Flash and his contemporaries invented the modern DJ through sheer hustle, imagination, and innovation is not simply *their* story; it is, in a very real sense, the story of hip hop. Like many in hip hop's first wave of innovators, Flash created a way out of no way and, in the process, transformed DJing into a serious art form and a lucrative profession.

Years later in an interview the man the music world now knows as Grandmaster Flash recalled turning down some of the earliest offers to do in a recording studio what he genuinely loved doing in area parks and dance clubs around New York. Like many of the young hip-hop artists in the 1970s, Flash was making a name for himself but not much else. He found it hard to believe that anyone would pay four or five dollars for music they were getting basically for free in the local community centers, on city blocks, and in gymnasiums that played host to those early hip-hop parties. His response to an initial offer to record the music he was helping to create was incredibly naïve: "Let's keep it underground. Nobody outside the Bronx would like this stuff anyway." And then he heard the Sugarhill Gang on the radio.

It was the autumn of 1979 and Flash could not believe his ears. "I heard this record on the radio almost every ten minutes on almost every station that I switched to," Flash remembered. "They said it was these boys out of Jersey." The success of the record haunted him; he realized that he had missed out on an opportunity to be the first to record the music he would eventually help introduce to the world. As he listened with equal parts of disbelief and amazement to rap's first commercial hit, he sensed that what he and others were doing might be on the verge of something big. Just how big no one could have ever imagined in 1979.

# PART ONE

# POP CULTURE
# and the STRUGGLE
# for HIP HOP

# CHAPTER ONE

# Remixing American Pop

*Rap has been around for a while now, it's really successful,*
*it's powerful and still vibrant, but something else is going*
*to happen soon.... The potential is unlimited.*
—BRYAN TURNER, founder of Priority Records, 1992

In 1989 *Billboard* magazine, the music industry's most important trade publication, held a briefing devoted to improving the way it collected sales data. Among the various people attending the meeting that day was a record industry executive named Michael Shalett. His primary areas of expertise included information technology, marketing, and market research. As Shalett listened to the various ideas being discussed, he could not believe what he was hearing. When the briefing was over, he left convinced that the methods used by *Billboard* were substandard and unreliable.

Next, he turned to Michael Fine, one of the nation's foremost research professionals and pollsters. Fine had distinguished himself as president of George Fine Research, a full-service, national and international market research firm adept at gathering public opinion. Established in 1935, the company developed some of the most widely used market research methodologies in the world. Exit polling, a technique the company helped refine, changed the way political projections are made and how election night results are reported. The collaboration between Shalett and Fine would have a similar groundbreaking impact on the business of pop music.

The same year that *Billboard* held its briefing the annual Consumer Profile of the Recording Industry Association of America

(RIAA) reported that rap music's market share was 6 percent. The numbers from the report could be read in at least two ways. For some, the market share was an indication that the genre, despite its relatively short career, had established itself on the pop music map. For others, however, the numbers suggested that for all of its noise and high jinks rap's popularity was still somewhat localized, if not ghettoized. In 1989, more than half, 57 percent, of all music purchased in the U.S. was purchased by consumers between ten and twenty-nine years old. Rap music's fourth-place share was an indication that the genre's impact, though commendable, was not necessarily formidable among its youthful audience.

Ten years later, however, rap's impact was undeniable as it was routinely producing some of the top-selling recordings of the year and establishing a prominent presence in the pop music landscape and beyond. Between 1990 and 2000 rap's market share more than doubled while its rival genres—rock, pop, and R&B—actually lost market share and the industry as a whole came face-to-face with declining sales. In the RIAA's 2000 Consumer Profile, rap's market share was second only to rock, roughly 13 percent compared to 25 percent. But even the most casual observers of pop music culture knew that rap's influence reached far beyond its own generic boundaries and official market share.

Rhythm and blues, a staple in American pop music for decades, had come under hip hop's spell as it began gravitating toward the grittier street-oriented beats and ghetto-theme lyrics that bolstered hip hop's aura and appeal. The resonance of hip hop was also detectable in more traditional pop fare. Just before the boy-band craze faded in the late 1990s, multiplatinum acts like N Sync and the Backstreet Boys adopted some of the edgier styles and lyrics typically associated with rappers. Even pop princesses Britney Spears and Christina Aguilera, in their bid to go from teen idols to more mature artists, began working with some of hip hop's most sought after producers, performers, and choreographers in order to stay relevant in the movement's widening orbit.

Still rap's impact was never a sure thing. In fact as the nineties began the verdict on the genre, especially from the perspective of music industry decision-makers, was still out. The earlier inroads made by groups like Run-D.M.C., Salt-N-Pepa, and Public Enemy notwithstanding, rap was still looked at with a certain degree of scorn and suspicion by industry executives. Though it was clear that rap had already established its bona fides among key segments of the youth marketplace, it was viewed by industry heads as a genre with limited and even uncertain long-term appeal. But as the nineties unfolded much of the doubt about rap was erased as a combination of pioneering labels, artists, and entrepreneurs transformed the genre into a spectacular music industry. Surprisingly, the most important factor in rap's rise was not, at least initially, an innovative producer, MC, or entrepreneur. Rather, it was the introduction of a new information technology that tracked music sales with unprecedented precision.

•••

Two years after they set out to improve how the music industry collected sales data, Shalett and Fine stood ready and eager to introduce their invention. They called the new data and information service SoundScan. Confident that they had created an improved scientific and reality-based method both men realized that developing the system was only half the battle. Now they had to convince the big record companies of the value of the new sales-reporting method. In 1991, the "two Mikes," as music industry insiders would later call them, began aggressively shopping their data intelligence to music retailers and record companies. Media accounts reported that the initial asking fee for the service was $800,000. SoundScan had to make an investment of its own because it paid retailers a fee in return for providing the company with sales-related data. The record companies, however, not accustomed to paying much if anything for sales data, responded coolly to the service.

SoundScan's big break came when the editors at *Billboard* decided to begin using the service to compile its music charts. Over the years the *Billboard* charts have become one of the most important gauges of success in the high stakes world of commercial music. *Billboard*'s listings of the top-selling albums and singles determine who is recognized as the industry's leading performers, which in turn impacts radio and video airplay, sales, industry accolades, and finally, of all things, chart position. The *Billboard* charts, in short, have the power to make or break careers.

SoundScan was a revolutionary idea. Prior to its introduction the methods used to determine sales and *Billboard* chart positions were archaic. Typically, music industry executives relied on the observations and hunches of record store clerks and managers who produced weekly reports that ranked sales trends. In order to determine chart position under the old system, *Billboard* would survey a jury of retail personnel and ask them to rank which albums they perceived to be the most popular or best-selling product. Under this system it was possible to gain a sense of which albums were "hot" but not how many copies were actually sold. The data was subjective and open to interpretation.

The subjective nature of the method created an obvious incentive for the music companies to try to influence the reports. There was rampant suspicion that the charts were affected more by hype than actual sales and may not have represented an accurate account of what product stores were actually moving. Over the years there were numerous stories about how reps from the major labels doled out free concert tickets, special promotions, and other perks as a way to encourage the kind of overreporting by stores that enhanced the profile and sales of their artists. Shortly after adopting SoundScan, then *Billboard* editor-in-chief Timothy White acknowledged that "Our old system was subject to manipulation and that people abused it. Store reporters could be bribed with clock radios and all sorts of amenities and favors."

Like film and television, the music industry has grown into a tenacious corporate machine powered by a few key numbers. The pressure to achieve commercial success has been an ongoing theme throughout the history of the industry, but new monitoring technologies, conglomerate ownership, and a global entertainment economy reinvented the business of selling music in the nineties. By the late 1990s four figures essentially dictated how the major music companies operate—the number of units sold, weekly radio spins, video rotations, and downloads. By providing new and more efficient ways of measuring those trends, new information technologies like Sound-Scan and Broadcast Data System (it measured weekly radio spins) changed the business of pop music. SoundScan became the most watched barometer for measuring commercial success and spotting key trends in the consumption of music. Thus, like the weekly box office results that have become such a major aspect of the business of film, the SoundScan data helped establish a blockbuster mentality that has made the pursuit of big opening-week sales, mega-hits, and multiplatinum albums an industrywide obsession.

Whereas the previous system relied on the hunches of store personnel, the computerized methods used by SoundScan provided what the corporate world refers to as "hard data." This information is perceived as manipulation proof and therefore more reliable. The genius of the system was that it used a simple bar code–recording format to transmit point-of-sale (POS) information to SoundScan's massive database located in Hartsdale, New York. SoundScan was able to take the POS information and supply the music industry with unprecedented data that told intricate stories about the market performance of specific albums, artists, and the companies that distributed them. In addition to tracking national sales, the new system could generate detailed data that measured an album's sales week by week, city by city, and even store by store. Within a few short years, the music industry executives would begin calibrating highly elaborate and specialized marketing strategies based on SoundScan's more meticulous reporting.

Early on, however, many of the major labels expressed concern about SoundScan. Most of the early complaints dealt with which stores and regions of the country were sufficiently represented in the SoundScan panel of national, multistate, and regional music chains. But others believed that the major labels' real concern was that the new method brought to an end a thirty-year-old system that allowed them to influence the all-important *Billboard* charts. The two Mikes knew that their service represented a threat to the established order. "There was definitely some reservation," Fine revealed years later. "They had a sense of control, and here we were trying to take that control away."

While the concerns expressed by the major labels may have been suspect, the new POS system generated genuine alarm among independent labels and distributors. The indie music sector knew that the so-called "mom and pop" stores were more likely to carry their product and also give a break to new artists the majors historically ignored. Their biggest worry was that while SoundScan could provide a more accurate account of music sales in the big chain stores it would underreport the sales activity in the smaller stores. In addition to endangering their financial health, underreporting could imperil the indies' ability to continue making music that cut against the grain of the hardened formulas and conservative taste preferred by the majors.

A few weeks before the introduction of SoundScan, the music industry, both majors and indies, held a collective breath—uncertain what would happen but fully convinced that things would never be the same again. Change was inevitable. Their concerns about Sound-Scan would prove to be both right and wrong.

• • •

In its May 25, 1991 issue, the music industry's most important trade publication announced, "This is a week of historic change for *Billboard* magazine," adding, "it's full-speed ahead into the future." That week both the *Billboard* 200 and Country Music charts began using the piece count data supplied by SoundScan. In a move intended to allay industry fears about the historic shift, *Billboard* wrote that the new system would likely "cause some drastic movement of titles up and down the two charts this week. This is a natural adjustment to a radically different methodology." *Billboard* declared the charts would eventually settle down to more gradual patterns of movement.

As expected, SoundScan's impact on the *Billboard* charts was immediate. But the actual impact produced by the new system was also unexpected. Within the first couple months of the new system's implementation, the *Billboard* charts began to tell an intriguing story. While the presence of rock and pop music near the top of the charts was predictable, the chart-rising performance of country and rap music was not. Immediately, SoundScan called attention to the commercial vitality of country and rap—two genres that prior to 1991 were widely viewed as having limited appeal. Both genres moved impressively up the *Billboard* charts, and by the end of the year were peppered throughout the *Billboard* 200.

The SoundScan data provided powerful evidence that the ranked reports produced by retail personnel had severely undervalued country and rap. Rather than reflecting actual sales, it turns out that those charts reflected the tastes, perceptions, and predispositions of store personnel that were unwilling or perhaps, more likely, unable to comprehend the cultural changes that were transforming the very meaning of American pop music. The underreporting of rap was a result of long-standing cultural sensibilities and racial assumptions that made it impossible to think of the genre as "pop music" in 1991. And yet, by the close of the 1990s that was precisely the case; rap, as much as any other genre, defined American pop.

In the post-SoundScan era the very notion of pop underwent a radical revision. Before SoundScan pop was largely defined by aesthetic attributes—sweet melodies, stylistic conservatism, and amicable lyrics. After SoundScan pop was just as likely to be defined by economics and marketplace resonance. The focus in this instance was on weekly sales figures and dollars. Under the latter definition, it became necessary to expand how the industry and the culture defined and experienced pop music. The shift meant that genres such as rap, despite an emotional and aesthetic core that ran counter to tradition, could now be added to the pop mix.

The instant beneficiaries of rap's newfound pop status were the independent labels and distributors that served as the primary province of rap music production in the early 1990s. The information provided by SoundScan supplied the momentum and credibility to enhance the profile of indie labels while also solidifying the foundation that enabled the rap industry to grow and prosper.

Indie distributors like Tom Silverman, the founder of Tommy Boy Records, realized immediately how the new data altered the high stakes world of pop music. Silverman was one of the first entrepreneurs to get into the rap game when many were unsure it had a future. He was on the scene when hip hop began to first break in the early 1980s. The music hit him hard. Back then it was all still raw, fresh, and pulsating with an aura of newness and independence that touched his core. He started Tommy Boy Records in 1981. His motto for success was simple. It also characterizes the historic role of indie music labels: "See what they [the major record labels] can't see—or find an area that's so minor they don't want to be bothered with it. The major labels tried to mechanize it like Henry Ford, but what works for cars doesn't necessarily work for music." Tommy Boy made its mark by introducing some of hip hop's truly groundbreaking artists, like Afrika Bambaataa, De La Soul, Queen Latifah, and House of Pain, one of the first successful, harder-edge white rap acts. These and other Tommy Boy recordings enlarged hip hop's aesthetic sensibilities and artistic possibilities.

Before SoundScan Silverman thought that indie labels represented roughly 5 percent to 7 percent of the U.S. sales market. About nine months after the introduction of the new sales-tracking system, Silverman gladly noted, "SoundScan's weekly reports show that... 11.7% of all records sold in the U.S. were distributed through independents." He added, "SoundScan is a great thing for indies—we realize we're a bigger part of the industry than we thought we were." Between May of 1991 and March of 1992 Tommy Boy went on to place several albums in the *Billboard* 200. Silverman, like many of his counterparts in the rap music industry, understood that SoundScan made his label's chart success possible. The new POS sales data was sweet vindication for indie distributors who knew that rap music was selling well but never had the "hard data" to support their claims or boost the standing of the genre they banked their financial lives on. Paradoxically, the chart recognition combined with the steady sales made labels like Tommy Boy more valuable and vulnerable. As a result of the success the indie labels were enjoying, the majors began to pay more attention to rap music.

Bryan Turner, president of another label that rode rap's rising tide, Priority Records, also understood the significance of Sound-Scan. Searching for the words to explain his phenomenal success as a record industry executive, the Canadian born Turner told the *Toronto Star* in 1999, "I can't explain how I got from there to here other than presented with certain choices and decisions, I made the right ones and worked my ass off." He went on to elaborate: "I got lucky in terms of establishing myself early on, connecting with a genre of music that became the cultural voice of the youth in the '80s and '90s. I don't know how else to explain it." Just twenty-eight when he co-founded the label, Turner made his mark by daring to distribute some of the most controversial and shocking fare in pop music history. His roster included hard core rappers like Eazy-E, N.W.A., Ice Cube, and the Geto Boys. After N.W.A. and Ice Cube reached the number one and number two positions, respectively, in 1991 Turner noted that the label "had those sales numbers before but never the chart position. We've probably had the sales for five or six top two albums before SoundScan."

The impact of SoundScan on the business of rap music was profound. While it is true that most culture industry executives neither understood nor respected hip hop, it is also true that they could not ignore the sales data SoundScan provided. In an industry that had long sold its soul to the guardians of capitalism, the commercial compulsions that operate among culture industry executives are a powerful force. In reality, only something as authoritative and compelling as the story SoundScan began telling could triumph over the racial inhibitions and cultural antagonisms that marked rap as a renegade genre. Though they still harbored ill feelings toward the genre, industry executives could no longer dismiss the huge financial payoff it offered.

Like many of his colleagues in the indie music scene, Turner sensed that things were changing in the world of commercial music. "I don't think there could be a better time than right now to be an indie, in terms of music," Turner said in March of 1992. "Rap has been around for a while now, it's really successful, it's powerful and still vibrant, but something else is going to happen soon and it's a wide open field right now. It's a good time to start a label if you want to be open-minded and just put out great music—it's an open-ended spectrum right now, and anything could break huge. The potential is unlimited." Turner's clear-eyed study of the emerging musical landscape, the potential role the indies would play, and rap's prospects, it turns out, could not have been more prophetic.

• • •

In 1990 Ted Field, the scion of the Marshall Field's department store fortune, decided that he wanted to develop his love of music into something more concrete. Since his arrival in Hollywood almost a decade earlier, the man described by the press as a ponytailed and wealthy socialite had already enjoyed a fruitful run in the film business. Though he had a long list of films under his producer's belt—*Three Men and a Baby, Jumanji,* and *The Hand That Rocks the Cradle* to name a few—he decided that the music business was his real calling. "You can have all the money in the world and be the unhappiest guy in the world," Field explained. "I wanted to do something that meant something in my life." Field had the money, connections, and drive necessary to make it in the music business but he lacked one other essential ingredient: experience. Luckily for him, he was smart enough to know that, if his dream of creating a competitive music label was to be realized, he needed a seasoned music industry insider as a partner. His quest to find someone who had both the experience and the mettle to launch an independent record label led him to Jimmy Iovine, a veteran record producer.

Iovine had been in the music business for more than three decades. Over the course of that time he worked as an engineer and producer for some of the biggest names in rock including: John Lennon, Patti Smith, Bruce Springsteen, and U2. The son of a long-shoreman, Iovine's tough Brooklyn upbringing served him well in the competitive business of commercial music-making. Around the time he was approached by Field, the weathered Iovine was in search of something new. Sensing that music and the world around him were changing, he was not sure where or even if he fit in any longer. Speaking about that crossroad period in his professional life, Iovine told a *Rolling Stone* reporter in 1997 that he believed: "Music is going to change. Young bands aren't going to be asking for me. But I love working with the new thing. I always liked the part of the business that's the first time you hear something, and I knew I wasn't in that business anymore."

Iovine may have suspected that Field's offer to help run a label may have been his last best shot at "working with the new thing." Many music industry insiders believed that the Iovine-Field partnership was destined to fail. After all, indie labels come and go. Even the two partners realized the odds were stacked against them. "We were looking at a long shot," Iovine said. "It was a guy with money from the outside and a record producer. Those two things couldn't succeed." One popular newsweekly characterized the Iovine-Field partnership as venture meeting capital, Flatbush meeting Beverly Hills.

They officially launched Interscope Records in 1990 just as several other indie labels announced their dreamy-eyed pursuit of music industry fame and gold. The nineties would prove to be a strange decade in the history of the music-recording industry. Over the course of the decade the business experienced some of its greatest profits and gravest dangers. Though the nineties proved to be a treacherous time for many in the music business, Interscope gained recognition as one of the industry's biggest success stories. Within its first three years of operation the label was turning a profit, and by 1997 Interscope was poised to gross somewhere between $250 and $300 million.

In December of 1996 the label pulled a coup when it claimed the first four spots in the *Billboard* 200. More than twenty years had passed since a label earned such chart distinction. Within a short period of time, Interscope was earning a reputation as an up-and-coming label that had its finger squarely on the pulse of music's changing tone. Just as impressive its success cut across different genres, making it a formidable opponent in the intensely competitive world of pop music. Over the course of its rise from indie label to industry powerhouse, Interscope played host to a star-studded roster filled out by Limp Biskit (metal-rap), Marilyn Manson (shock rock), No Doubt (pop rock), Eminem (pop rap), and 50 Cent (hard core rap). The diversity of its success positioned Interscope as a trailblazer in the rapidly changing world of pop music. Referring to Interscope's rising influence, Russell Simmons, former CEO of chief rival Def Jam, noted, "Jimmy has become a real thorn in my side in the [black music] business," adding, "he's got the alternative rock world, the alternative black world, and he's just starting. It's pretty scary."

Despite its remarkable diversity, and the success Interscope enjoyed, it was difficult—in fact impossible—to deny that it was the label that hip hop and one of the music industry's most notorious imprints built.

• • •

The initial freedom that Iovine and Field enjoyed at Interscope in the early nineties allowed them to play the music business game by a less conventional set of rules. The relative independence they had made it possible to experiment with a wide palette of musical styles and genres. While they lacked the deep pockets of the majors, Interscope's small size provided the insulation and freedom to make music with virtually no fear of corporate interference or censorship. Still, like all start-up labels Interscope needed to find a musical niche, signature artist, or song that could deliver visibility, credibility, and, most importantly, financial stability.

Like most good fortunes in the zany and uncertain world of pop culture, Interscope's rise was a matter of fortuitous luck and good timing. The record label's home, Los Angeles, just so happened to be the fertile quarters for gangsta rap, one of the nineties most influential and controversial styles of music. Though it became closely and most notoriously associated with the West Coast, gangsta rap's humble beginnings originated in the 1980s from the streets of Philadelphia and New York. Compared with earlier styles of rap, gangsta was much more strident in tone and graphic in its storytelling. This particular subgenre of rap, similar to most new music styles, was nourished in that great reservoir of musical innovation: the cultural underground. Far from public view and completely disconnected from the corridors of media and corporate power, a group of young music producers, artists, and entrepreneurs engineered a musical style that was the antithesis of what most believed was commercially viable music at the time. Whereas conventional wisdom suggests that most marketable music genres are inspiring, "feel good," or romantic, gangsta rap was incendiary, self-consciously profane, and ruthlessly unsentimental.

As the gangsta style evolved throughout the decade it became, for some, the unfiltered voice of a generation of angry and alienated young black men who inhabited America's abandoned ghettos. For others, the gangsta style was a meticulous pose, a shrewd, market-driven performance that craftily exploited America's fear of poor, ghetto youths. Perhaps Ice-T, the self-proclaimed "Original Gangsta," put it best and as only he could, "Man, everybody in the hood is trying to get the fuck out. I mean, before I was a rapper, what in the hell do you think I was robbing for?" he asked a London reporter in 1993, "to stay broke?" Following their own ambitions and commercial instincts, gangsta rappers created their own world and, in the process, emerged as an unlikely group of music makers who turned the blighted conditions of ghetto poverty into an oasis of adolescent fantasy and popular entertainment.

Los Angeles, in addition to serving as the home for a growing collection of hard-core performers, had already produced the most ill-famed gangsta rap crew, N.W.A. (Niggaz With Attitude). Their combustible lyrics and profane gestures earned them public scrutiny and even a warning from the FBI after the group recorded its anti-authority street anthem, "Fuck Tha Police." But their reputation as truth-telling street reporters and ghetto ethnographers also gained them a national following and, eventually, platinum-level music sales. When the chiefs at Interscope were introduced to Marion "Suge" Knight and Andre "Dr. Dre" Young, co-founders of Death Row Records, they were certainly aware of the potential upside of getting into the gangsta rap game. There was, too, as Interscope would learn in 1996 during the backlash against hard core rap, and Time Warner in particular, a serious downside as well.

•••

In an industry that has produced its share of unlikely moguls and intriguing personalities Suge Knight stands out in true ghetto fabulous fashion. Standing taller than six foot five and weighing more than three hundred pounds, nothing from his background suggested, at least at first glance, that he could run a powerhouse record label. He had ties to the infamous Bloods, a gang in Los Angeles. After a brief and undistinguished career in pro football, he used his size and intimidating presence to work as a night club bouncer and security guard.

Although he decided that he wanted to run his own music label, there was no real reason to believe that he could succeed. Fittingly, Suge's rise in the music industry was straight out of a Hollywood gangster movie. His short but scintillating run in the business of selling music blurred the lines between real life and theater, eventually reaching tragic consequences that touched close to Death Row's inner sanctum when Tupac Shakur, one of the label's brightest and most beleaguered stars, was gunned down in Las Vegas. His strong-arm tactics and no-nonsense approach to staking out his own territory actually made Suge one of the most feared and, strangely enough, revered men in the music industry.

But underneath his thug-tough swagger and gang affiliations, he possessed a shrewd business mind. In her profile of Suge and Death Row in a 1996 cover story for the *New York Times Magazine*, Lynn Hirschberg wrote that Suge's real genius was in "shaping street culture for consumption by the youth of America." From the outset Suge knew that he wanted Death Row to be bigger than a run-of-the-mill rap production house. Despite his checkered past and nasty rumors about how he actually got the money to enter the music business, he patterned himself after one of America's greatest music moguls, Motown Records founder Berry Gordy.

Though the differences between Suge and Gordy were more than apparent, there were some striking similarities. Like Gordy, Suge's ultimate goal was to package black culture and style for mainstream America. And like his predecessor, Suge understood that his artists needed to develop songs that captured the mood of their respective times while also fashioning personalities that played well on radio and television. Although Gordy instructed his artists to cultivate personas that were respectable, well-mannered, and graceful, Suge put together a roster of performers that relished being disreputable, unpolished, and raw. Whereas Gordy developed artists that white America found pleasing and assimilable, Suge developed artists that America's bourgeois sensibilities found objectionable and threatening. Still, despite the sharp contrasts, they both managed to produce a body of music that recorded in sound and song the mood shifts that captured their respective generations of young music lovers.

Iovine, perhaps because of his own street-tough background or sheer desire to make Interscope a success, looked past the hazardous baggage that followed Suge. "Nobody," he says, "wanted to be in business with Death Row, because, unfortunately, they [other music industry executives] felt there was an element there that could be dangerous. But I knew they had great music and that they were a bunch of guys who wanted to make it out of the ghetto. That's something I can understand."

While Iovine tolerated Suge, he was clearly captivated by Death Row's other half, Dr. Dre. If Suge was the business mind and muscle behind Death Row's assault on the music world, Dr. Dre provided the creative vision and punch. The albums that he produced with N.W.A., rap's first big crossover gangsta act, achieved platinum-level sales without the benefit of radio airplay or heavy marketing. It was a feat that until N.W.A. and other rap acts began accomplishing it in the early nineties was considered virtually impossible. But then again who would have thought that Dre's first album with Death Row, featuring tracks like "The Day the Niggaz Took Over" and "Bitches Ain't Shit" would become a pop classic?

• • •

Late in 1992 Interscope and Death Row released their first album, a Dr. Dre vehicle simply titled *The Chronic*. The album's title was a reference to an especially potent blend of marijuana that many of Death Row's key figures enjoyed smoking while they worked and played. Led by Dr. Dre, Death Row's artistry, like the concoction its first album celebrated, was a blistering blend of different musical stylings, kitsch, and dark humor that brought an aura of pop sophistication to gangsta rap. *The Chronic* created an elaborate texture of sounds and images comprised of blaxploitation and documentary films, seventies television sitcoms, local news, comedy skits, game shows, and the sometimes profound, sometimes profane world of ghetto street culture. Nine months after its release *The Chronic* was double platinum and still in the *Billboard* Top Ten. During its run it was the biggest-selling hard core rap album of all time.

From the date of the album's launch, Interscope and Death Row aggressively pursued their bid to enlarge gangsta's appeal and presence in American pop culture. Dr. Dre, the consummate artist, took creative control of the album's musical direction and the videos that made regular appearances on MTV and BET. His use of samples from George Clinton, Bootsy Collins, and Donny Hathaway evoked a more upbeat era in black American life even as it reveled in the downtrodden and profane world constructed in the gangsta imagination. The videos he directed were at once homespun, hilarious, and hard-hitting. Shot in homes and hoods across South Central Los Angeles's vast summery ghettoscapes, the videos were intimately connected to the passion, pleasure, and pain that reverberated throughout the hip-hop movement. Dre's directorial nuances expanded his creative repertoire and reputation as a boundary-crossing artist. Talking from the set during the making of the "Let Me Ride" video, Iovine boasted: "There aren't three people like him in the music business. He can rap, he can produce...and he can direct a video with humor. Do you know how hard that is? Famous movie directors can't do that."

*The Chronic* was clearly the high-water mark in the strange career of gangsta rap. The album's G-funk grooves, success with radio, and crossover appeal make it the most memorable recording from the tremendous output of gangsta inflected titles that, between 1988 and 1994, defined rap and a significant aspect of youth pop culture in America. *The Chronic* came complete with all of the fixings—drugs, death, money, sex, misogyny, and commentary about racial abandonment and oppression—that made gangsta rap delicious and distasteful. But Dr. Dre successfully blended the fantasy-driven motifs in hard core rap—sensational stories about drug dealing, murder, and life in the streets—with the familiar and therefore more friendly tonalities of soul, funk, reggae, and black pop. Though gangsta rap had been popular before the release of *The Chronic,* pop radio formats avoided it like the plague. According to Step Johnson, Interscope's head of promotion, "There were always people who wanted the music. The problem was getting PD's [program directors] and MD's [music directors] to play it."

But the tastes, trends, and sensibilities that govern youth culture would undergo a profound shift sparked, in part, by the coming of gangsta. *The Chronic,* and what Death Row offered in the immediate aftermath—Snoop Doggy Dogg, Tupac Shakur, The Dogg Pound—proved to be the perfect potion for a commercial radio broadcast industry that was coming under greater corporate control, supervision, and pressure. The dramatic changes that occurred at WQHT (Hot 97) New York illustrate how the landscape of America's pop culture shifted in a way that fortified rap's pop status.

Created in 1986, Hot 97 featured a freestyle Latin dance music format, but had shifted to rap music by 1993. Like a lot of radio stations around the country, Hot 97 tested songs before including them on its playlists. The station's then musical director explains: "When we test records, we're testing the hooks. The records with the catchy hooks you can sing along to test better." In 1993, Hot 97's audience was about half white, a third Latino, and about a fifth black. Nevertheless, the decision makers at Hot 97 believed that because of its infectious melodies, not to mention MTV's embrace, *The Chronic* was well suited for radio airplay. Tracks like "Nuthin' But a 'G' Thang" and "Dre Day" became staple tunes across America's airwaves and catapulted harder edge rhymes to the forefront of radio.

But the danceable grooves and hummable hooks that made Death Row's music a favorite among radio programmers also smoothed over the deeply ingrained misogyny and sexual violence that throbbed throughout the music. Even as the producers of gangsta struck a rebellious pose that threatened to unleash its wrath on the dominant culture, it was often women, and especially black women, who bore

the brunt of its wrath. Gender and sexual tensions have always existed in popular culture, but the gangsta sub-genre took hip hop's
misogyny to the extreme. What the producers of gangsta discovered
was that the more outrageously they performed, the more success
they accumulated. That success produced mixed results—it simultaneously propelled the movement to new heights while undermining
the claim that hard core was the unfettered voice of ghetto America.

• • •

*The Chronic* did all of the things that Interscope needed it to do and
more. It gave the label a distinct, if not distinguished presence in
American pop music. The album also formed a definitive musical direction for the label while providing the financial momentum necessary for stability and growth. The rise of Interscope and the coming
of hard core rap signaled, yet again, another shift in the ongoing saga
of the hip-hop movement. No longer could the movement, in all of
its splendor and squalor, avoid the spotlight and the temptations of
"big media" and "big money." Thus, the next phase in hip hop's journey from the margins to the mainstream was easily predictable to
those who understood the historical trajectory of pop music and the
jerky currents of pop culture.

The scenario that was unfolding was essentially the same one that
had come to define the history of American pop: A small and independent sector had gambled on an unproven style of music and won
only to eventually lose. Even as he was enjoying the ride, the success,
and the money, Tommy Boy Records' founder Silverman saw the
writing on the wall, "The majors," he warned in 1992, "will pick up
the big indies, and jump on independent records which are breaking." Within a few short years Interscope, once a bit player in the
music business, grew to become a major label and key entertainment franchise in one of the world's biggest media conglomerates,
Vivendi/Universal.

When it was all said and done Interscope, Death Row, and *The*

*Chronic* left an indelible mark on the face of pop culture. Their debut effort did not invent hard core rap or establish its popularity. However, it did give the hard core presence in hip hop a more prominent profile and commercial identity. After gangsta something changed in American culture, especially in the symbolic and everyday milieus inhabited by youth. In the aftermath of the remixing of American pop, young people talked and looked at the world differently. Along the way their media—everything from music to television, video games to film, and advertising—developed a more contrary tone.

Hip hop's journey from the cultural margins to the cultural mainstream marks a pivotal moment in American history. Though hip hop has long been made up of various expressive elements, rap music stands out as the public face of the movement. Thus, the state of rap has become a key indicator of the state of hip hop. Despite its street credentials and ghetto-tough creed, it was difficult to deny that by the late 1990s rap had not only become part of the pop music establishment, it was the establishment.

Rap was one of the most lucrative musical forms in the business and, for better or worse, a prominent trendsetter and cultural sign of the times. The "pop" status of rap is peculiar precisely because the producers of the genre have long positioned it as the appropriate antidote to the syrupy style and mundane melodies that usually define pop music. Rap artists and producers carved out a successful niche in the music industry by introducing a gritty urban realism, frenetic style, and bombastic approach to music that broke away from the ordinary ways of the pop music machine. As the genre went on to experience unprecedented appeal in the 1990s, it would be accused of the very things—tediousness, stylistic conservatism, and formulaic trends—it once stood firmly against.

That's why Silverman, head of one of rap's first successful and most innovative labels, got out of the rap game twenty-two years after he first got in. In 2002 Silverman sold his remaining share in Tommy Boy Records to the Warner Music Group, a longtime distributor and partner. His reasons highlighted the contradictions that defined rap's margins-to-mainstream passage. "We [Tommy Boy Records] were hip hop history, and unfortunately a lot of hip hop is history at this point," Silverman said, after the deal with Warner was complete. "I'm interested in hip hop only if it can reinvent the future, not if it's a reflection of the past. Much of the hip hop that's out there right now is closer to what mainstream R&B was in 1981—when we started—than the true essence of hip hop." Rap, Silverman believed, had become too comfortable with success, too good at the corporate machinations that sold 80 percent of the music consumed in the world. Looking ahead, he added, "I'm still interested in hip hop, but I want the next shit." What exactly the next shit would be and what it said about the state of the hip-hop movement was not only of interest to Silverman. It was, ultimately, a source of great debate, tension, and speculation in the hip-hop movement.

CHAPTER TWO

# A Great Year in Hip Hop

*The streets have spoken.*

—DEF JAM RECORDS

In 1997 a small but determined group of publishers launched a new music magazine. They named it *XXL* with the tagline "Hip Hop on a Higher Level." Some of the key players involved with the new book were former staff members of *The Source*, one of the earliest and most successful news and entertainment monthlies dedicated to covering the vital world hip hop was creating. *The Source* was the idea of two Harvard students, Jon Shecter and Dave Mays. It began as a one-page photocopied newsletter that Mays produced for the listeners of a radio program he created. Though the program was hosted at Harvard, most of his listeners were young people from in and around the Boston area. When they graduated, Shecter and Mays moved to New York, where they began working to turn the newsletter into a glossy monthly.

Despite growing up white and relatively comfortable in a Washington, D.C., suburb, Mays developed a strong connection to the urban-based youth culture. He cut his teeth on Old School hip hop, growing fond of the Sugarhill Gang, Kurtis Blow, and Run-D.M.C. Years later, he would say, "hip hop made me respect black people." The debut issue of *The Source* was published in 1988. After a bumpy beginning the number of ad pages in the new publication doubled between 1991 and 1992. While its rate base was substantially lower than the more established music magazines like *Rolling Stone* and *Spin*, *The Source* earned recognition as the best-selling music magazine on newsstands by the middle nineties. Like the movement it covered the magazine touched a nerve. As hip hop's profile and audience grew so did *The Source*, and soon it began promoting itself as "the bible of hip hop culture, music, and politics." But *The Source*'s success also came with a cost; it inspired a host of competitors.

In 1993 music legend Quincy Jones entered into a joint venture with the Time Warner media conglomerate to create *Vibe*. From the beginning, Jones envisioned a magazine that would be to urban music and urban culture what Jann Wenner's *Rolling Stone* magazine was to rock music and the generation that defined it: the literary heartbeat and voice of a cultural movement. Whereas *The Source* positioned itself as a must-read for hard core hip-hop heads, *Vibe* aimed for a bigger, more multicultural and affluent readership. Former *Vibe* Venture CEO Keith Clinkscales explained: "We don't think of ourselves as a hip hop or R&B magazine. *Vibe* is a music magazine, the way *Rolling Stone* is a music magazine." He added that *Vibe*'s goal "is to be as important as if not more important than *Rolling Stone*. What we want to emulate is not just their music coverage but also everything else they do."

Because of its deep pocket connections to Time Warner, *Vibe* benefited from one of the most aggressive launches in the history of magazine publishing. By 1998 *Vibe*'s rate base of 600,000 also made it one of the fastest growing magazines ever. By 2003 its rate base of more than 800,000 placed it second only to *Rolling Stone* (1.3 million) among music magazines. *Vibe* posed a serious challenge to *The Source*'s position as hip hop's leading journalistic voice. But *Vibe*'s rapid rise also produced its share of growing pains.

From the very beginning questions about who—and what sensibilities—should define the magazine's editorial mission generated serious tensions. When Jones named Jonathan Van Meter, a former editor at *Vogue* who was also white and gay, as *Vibe*'s first editor-in-chief, hip-hop mogul Russell Simmons withdrew his involvement. "I would like to see some straight black men involved in the editing of this magazine, someone whose experiences are similar to that of the rappers," he said. In 1994, Van Meter resigned after he and Jones reportedly clashed over his decision to put Madonna on the cover of the magazine.

The tensions at *Vibe* were not unique in the world of hip-hop publishing. Both *The Source* and *XXL* had their share of problems, too. All three had to deal with staff walkouts and squabbles over editorial vision and content. Though the rise of hip-hop magazines was driven by a passionate belief that the movement deserved its own voice, there was virtually no consensus regarding how that voice should be defined or how hip hop should be documented. Discussing the tensions that hovered over *Vibe* during his run as editor-in-chief, Alan Light maintained, "Given the culture we cover and the composition of our staff, issues of race were never far from the surface of our mission—nor should it have been—which also led to conflicts inside and outside the office on a regular basis." These battles reflected the escalating tensions and passionate debate within hip hop about its own identity and purpose.

By the time Elliot Wilson, *XXL*'s editor-in-chief and former music editor for *The Source,* took out an ad in *Billboard* urging *The Source*'s advertisers to switch to his magazine, the publishing wars in hip hop had turned personal and bitter. At stake, of course, were the usual industry concerns: a desire to capture a competitive share of a readership and advertising revenue that was steadily growing and industry recognition as a "well-run book." But this struggle was also about something else. If the old adage that journalism is the first draft of history is true, then this particular struggle for hip hop highlighted the intense battle to become the initial and most trusted voice of record for a movement that was growing more vital every day.

The magazine publishing wars in hip hop reflected the vast cultural and economic developments that were remaking the movement. In the 1990s the vibrant world of hip hop grew into a gold mine of entrepreneurial activity. Along with that growth came the inevitable questions about race, commerce, and perhaps most importantly, ownership of the movement. Hip hop, dating back to its humble beginnings in the seventies, had always spawned its own economy. Back then hip hop's mostly informal economic activity consisted of mix tapes, local parties, local concerts, tours for break dancers, or the occasional showcase for talented graffiti writers. The entrepreneurial spirit in hip hop and the hidden economy it built were enlivened by a generation of youth who had little, if any, access to the corridors of corporate power and modern industrial image-making.

But all of that changed in the nineties. Emerging alongside the growth and popularity of the movement was a more formal hip-hop economy, one that developed surprisingly strong synergies with corporate America. In this corporate-driven climate hip hop's influence widened considerably as a generation, who in another time and place would ordinarily be confined to society's margins, gained unprecedented access to print, music, video, and other media. But with the greater access to corporate capital came even greater difficulties in maintaining control over the movement and the values that shaped it. Nevertheless, hip hop's economy raged forward. In addition to the vibrant music and magazine-publishing industries, the gold rush in hip hop produced a seemingly endless sea of opportunities in other industries like apparel, film, art, music video, and marketing.

This was the world that *XXL* entered. Realizing the tough challenge that they faced in hip hop's thriving but hypercompetitive economy, the editors at *XXL* searched for a way to distinguish their "book" from their rival's while further enhancing the profile and the legacy of the movement that had made their mission possible.

• • •

Early in 1998, during a meeting to discuss the year's publication plans, someone at *XXL* mentioned re-creating the now famous 1958 *Esquire* magazine "A Great Day in Harlem" photo of jazz legends. About forty years earlier, *Esquire* had assigned photographer Art Kane to take the picture that included fifty-seven artists, among them jazz giants Thelonious Monk, Dizzy Gillespie, and Count Basie. The re-creation idea was initially shot down, but Sheena Lester, *XXL*'s editor-in-chief at the time, insisted that they could do it. She sensed that the idea would not only make a powerful statement about hip hop but also signal the arrival of *XXL* as a viable and smarter alternative to the other hip-hop magazines. Next, she set her sights on Gordon Parks, the legendary photojournalist and artist extraordinaire.

One day while she was meeting with Harry Allen, a longtime hip-hop journalist, in uptown New York, she received a phone call from a staff member. She was told that Parks had declined their invitation to photograph the event. Friends and *XXL* staff persuaded Lester to make a personal plea to the famous photographer. She phoned and, again, he politely declined. Then, Lester made her last and what turned out to be best pitch, telling Parks, "Not only do we want you take this picture, we believe that no one else should take the picture but you." After hearing that, Parks relented and agreed to come on board.

Though there were several photographers the magazine could have assigned to the shoot, the choice of Parks issued an important statement about hip hop's respect for and grasp of American history. Parks had emerged from obscurity in the 1940s to earn a reputation as a rare storyteller. His pictures brilliantly captured the texture of everyday black life and have since become a treasured historical record of America's ongoing quest for racial justice. Parks's emergence as a world renowned photographer symbolized an important turning point in America.

Early in his career Parks viewed the camera as his weapon against racism. When he stepped behind the camera, he produced almost magical photos with a new gaze, a new way of seeing and portraying black American life. It was, after all, his stylish and even innovative approach to American cinema that brought to life the generation of pop culture icons like Shaft that so many of hip hop's MCs, filmmakers, and artists turn to for creative inspiration. Though the eighty-five-year-old Parks was several generations removed from the subjects he photographed, *XXL*'s decision to choose him was fitting.

Managing the various schedules and setting up a date for the shoot proved to be a serious logistical challenge. But after a series of "reschedules" several of hip hop's most notable figures came together on September 29 for the event. Billed as "A Great Day in Harlem '98," the photo shoot paid homage to one of the most famous pictures taken in modern music history. Now, a bit more than forty years later, a new generation of cultural icons posed for pictures on the same brownstone steps at 17 East 126th Street in Harlem that was the site of the jazz photo. Much had changed in Harlem in the world of music and in American culture since that summer day in 1958. The Harlem brownstone was now vacant, and jazz, once a cutting-edge and popular musical genre, no longer defined what young people considered hip.

The photo shoot represented a unique moment to reflect on hip hop's phenomenal growth and undeniable impact on the world around it. Grandmaster Flash and DJ Herc were among those who represented hip hop's pioneering days. Deborah Harry, of the rock group Blondie, symbolized hip hop's reach and its influence on the avant-garde art world. Shaquille O'Neal signaled hip hop's synergy with other arenas of entertainment like sports. And the collection of artists from different parts of the country highlighted the geographic and aesthetic diversity that made hip hop first a regional, then national, and finally a global phenomenon.

As the day unfolded a number of those who participated in the photo session were touched by the opportunity to experience hip hop's past, present, and future. Grandmaster Flash was full of pride as he basked in the pivotal role he'd had in the making of the hip-hop movement. "This is beautiful," proclaimed Flash. "I get to see a whole lot of my old friends, new friends, people who were just pedestrians and now are superstars. God says if you remain humble, all your blessings will come to you. Look at all my blessings!" Ahmir Thompson, a member of one of hip hop's most original bands in the nineties, The Roots, documented the event with a hand-held video camera. Like many who gathered that day he understood and appreciated the significance of the occasion. "I've been doing this for six years, and I've never met the essential people of hip hop," he said. Many described the atmosphere as electric. It was a day when Young and Old School hip hop came together in a way that had become virtually impossible in a movement that had grown exponentially over the years and produced its share of rivalries and competing interests.

But even as it paid homage to jazz and the prodigious talents of Parks, the 1998 photo shoot also pointed forward. Much like the picture that preceded it, the photo delivered a powerful message about the changing of the cultural guard in America. As jazz did in an earlier age, hip hop was embodying and defining the changing rhythm of American life. Its most profound impact was visible in the exuberant worlds created and inhabited by youth. It was visible in the music that provided the soundtrack to their daily lives, the clothes they chose to wear, the identities they crafted, and the worldviews they fought to express.

Perhaps more than anything, "A Great Day in Harlem '98" signified the degree to which the hip-hop movement was beginning to come to terms with itself: its rise and the enormous influence it wielded in America and beyond. "This is definitely historical and memorable," said Wyclef Jean, a member of the groundbreaking group the Fugees. Jean added, "This is America today. However you look at it, hip-hop is what's influencing little kids right now." In his assessment of the power of the moment, the music, and the movement, John Forté, a successful rap producer, explained that "[hip hop] has endured so many things, from being spit at by mainstream media and musicians to the deaths of Eazy-E, TuPac, Scott La Rock, and Biggie. And here it is, still standing, still powerful, having even more influence."

• • •

In reality, the "Great Day in Harlem '98" photo shoot was merely a snapshot in a year in which the Record Industry Association of

America declared, "Rap was the biggest story of the year in the music industry." Though the genre's journey toward the mainstream began as far back as the middle 1980s, its most important and impressive gains came in the late nineties. In particular, 1998 proved to be a great year in hip hop. It was the year that rap music's ongoing flirtation with the mainstream became real and undeniable for the players that really matter, the executives who run the major music groups. That year rap's certified numbers—units sold, multiplatinum status, and chart-topping performances—confirmed that the genre, long considered a cultural force, had become a major economic force, too.

Over the course of 1998 a total of eighteen albums occupied the top spot on the *Billboard* 200 list. Three of the albums belonged to sets by Garth Brooks. Two Celine Dion vehicles, a solo album and the monster soundtrack from *Titanic* that owed much of its success to the Canadian-born singer, also topped the charts. Six different rap artists—DMX, Master P, Beastie Boys, Snoop Dogg, Lauryn Hill, and Jay-Z—climbed to number one on the *Billboard* 200 that year. Insiders at *Billboard* referred to the top 200 chart as "the big chart." Among music industry insiders "the big chart" represents the most important and influential gauge of popular music tastes.

The first real sign that rap would have a breakout year occurred the last week in May. That week Garth Brooks saw his two-week run atop the *Billboard* 200 come to an end. Brooks was knocked off the top spot by a little known rapper from the New York suburbs, Yonkers, named DMX (Earl Simmons). Two weeks earlier Brooks's six-CD boxed set titled "The Limited Series" became only the second multi-CD set to debut in the number one spot. The man one *New York Times* reporter called "the Real King of Pop" had spent more time at number one on the big chart, forty-four weeks, than any other artist in the decade. His success bolstered Nashville's claim as America's music. But times were changing. That week DMX's debut album, *It's Dark and Hell Is Hot* (Def Jam/Mercury) sold more units than Brooks or anyone else in the nation. Because most music critics and industry observers had no idea who DMX was, they spent the next week scurrying around to acquire more information about the rapper. The following week DMX's label, Def Jam, took out a full-page ad in *Billboard* to celebrate the occasion. The ad featured a waist-high close-up of DMX, eyes closed, head tilted slightly upward in a prayerlike position and read:

DMX

TO LYOR, RUSSELL & THE ENTIRE DEF JAM STAFF

ONE WORD—PLATINUM!

THANKS

AND NOW THE WHOLE WORLD IS SINGING THE RUFF
RYDERS ANTHEM!

The ad exuded an air of confidence that called attention to rap's rapidly rising status in the music industry. Perhaps more important the ad served notice that the movers and shakers in the rap game were for real and that hip hop was a formidable player in the high stakes world of commercial music. Overcoming Brooks, by now a crossover and country megastar, was no small matter. Since the introduction of SoundScan in 1991, country music, and Brooks in particular, had become one of the music industry's biggest triumphs. In 1998 country, according to the Record Industry Association of America, held a market share of 14.4 percent. Though the share was down from an all-time high of nearly 19 percent in 1993, it was still a strong showing.

Buoyed by its steadily rising market share, rap, a genre long vilified as "street music," found itself poised to challenge Nashville's claim as America's most popular music. Def Jam's ad, as time would soon reveal, was right. Over the next six months, and in the ensuing years, hip hop's steady charge toward the mainstream turned into an all-out assault as a worldwide audience tuned in to rap as never before.

• • •

Three weeks later, in its June 20 issue, *Billboard* reported that Master P's album *Da Last Don* sold 495,000 units in its first week. That was a bigger debut than any other record in the U.S. that year. According to *Billboard*, in its 1998 end-of-the-year pronouncement regarding the music industry's highs and lows, "Not only are these artists selling to their street base in the first week; they're appealing to a much broader audience than ever before." Master P, the New Orleans–based head of No Limit Records, came out of nowhere to become one of the industry's biggest stories in 1998. P's No Limit Records captured the big bass, bouncy beats, and raucous rhymes that fueled the creation of a number of recording studios and production houses across states as varied as Louisiana, Texas, Georgia, and Florida.

Born Percy Miller, Master P grew up in the Calliope projects on New Orleans's South side in the 1970s. As a youngster he had shared the oftentimes fruitless hoop dream that grabbed the hearts and minds of so many poor black boys. When he and his wife, Sonya Miller, received a $10,000 check as part of a family settlement involving the death of his grandfather, they pondered their future. After careful deliberation they decided to open a record store. While selling kids rap music that most of the major music retailers did not stock, they stumbled upon a niche and discovered an opportunity. Percy began recording songs he sensed could sell well throughout the South. He spent a thousand dollars to produce the album *The Ghetto's Tryin' to Kill Me* and then journeyed across Louisiana, Texas, and other parts of the South selling that first recording out of his car. Amazingly, he sold 100,000 copies. Like a number of upstart rappers, Master P had to rely on his own instinct, talent, and energy to establish his product and his dream.

His career in the music business turned more intriguing when Dave Weiner, West Coast sales manager for Priority Records, saw him selling records out of the trunk of his car. Priority monitored Master P's success and made him an offer. Here, finally, was what any small record producer dreamed of: a deal with a company that could market your product and get it into retail. But Master P wanted something more. As he weighed Priority's offer, Master P studied the plight of other rappers, looking below the glamorous image typically portrayed in songs and music videos: "I looked at the way these guys live. I did some research. These guys sell all these records, but none of them really owned houses or anything. I figured, One day, I'm gonna change the game. I'm just gonna start off small."

Rather than settle for the typical boutique deal that would have given Priority the upper hand in the partnership, Master P, along with his lawyers, negotiated a unique arrangement. Priority's Weiner explains, "We took no equity in his company, took none of his publishing; it was strictly a distribution-only deal." Though it did not get an immediate infusion of cash, No Limit maintained control of its product and, just as important, its vision. In his 1999 feature of Master P for *Fortune* Roy Johnson Jr. wrote: "Unlike other artists, who earn only royalties on their record sales, Master P's No Limit retains eighty-five cents on each dollar generated. Priority gets the other fifteen cents plus marketing expenses. More important, No Limit owns the masters to his music." No Limit produced twenty-three albums in 1998; fifteen went either gold or platinum, with sales reaching $200 million.

Master P's success that year delivered a sharp message about the changing state of the rap game. In an industry that takes great pride in "keeping it street," the down- home, rowdy image that Master P's No Limit label cooked up played well, struck it big, and established the "Dirty South" as a vital region in hip hop. After observing the success of No Limit as well as Atlanta's LaFace Records, which featured acts like Goodie Mob and Outkast, Def Jam—a perennial power in the rap music industry—and even Sean P. Diddy Combs set up shop in the South, looking to move in on the region's untapped talent and lucrative market. The focus on the South not only signaled the region's rise, it also symbolized the movement's spreading influence, multiple accents, and continuing fragmentation.

Master P's assault on the big chart came at the midway point of the year and signaled to *Billboard* that the state of American popular music was in the midst of a historic shift. Geoff Mayfield, a senior writer at *Billboard*, wrote: "A closer look at the numbers suggests that the genre has played a bigger role in the first half of this year than it did in the first six months of '97." Mayfield went on to report that in the first half of 1997 eight rap albums had debuted in the big chart's top ten. By comparison, seventeen rap titles debuted in the top ten in 1998. While a majority of the rap albums that reached the top spot spent about one week in that position, the sustained presence of the genre in the top ten throughout the year made a much more comprehensive statement about the music's popularity. Rap, along with film soundtracks, took home the honors in 1998 as the genre that collected the most weeks at number one. While rap occupied fifteen weeks in the top spot, motion picture soundtracks held on to the top spot for sixteen weeks. The soundtrack to the blockbuster movie *Titanic* occupied the number one position for an incredible fifteen weeks. Nevertheless, once you accounted for the *Titanic* soundtrack, rap, in terms of chart-topping performance, was by far the most dominant genre of the year.

When DMX knocked Brooks from atop the *Billboard* 200 in May his label, Def Jam, simply declared, "The streets have spoken." But more than the streets had spoken. In reality, it was more like the streets, the suburbs, and the entire world had spoken and what they had to say reverberated throughout the pop culture landscape. Still, despite all the noise rap music made in the first half of 1998, the hip-hop movement would have much more to say over the course of the next six months.

• • •

Hip hop's widening sphere of influence reached far beyond the music industry. In September 1999 *Advertising Age* listed its "21 Brands To Watch In The 21st Century." Listed alongside power brands like MicroSoft, General Electric, AT&T, and Wal-Mart was FUBU, a seven-year-old urban fashion-apparel label. Noting FUBU's appeal with white, suburban teens, *Advertising Age* wrote, "As hip-hop roars as a social force, FUBU is poised to become its first mainstream brand." A year earlier FUBU's revenues more than doubled what the company generated in 1997, reaching well beyond $200 million. FUBU had recently exploded onto the scene after becoming the first African American design house to gain a window display at Macy's famous New York store. At a time when "branding" has become the name of the game among advertising and marketing gurus, the street-savvy handling of the FUBU brand attracted considerable media attention and admiration in 1998.

FUBU's rise to prominence was a real life rags-to-riches tale. One day in 1992 Daymond John and Carl Brown were shopping in Manhattan for a tie-top hat, a popular accessory piece worn by young black men. After an exhaustive search in Manhattan, they eventually found the style they were looking for. Both men were shocked by the $20 price tag for what they knew was a simple knit job. Daymond thought, "For $20, I could make 20 of these a day." Soon, he was doing just that.

At the time Daymond worked as a Red Lobster waiter. "I would get up at 8, go buy fabrics, make some hats until 2 p.m., call stores or go try and sell them until 4 or 5 o'clock, go to work the dinner shift, get home about 12 and make hats until around 5 in the morning," he said. Daymond and Carl partnered up with two neighborhood friends, J. Alexander Martin and Keith Perrin. They began making and selling hats at concerts, dance clubs, anywhere they could find style-conscious young black men. One day they made $800 selling hats near a mall in Queens.

Next, they expanded their homemade operation by making T-shirts, rugby jerseys, and baseball caps. When the orders began to come at a rate that required their full-time attention, they had to make a decision: turn the after-hours gig into something real or give it up. Daymond had always wanted his own company, so the idea of surrendering his dream was never a real option. Realizing they had far more to gain than to lose, the other three men decided to jump onboard. And so it was that Team FUBU, as the four men began calling themselves, came together to start their own design house.

Daymond's mom, an American Airlines employee, let them set up shop in the basement of her home in Hollis, a working-class neighborhood in Queens. Later, she allowed her son to take out a $100,000 mortgage on the home to provide start-up funds. With sewing machines stationed throughout the house, they hired friends and acquaintances to help them keep up with a rising workload. One day in the middle of cutting, sewing, brainstorming, and dreaming out loud, they began to think about a company name. According to Daymond, the group "wanted to come up with an acronym meaning something. It had to be a name, a name that you hadn't heard before, but a name that you would definitely remember. You didn't know if it was Italian or Japanese or American. So that's how we came up with the name."

They agreed on FUBU, which was short for "For Us, By Us." The name symbolized hip hop's commitment to its urban origins and cultural roots. As the company's visibility grew and its customer base expanded well beyond young, black men, the name posed a slight dilemma for Team FUBU. Like the movement, in general, FUBU faced the problem of balancing its fidelity to urban street culture with carefully managing its appeal to suburban white youths.

Team FUBU was smart, industrious, and passionate. Each member possessed particular sets of skills, which as a whole drove the brand toward great growth. Daymond was widely regarded as the leader and visionary figure of the group. Carl directed his talents toward expanding the FUBU brand beyond retail, scouting out opportunities in the entertainment media. J. Alexander, a former Navy radioman in the Gulf War, had gone to design school at New York's Fashion Institute of Technology and developed a finely tuned antenna for fashion trends. Keith Perrin was savvy in the ways of product placement and business management. Despite their varied talents, education, and retail experience there were no real opportunities for young, lower-middle-class blacks in an industry overwhelmingly dominated by whites. But like many entrepreneurs from their generation, they strongly believed that hip hop's economic potential should be mined by young people like them, who had a connection to the everyday rhythms of the culture. This fact, Team FUBU believed, gave them the kind of psychographic insight into their market that advertisers and the big design houses like Ralph Lauren, Tommy Hilfiger, and Calvin Klein did not possess. They were so confident about their understanding of hip-hop tastes, sensibilities, and style trends that they did their own advertising rather than hire an established shop. According to Daymond, Team FUBU was "the consumer making for the consumer."

The rise of hip hop–influenced design houses began in 1989 when a few black designers began making clothing that captured the modish flourishes and bold attitudes present in rap music. Inspired by hip hop's sense of big style and do-it-yourself attitude, young designers like Carl Jones, T. J. Walker, and Carl Williams laid the foundation for what is now known in the men's apparel market as "urban sportswear." When Cross Colours, the first full-fledged African American–run hip-hop design house, failed after its distributor went bankrupt, Williams established Karl Kani. The boutique label set a new standard for young, black-owned design houses. Williams recalls: "At first, we [blacks] were just used as models. We didn't have our own stores, [were] not in major stores, and didn't even have our own companies. It was my vision to see the business blossom like this. . . . The growth has been, and will continue to be, phenomenal." Between 1992 and 1998 the urban sportswear industry skyrocketed, growing into a multibillion-dollar industry.

When FUBU began in 1992, it had neither the money nor the connections to place its product in key retail sites. But that did not stop the urban apparel label from making noise. The company's first big break came in 1995 when, desperate for money, Team FUBU placed an ad in the *New York Times* that simply read: "Million Dollars in

Orders. Need Finances." Although several companies responded to the ad, the group decided that Samsung America, one of the world's largest distributors, could best boost their profile and money-making potential by getting them into retail stores. The distribution deal with Samsung gave the design house financial strength as well as an aura of legitimacy.

FUBU's next big break came two years later in 1997. That year the Gap was engineering its own re-branding campaign as company executives looked to establish a younger, more hip lifestyle image. One of the company's spots featured LL Cool J, one of hip hop's most enduring personalities. Like the members of Team FUBU, he grew up in Hollis, Queens. Predictably, LL wore a Gap T-shirt and jeans for the spot. But he also wore a brightly colored baseball cap with an unfamiliar logo. The logo, it turns out, belonged to FUBU. Midway through the lightning-quick rhyme he performs in the thirty-second spot LL dropped the line, "For us, by us, on the down low." Unbeknownst to Gap and the hip hop–impaired, LL was promoting FUBU even as he appeared in an ad for Gap. The move was classic hip hop: slick, bold, and traced with the guerrilla instinct that made hip hop so appealing to youth.

Within a year of the spot the FUBU brand, once unfamiliar enough to sneak in a national ad campaign, was visible in malls across America and upscale FUBU retail stores throughout Europe and Asia. Hip hop's regular presence on MTV and BET, its frequent use in various ad campaigns, and near omnipresent status in the pages of pop music magazines provided the ultimate runway for publicizing the culture's sartorial splendor.

The impact of hip hop was, at once, obvious and obscure. Though hip-hop brands like FUBU were making a loud statement about youth's style trends, something far more subtle was also happening: Hip hop was redefining America's racial vocabulary and cultural landscape. This was detectable in the way hip hop transformed the meaning of *urban* in America's cultural imagination. Whereas *urban* once meant poor, marginal, and untouchable, under the sway of hip hop, it also symbolized what the commercial marketplace construed as vital, hip, and desirable; in short, many of the things that marketing specialists spend millions of dollars to have associated with the brands they promote.

Young hip hoppers from some of the poorest and richest places in the world had at least one thing in common: the identities they took great pride in were clad, quite literally, by the creative inspirations that fashioned hip hop's body and soul.

• • •

Meanwhile, as the hip-hop economy continued to grow, rap's popularity only intensified during the second half of 1998. In the first week of August five rap albums, each backed by a major label, made their debut. Writing about rap's accomplishments that week, Datu Faison, a *Billboard* rhythm and blues editor, noted that he could remember a time when releases by big-name rappers were "few and far between, like treats for a nation of starving consumers. Now, years later, five highly touted rap albums are all hitting retail during the same week." Just as impressive, of the nineteen albums that debuted on *Billboard* that week the rap titles were among *Billboard*'s nine highest debuts. Starting with the Beastie Boys on August 1 and ending with Snoop Dogg on August 29, a rap album held on to the nation's top spot for five consecutive weeks. Equally extraordinary, according to *Billboard*'s August 8 chart, an unprecedented ten of the nation's top twenty albums were rap.

One of the most eagerly anticipated albums in 1998 was Lauryn Hill's debut as a solo artist from the Columbia imprint Ruffhouse Records. Even before the release of her album, Hill had earned a reputation as a smart and supremely talented artist who, despite a fierce and savvy flow, evoked an earlier and more socially conscious era in soul music and R&B. Prominent in her solo album was the mixture and unparalleled mastery of intelligent hip-hop lyrics, soul-soothing ballads, foot-stomping R&B, and radio friendly grooves. The album was a remarkable display of her range as a songwriter, co-producer, artist, and entertainer. Despite all the pre-release excitement, no one was prepared for the kind of success the album would achieve.

*The Miseducation of Lauryn Hill* hit the streets the first week in September and immediately claimed the top spots on both the *Billboard* 200 and Top R&B Albums. The first-week sales were off the charts and the 422,500 units sold set a record for a female solo artist. For four straight weeks the album dominated the charts and established Hill, despite her own reluctance, as a pop superstar.

Hill's spectacular solo debut was a breath of fresh air for the music genre, rap, and the cultural movement, hip hop, both growing stale even during or perhaps because of their commercial triumphs. That she was a woman made her accomplishments in a genre dominated by men all the more significant. One of the dominant tendencies in hip hop's rise was a hypermasculine style and exterior that provided little, if any, room for women who were strong, independent, and competent producers or performers. By 1998 few women dotted rap's corporate landscape.

Back in the day, the male-dominated industry had its share of female MCs as names like Roxanne Shante, MC Lyte, Salt-N-Pepa, and Queen Latifah were notable fixtures in hip hop. As the music and the formulas that shape rap harden, female MCs are fading from the bright lights that promote the game's biggest names. Hill stands out in sharp contrast, breaking through the strict gender barriers that often restrict the female body and voice to the male sexual fantasies that pervade the world of hip hop. Significantly, Hill does not shy away from female sexual power and pleasure; she simply does not make such issues the only attributes in her appeal and self-presentation. Her strong lyrics, beautifully arranged compositions, and inspiring lessons about relationships, self-pride, and community break the mold in an industry that typically requires women to accentuate their sexual selves rather than their musical selves.

Because *The Miseducation* cut across several genres—including rap, R&B, reggae, soul, and pop—some of her detractors question if it is hip hop. Hill shines as a brilliant symbol of hip hop's phenomenal evolution and musical maturation. In addition to her groundbreaking recordings with the Fugees, the rap-inflected tracks on *Miseducation* place her solidly within—and even expand—hip hop's ever-widening aesthetic.

As 1998 entered its final three months, hip hop's takeover of the mainstream continued virtually unabated. On October 17, four of the six new albums that debuted in the top ten were rap sets. The top three albums in the country were new hip-hop releases, Jay-Z's *Volume 2 . . . Hard Knock Life*, Atlanta-based Outkast's, *Aquemini*, and *The Love Movement* by one of hip hop's most appreciated groups, A Tribe Called Quest. Half of the albums in the top ten that week were rap. In his weekly assessment of the numbers game in the music biz, Mayfield wrote in the October 24 issue of *Billboard:* "For the second week in a row, hip hop owns the top three slots on the *Billboard* 200." If you included Hill's *Miseducation*, the four biggest albums in the nation for two consecutive weeks in October were hip-hop releases.

Mayfield, like several of his colleagues at *Billboard*, was a highly sought after expert for the many reporters seeking to get an angle on music industry trends and forecasts. Despite rap's consistent success on the charts in 1998, many reporters could not believe the tide change that suggested America's music tastes had shifted. In a move that was designed to deliver the message as clearly as possible, Mayfield went on to write in his column that week: "If you're one of the many people (mostly reporters from the consumer press) who have asked me over the last five years whether rap is on the verge of a fade, wake up and smell the coffee . . . rap is here to stay."

Jay-Z's takeover of the big chart was a significant and even historic move. For five straight weeks *Volume 2 . . . Hard Knock Life* was the number-one-selling album in the nation. Since *Billboard* had modernized its charting system in 1991, only four rap albums had held down the top spot on the big chart for four weeks. The only other album to hold down the top spot longer than Jay-Z in 1998 was the soundtrack to *Titanic*. Prior to his success in October, Jay-Z had never spent more than one week on the *Billboard* Top Ten. It was, as Mayfield wrote, "a world gone mad."

•••

The life and times of Jay-Z reveal much about the rise of the hip-hop nation in the late 1990s. Born Shawn Corey Carter in December of 1969 Jay-Z came of age in the rough-and-tumble world of the Marcy projects in Brooklyn. The last of four kids Jay-Z grew up shy according to his mother, Gloria Carter. Though he brought her very little pain at birth, Shawn would manage to bring her considerable pain and anxiety later as a teen. He grew up admiring the swagger and style of local street hustlers. Despite a sharp mind, he opted for the lessons offered by the streets instead of school. His baptism into the merciless waters of street hustling came as the crack cocaine economy hit poor ghetto communities hard, making an already bad situation even worse.

"Back then," Jay-Z remembers, "I would say it was, like, two things. It was either you're doin' it or you was movin' it." He chose to move it. But even as he labored in America's underground economy Jay-Z also mapped out rhymes, songs, and even concepts for albums. His ideas capture the tensions and the texture of the troubled world he was immersed in.

When it came time to record his first album Jay-Z, like all artists, had to figure out what he wanted to say to the world. On his debut album *Reasonable Doubt* (1996, Roc-A-Fella Records/Priority), Jay-Z tapped into the street experiences he knew so well. To the outside world his rhymes about living and dealing in the streets might easily mark him as yet another studio gangsta seeking cheap thrills. But he approaches the rap game with a style that, in many respects, is notably refined.

Whereas most hard core rappers strive for excess—excess violence, glamour, and sex—Jay-Z's understated but self-confident style and intricate rhymes, in his words, "kept it realer." What separates him from other hard core rappers is his attention to narrative detail. Though not as shocking as his hard core rivals', Jay-Z's rhymes are harder hitting, more believable, and, as a result, much more powerful. His rhymes probe the psyche, pleasures, and paranoia of the street hustler, and he composes lyrical vistas that champion the "good life," even as he carefully portrays the grim realities of a life he vows never to forget. In his best rhymes Jay-Z combines intricate life stories with a delivery that is precise and perceptive. Listen to him at his best, and you not only believe him but feel as though you are there with him. The lyrics he crafted are confessional, clear, and clever earning him a reputation as a top-notch ghetto chronicler.

The introspective rhymes he arranged add an important dimension to the "bad man" figure that has a rich and enduring legacy in African American culture. Historically, the figure has stood out by standing up against racial oppression. From Stagger Lee to Bigger Thomas, Jack Johnson to Muhammad Ali, blaxploitation to ghetto action films, blues to hard core rap, the bad man figure has raised more than a little hell in the black popular imagination.

His willingness to reach for the subtle and the sublime also explain why Jay-Z found inspiration from such an improbable source as the Broadway musical *Annie*. The story, based on an orphan girl in Depression-era America and her struggle to maintain her dignity while searching for a brighter tomorrow and the parents that gave her up, struck a chord with Jay-Z. When he heard DJ Kid Capri on tour playing a song from *Annie* Jay-Z decided he had to have it. He even watched the movie and afterwards found himself mesmerized by the small band of rag-tags. "[I]n the chorus they're not singin' 'It's a hard-knock life' and cryin' about it," he explains. "They're singin' like they're rejoicin'. Like they too strong to let it bring them down. That's why I call that the ghetto anthem." The sample from his hit single, "Hard Knock Life (Ghetto Anthem)," as well as the title from his breakthrough album, *Volume 2 ... Hard Knock,* bore the marks of the little redhead moppet.

The release of *Volume 2 ... Hard Knock* revealed a savvy blueprint that would transform Jay-Z from an agile and respected MC to hip-hop wunderkind and one of the most prolific and successful recording artists of his generation. While a track like "Hard Knock Life (Ghetto Anthem)" was designed to gain him the wide radio and video airplay necessary to achieve crossover celebrity, other less publicized and less radio-friendly songs maintained the ghetto-strident tone that spoke to his hard core base. Whereas the party anthems dropped hits, the more introspective musings dropped keen insight about race, poverty, and the view of the world from the other side. Jay-Z, as much as any of his contemporaries, mastered this strategy and effectively balanced the seemingly incompatible demands of pop celebrity and street credibility.

Along with his partners, Damon Dash and Kareem "Biggs" Burke, Jay-Z leveraged their historic success in 1998 into a diverse lifestyle brand. Between 1999 and 2003 they built a lucrative urban sportswear label, Rocawear, a film and video production outfit, Roc Films, and an elite sports bar, The 40/40 Club (hip hop's version of a theme park), while also becoming a distributor of Armadale, a premium vodka. The success they enjoyed parlaying their street-savvy ways into a mini-conglomerate operation was yet another example of how hip hop had become, at least for the elite creative class of artists, entrepreneurs, and executives it gave rise to, a fast-moving elevator up the social and economic ladder. It showed how hip hop, when virtually nothing else could, provided opportunities for young people stranded in America's ghettos to translate their entrepreneurial skills into vibrant economic opportunities.

The Roc-A-Fella brand was an obvious nod to the wealth and privileged status of the Rockefeller financial dynasty. In the end, it was as much an expression of resilience as it was opulence. The making of the Roc-A-Fella juggernaut represents in brilliant fashion, what historian Robin D. G. Kelley persuasively argues is the greatest contradiction in hip hop's rise: how capitalism has become black youth's greatest friend and greatest foe. Shawn Carter, the young Marcy projects' resident, had three pair of pants growing up; Jay-Z, the hip-hop celebrity and mogul, owned a clothing line that earned more than $200 million a year. Capitalism had a hand in both.

When Roc-A-Fella released Jay-Z's *Black Album* in 2003, the six foot two rapper stood tall as a full-size celebrity. As he made the rounds promoting the album, he talked at great length about why he was retiring as a solo artist and about the state of the rap music industry. After ten consecutive platinum-plus studio-recorded albums, he believed he had said and done it all in rap. As he looked out over the hip-hop landscape, a world that bore his imprint, Jay-Z felt a sense of honor and humility. In 2003, Jay-Z, Outkast, 50 Cent, and Eminem led a Grammy nomination charge that signaled rap's ascendancy in 1998 was no fluke, that indeed a real power shift in the music industry occurred that year. But he also wondered out loud about the young lions coming up in the rap game.

Though hummable dance club anthems like "Can I Get A" and "Big Pimpin" celebrated the hedonistic pleasures of sex, wealth, and patriarchy, Jay-Z believed he also strove for balance and artistry. "People always say [my music] is about one thing or about bling-bling, but since my first album I've always [given] you the good side—the high life, because that was real for me—but also [given] you the tracks that come with that life. For every 'Ain't No Nigga' there was a 'D'Evils' on the album. There was a 'Can I Live' for every 'Can't Knock the Hustle.' For every party song, there's always that balance." But now he feared that with so much money at stake up-and-coming artists were only interested in the party anthems and "thug life" records that produced most of the lucrative radio and dance club hits in rap music. In this environment there was little interest in the dramatic, story-driven rhymes Jay-Z produced throughout his run.

At the height of his popularity in 2003 and just as R&B princess

Beyonce Knowles's career as a solo artist was set for takeoff, Jay-Z did a feature rap on her breakout single, "Crazy in Love." Midway in the rhyme he slipped in a bit of history about how ever since his platinum hits, rap has changed the business of pop. Only a few people likely realized that Jay-Z was speaking about 1998, the year rap made its greatest surge. But after the "great year in hip hop" the rap game, too, would never be the same.

• • •

Even as rap music was breaking through the barriers maintained by the music mainstream one final barrier remained: the black music establishment. Since the late 1950s rhythm and blues had been the heart and soul of black popular music. Over the course of that period, radio programmers, industry executives, successive generations of artists, the music press, and a legion of fans became part of an elaborate machine. The R&B dynasty produced professional comfort and a small fortune for some, an evolving stable of stars for others, and considerable pleasure for generations of music lovers. But the world of R&B extended well beyond music. As Nelson George, author of *The Death of Rhythm and Blues,* writes: "R&B—and music in general—have been an integral part of a black community forged by common political, economic, and geographic conditions." The arrival of hip hop not only threatened R&B music and the world it created, it also questioned for the first time in roughly four decades who and what kinds of sensibilities would define the most important cultural industry in black America: popular music.

From the very beginning key sectors of the black music establishment shunned hip hop and the music it produced. The reaction in the late 1980s and early 1990s of urban contemporary radio is a clear example. It was not uncommon in the late 1980s to hear "no rap" promos on radio formats that appealed to black audiences. From the perspective of the executives who ran urban contemporary radio, R&B was still preferred in the early 1990s. The resistance to rap was

fueled by concerns that the music's youthful exuberance, street inclinations, embrace of ghetto authenticity, and complete disregard for
mainstream notions of respectability would alienate older and more
affluent black listeners and, thus, taint how advertisers perceived and
valued black stations. The cool attitude toward rap reflected the attempt to guard an urban radio institution that had spent the better
part of its career struggling to gain respect and favorable billings
from advertisers.

In 1998, when a damaging memo from the Katz Radio Group, a
New York–based company that sells national advertising for radio,
was leaked to the media it confirmed black radio programmers' worst
fears. In the memo, according to news reports, "sales representatives
were instructed to discourage corporations from placing commer-
cials on [black and Latino stations] by telling them that 'advertisers
should want prospects, not suspects.' " It was precisely that kind of
stigma and the punitive economic consequences it produced that
compelled many black stations to avoid rap music.

But other factors also influenced black radio's chilly response to
rap, namely, generational tensions. R&B represented tradition, stability, and business as usual while rap, the new cultural expression on
the block, represented innovation, change, and business as *unusual*.
In their resistance to rap the R&B vanguard moved to stem the onrushing tide of generational change. Their desire to do so was as much
about the politics as it was the music of black America. Despite the
resistance, a number of maverick DJs, program directors, and radio
entrepreneurs began to feature rap across America's radio airwaves.

In New York, Mr. Magic and DJ Red Alert were credited with establishing the genre's presence in the nation's largest media market.
In the early 1980s Mr. Magic hosted "Mr. Magic's Rap Attack" show
on Saturday nights from two to five in the morning on WHBI New
Jersey. By the mid-1980s two stations, KISS and WBLS, featured one
or two rap recordings every half hour. Even in New York, the cradle
of hip-hop music, program directors had to showcase the genre during the least lucrative day parts so as to avoid costing their station

adult listeners and ad revenue. The few stations that did play rap usually restricted it to late nights, mix shows, weekends, and the summer months.

By the late 1980s and early 1990s rap's presence across America's radio airwaves began to appear more sporadically. Alongside Mr. Magic came other radio mavericks who believed in the music and the constituency of listeners they knew existed. This free mix of DJs, entrepreneurs, and programmers dared to experiment with a heavier, less guarded rotation of rap music. In the 1980s KDAY Los Angeles began featuring local MCs paving the way for the West Coast explosion in rap. In 1991, WOWI Norfolk, Virginia, became the first station to play rap throughout the day. Steve Crumbley, the station's program director, used the format to drive adult listeners to a sister station. Recalling that decision, Crumbley says, "Everybody I knew—all the PDs—called me and said, 'This is not going to work.' But they all called back and said, 'You were right.'"

In 1992, WJPC-AM (950), the flagship station of the Robert Johnson publishing magnate, based in Chicago, became that city's first station to prominently feature rap. Shortly afterwards Houston's KYOK-AM began to play up rap. Though these stations occupied low-power AM frequencies, they helped to establish rap's early presence on radio. According to Sean Ross, vice president of Music and Programming for Edison Media Research, a leading entertainment media research company: "These stations forced everyone else to come on board—the audience already existed."

Urban contemporary radio's effort to preserve its way of life by keeping rap under wraps soon gave way to an irresistible force, widespread industry change. Throughout the 1990s the broadcast radio industry experienced a dizzying degree of change marked by acquisitions, mergers, and consolidation. The shifts led to greater market segmentation and format fragmentation. Many of the new formats were designed not only according to genre—pop, rock, R&B, country—but also by age of listeners. By the middle 1990s radio started to, in industry parlance, "superserve its audience" by developing formats, playlists, giveaways, morning shows, and advertising that catered to finely defined demographics. The black radio audience found itself split into a broad cluster of listeners. Thus what was once urban contemporary splintered into several different formats—R&B Adult Contemporary, Classic R&B, R&B/Hip Hop, and Hip Hop.

Rap's growing presence across America's radio airwaves can be attributed, in part, to good luck. The genre began to position itself as the voice and lifestyle choice of a new generation just as radio began developing formats specifically for young listeners. Many program directors and executives vying for the youth market turned to rap to draw young listeners and deliver advertisers a highly desirable demographic. From the middle nineties to the first few years of the new millennium, stations playing rap grew wildly. In the mid-1990s roughly six to eight stations around the country featured rap as a regular part of their playlist. However, by 2000 several markets—big, medium, and small—found themselves faced with as many as two and sometimes three rap stations. Dana Hall, the urban contemporary editor for *Radio & Records*, an industry trade publication, maintains that "in the top twenty to twenty-five markets what is usually referred to as urban or 'rhythmic radio' usually ranks among the top two or three formats in terms of audience share."

In 2004, according to Inside Radio, an industry data and information company, there were about one hundred seventy R&B stations in the country and roughly five hundred Top 40 formats. As Sean Ross explains: "[Rap] has certainly become the dominant music style on a contemporary R&B hits station and was, for a moment, becoming the most prominent music on Top 40 as well, although we've seen some signs of those program directors backing off (although not eliminating) hip hop." Some of the more notable stations went beyond playing the music, going so far as to develop a language, style, and station persona that embraced the culture's edge and irreverent worldview. "In the middle 1990s," Ross maintains, "WQHT (Hot 97)

New York became one of the first stations to devote itself to the hip-hop lifestyle as well as the music." In an effort to stay true to hip hop's street aura and in-your-face style, the boldest stations boasted that they played rap music, in their words, "all the damn time."

• • •

Slowly but surely the sonic shifts that were altering the sound of urban- and youth- oriented radio began to register on the black music charts. The retailers and record industry personnel that influenced the R&B *Billboard* charts, like the handlers of urban contemporary radio, resisted rap music. Though *Billboard*'s pop and country charts began using the "hard data" provided by SoundScan in 1991, it was a few years before the R&B charts fully adopted the more modern reporting methods. Until then, the indie rap labels had to deal with a revealing paradox.

Amazingly, even as rap music was climbing up the pop charts, the surge in popularity was not reflected on the R&B charts. Many indie labels understood that the discrepancy between the pop and R&B charts was, more than anything else, a result of the continued use of outdated sales-tracking practices that maintained a bias for R&B. Tommy Boy's Silverman explained it this way: "In the past, the major labels gave away refrigerators and microwaves to retailers in exchange for store reports. Now that's over on the pop side, but it still happens on the R-and-B side. We still have to play that game on the black singles chart." He continued, "I have to hire a guy for $1,000 a week plus giveaways of $5,000 of free product to the 140 stores that report to that chart, in order to get reported what I am actually selling."

Bryan Turner, the founder of Priority Records, expressed similar concerns when N.W.A., one of the indie rap label's hottest acts, found itself caught in the old guard's fight against the coming of rap music. "N.W.A. was #1 on the pop chart, but never went #1 on the black chart," Turner pointed out. "The same week it was #1 pop, it was #50 on the R&B chart. The black album chart is still [compiled] via subjective reporting from a certain number of retailers."

Labels like Tommy Boy and Priority Records experienced firsthand the uphill battle the rap industry faced against the R&B old guard. Though it was never publicly acknowledged, hip hop's battle against the black music establishment, for respect and recognition, was just as intense as the battle it waged against the music industry at large. In this case, though, the struggle revolved around what kinds of music, images, and sensibilities were most suitable for depicting modern black life. It was clear that R&B executives used their experience, networks, and relatively deep pockets—compared to the rap industry—to influence the charts that presumably reflected the musical tastes of black America. It is also likely that the retailers charged with the responsibility of reporting black music sales were unable and unwilling to acknowledge that a genre as notorious as rap was, in all likelihood, more popular than R&B. But as the charts slowly began to generate what industry executives interpreted as a more accurate reflection of black music sales, the rise of rap was all but assured.

When *Billboard* began using SoundScan data in the spring of 1991, traditional R&B style artists like the O'Jays, Teddy Pendergrass, Alexander O'Neal, and Whitney Houston ruled the black music charts. But the roaring tide of change, once held back, reached shore in 1998. That year the *Billboard* R&B charts began to reflect just how thorough rap's ascendancy in the world of pop music was. By the end of April the top ten R&B albums in the country were all rap. Equally impressive was that more than half of the chart, 53 percent, consisted of rap albums suggesting that the transition was, in all likelihood, long term. Of the twenty-three albums that topped the *Billboard* R&B charts in 1998, nineteen were rap albums and at least two others were heavily influenced by rap. As late as 1997 R&B still maintained a slight edge over rap in terms of market share, 11 percent to 10 percent. Three years later their respective market share showed a decisive flip-flop; rap posted a 13 percent share compared to 10 percent for R&B.

• • •

And so it was, after years of scrutiny, struggle, and its share of scandals rap music reached another milestone; according to *Billboard* in 1998 it officially became black America's music of choice. The takeover was in full force. For some the official recognition was late in coming. Grudgingly and despite years of repelling rap's charge, the old guard in black music had no choice but to give in to the shifting seas of cultural change. In the arena of music the changes meant that a new generation of artists, executives, and entrepreneurs would become the vanguard of a new era in the cultural industry that, more than any other, embodied black America's brilliance and blemishes.

The ascendancy of rap was also a harbinger of bigger things to come, namely the remaking of black American social and political life. Hip hop's dramatic influences in the musical world of black America were not nearly as pronounced in the worlds of black political or intellectual life. But change in those arenas and the kinds of struggles that were sure to ensue were not nearly as far off as they appeared in 1998. In fact, those changes were steadily making their way toward shore.

CHAPTER THREE

# *Fear of a White Planet*

*Rap forfeited whatever claim it may have had
to particularity by acquiring a mainstream white
audience whose taste increasingly determined the
nature of the form. What whites wanted was not
music, but black music, which as a result stopped
really being either.*

—DAVID SAMUELS

For much of its history hip hop has defied the racial and class boundaries that shape life in America. No figure symbolizes this fact more
than Eminem, rap music's first genuine white superstar. His meteoric
rise to celebrity was yet another indication of how the hip-hop movement was rewriting America's racial and cultural history. The social
changes wrought by hip hop were part of an all-important makeover
in youth and American pop culture that generated deafening debates
about the state of the movement and what it revealed about the state
of race in America.

No dispute about hip hop's racial significance was more ruthless
or revealing than the 2003 "beef" between *The Source* magazine's
Raymond "Benzino" Scott and Eminem. In a battle rap he recorded
that year titled "Die Another Day," Benzino compared Eminem to
David Duke and called him "a culture stealer." Not to be outdone,
Eminem fired back with his own "dis track" charging that Benzino
was a fake gangsta. The duel escalated in November when *The
Source*'s two chief executives, Benzino, listed on the magazine's mast-
head as Founder and Brand Manager, and Dave Mays, one of *The*

*Source*'s original founders, announced they had discovered old tapes of Eminem using racial slurs in a rap recording. Benzino and Mays planned to unveil the tapes at a press conference they hoped would send shockwaves throughout the worlds of hip hop and pop culture.

On the evening of November 17, a pack of curious reporters made their way to the Millennium Broadway Hotel in midtown Manhattan for what *The Source* described as one of the most important media listening sessions in hip hop's history. While the reporters knew that they would not be listening to a new recording artist or album, the buzz that evening was still intense. Once the gathered bodies settled down, Scott and Mays went on the offensive.

"Bringing this tape to the public," Mays stated, "is the latest chapter in *The Source* magazine's ongoing effort to expose influences corrupting hip hop, including racism." That evening Mays and Scott played pieces of two recordings that sounded like a free style or improvisational live rap. Both rhymes descended into an adolescent rant about good and bad girls that developed an ugly racial slant. In one of the songs a rapper identifying himself as Eminem and referring to the anatomy of black women quips, "I don't like that nigger-shit." The second recording and its references to good white chicks and dumb black chicks was just as crude.

Many of the reporters on hand for the press conference wrote afterwards that in addition to the racial and gender slurs that marred the recording, the production quality, described by one reporter as "a primitive drum machine," and amateurish rhymes were seriously defective. The tapes were newsworthy for one reason: *The Source*'s charge that the voice reporters heard was Eminem. In a statement released during the press conference *The Source* claimed: "The tape contains what is clearly identifiable as Eminem's voice, reciting racial slurs targeted against black women, and it proves Benzino right after a year of being vilified by the media for bringing such questions surrounding Eminem to the fore." Benzino and Mays colored Eminem as a racist interloper who embodied the corrosive forces that were undermining hip hop's integrity and social value.

Eminem was no stranger to controversy. The first two years of his march to superstardom were paved, in part, by assertions that he was a loathsome performer who spewed rapid fire hate-speech draped in wordsmith rhymes, with a twisted sense of humor, and elaborately crafted studio beats. Nevertheless, the legacy of racism in America combined with hip hop's intimate connection with black and Latino communities made *The Source*'s allegations against Eminem, rightly or wrongly, potentially far more damaging than the previous accusations of homophobia and misogyny. Both Mays and Scott understood this. Eminem did too. The evening of the press conference he released a statement admitting that it was his voice on the recording denigrating black women. Significantly, he did not claim the recording that included the use of the racial epithet. "The tape they played today was something I made out of anger, stupidity and frustration when I was a teenager," Eminem explained. "I'd just broken up with my girlfriend, who was African-American, and I reacted like the angry, stupid kid I was. I hope people will take it for the foolishness that it was, not for what somebody is trying to make it into today."

Eminem was fully aware of the precarious nature of his celebrity and the racial fault lines upon which it stood. Throughout his rise Eminem made it a point to show respect for black music, hip hop, and the history and people that produced both. In a 2000 interview with *Rolling Stone* Eminem was asked if he would use the word *nigger* on a record. His response demonstrated the fine line he knew he was walking. "That word is not even in my vocabulary," Eminem told the reporter. "[I] do black music, so out of respect, why would I put that word in my vocabulary." It was an interesting response given the fact that *nigga* has become such a common part of rap's everyday "keeping it real" vernacular. It indicated that—despite a tendency toward the contemptible—even Slim Shady, Eminem's wildly controversial alter ego, knew certain lines were not to be crossed. Eminem's unusually quick response to *The Source*'s charges confirmed their seriousness. Once again, the stakes in hip hop were high.

In the end, the personal animus between *The Source* and Eminem dramatized something that, in reality, was much bigger than the two principals. As their battle unfolded, it shed light on what arguably was the most important factor in hip hop's brief but stirring history: the steadily growing impact of whites in the movement. Eminem's ascendancy punctuated the extraordinary changes that created an enormous sense of anxiety within hip hop regarding the degree to which whites—white-controlled corporations and white consumers —had become the dominant force in the movement. It was a development, some feared, that threatened the very soul and survival of hip hop.

•••

Eminem's emergence in American pop culture came during a time of sweeping change in the music industry. By 1999, the year of his major label debut, the music industry began grappling with a cultural and technological upheaval that raised serious questions about its future economic health. According to the RIAA's 2002 year-end statistics, the number of CDs shipped between 2000 and 2001 dropped more than 6 percent. Between 2001 and 2002 the RIAA reported another decline, nearly 9 percent. The declining number of CDs amounted to just over one billion dollars in lost revenue. During the same period the industry also experienced the shutdown of thousands of retail stores and widespread layoffs. Several reasons combined to explain the industry's economic woes—consolidation, skyrocketing production and marketing costs, disposable music, big advances to superstar artists, stiff competition from new media such as video games and the personal computer, and music downloading.

In September of 2002, Hillary Rosen, then serving as chairperson and CEO of the Record Industry Association of America, told the U.S. House of Representatives Subcommittee on Internet and Intellectual Property, "It is estimated that more than 2.6 billion files are copied every month—and no creator, no property owner is compensated for these copies." According to Rosen, "Taking music on the

Internet is no different than taking it from a store." After a few years of denial, the music industry began to acknowledge that in the face of immense change it would have to reinvent its way of doing business. In the meantime, however, it needed to figure out a way to weather the digital storm. The rap music industry became an unlikely beacon of light posting huge sales numbers despite the sagging sales that troubled Rosen and her industry colleagues.

No figure loomed larger in the music business than Eminem. In 1999, his debut album, *The Slim Shady LP*, sold more than three and a half million units. Released fifteen months later his second album, *The Marshall Mathers LP*, sold more than 1.7 million units... in six days. After his breakout success Eminem used his newfound power and sway with young music buyers to negotiate the development of his own imprint, Shady Records. In 2002, his third album, and the first released under Shady Records, *The Eminem Show*, sold more than six and a half million units at a time when the industry was launching an all-out legal assault against music downloading. *The Eminem Show* was the biggest selling album of the year and established the "Real Slim Shady," a popular Eminem alias, as a real player in American pop culture.

Shady Records launched another mega-hit album, 50 Cent's *Get Rich or Die Tryin'* in February of 2003. When the album sold 872,000 its first week, based in part on 50's connection to Eminem, it pumped much-needed life into an industry that was suffering from anemic sales and disappointing headlines. In 2003 three of the four biggest opening-week sales totals in the music industry were Eminem-related projects. Eminem was leading a charge that saw rap music doing what few other genres were reliably doing in 2003: bringing young music buyers into the brick and mortar stores that were once the financial backbone of the business. In just four short years, Eminem was well on his way to selling more albums than any other rapper in history. It was an incredible run. In that short period of time, Eminem, as *Rolling Stone* reporter Anthony Bozza wrote, "had gone from white trash to white-hot."

• • •

In virtually every interview granted during the whirlwind of publicity that accompanied his major label debut in 1999, Eminem and his distributor, Interscope Records, moved with purpose and precision. During that first year, the most crucial period in the launch of a new musical career, the foundation for Eminem's superstardom had to be laid carefully. A key feature in the marketing strategy was the emphasis on his downtrodden past. Eminem's harsh upbringing fed a myth-making machine that culminated in multiplatinum sales, industry accolades, and a kind of visibility that supercedes most of the black MCs he is often compared to. From the very beginning the Eminem show, a vast marketing endeavor, was skillfully orchestrated to play up the rapper's beleaguered past in order to play down the one issue Eminem and Interscope feared most, his whiteness.

Eminem was born Marshall Bruce Mathers III on October 12, 1972, just outside of St. Louis to a teenage mother on welfare. His young life, despite the aristocratic-sounding name, was defined by one disappointment after another. That life became the cornerstone in the making and marketing of Eminem. Without fail, certain key (and occasionally fabricated) facts about his life appeared in every newspaper and major magazine around the country that profiled his major label debut. Eminem's personal demons became an open book as readers learned about his itinerant childhood; the blood feud with his mother, Debbie Mathers-Biggs; his decision to drop out of high school after failing ninth grade three times; how he came of age in a predominantly black Detroit housing project (not completely true); recollections of the schoolyard bullies and beat downs he endured as a kid; the strained relationship with his girlfriend, Kim Scott; the professed love for his daughter, Hailie Jade Mathers; and the degree to which he toiled in Detroit's underground hip-hop scene as a battle rapper. It was this past, so the publicity machine asserted, full of dysfunction and deprivation, which made his embrace of hip hop legitimate and compelling.

By selling Eminem's class and personal struggle, Interscope hoped to draw attention away from the more troubling questions regarding his status in hip hop as a racial outsider. Both Eminem and Interscope understood that his whiteness threatened to rob him of the most important credential in hip hop, street authenticity. When Benzino referred to Eminem as "Vanilla Ice 2003" it was a deliberate attack on the rapper's whiteness, a calculated attempt to reestablish hip hop's racial borders. In 1990 Vanilla Ice had the best-selling rap album ever up to that point. But when it was revealed that his much publicized hardscrabble background was a fabrication, it only confirmed what most suspected: white rappers had neither the skills nor the requisite perspective gained from life on society's margins to truly be down with hip hop. Not only was his credibility destroyed, his name and fame became the butt of jokes. Vanilla Ice, and by extension all white rappers, became a symbol of cultural theft, thus severely weakening their status in hip hop.

Like many white teenagers across the U.S. in the nineties, Mathers found himself drawn to the magnetic world of hip hop. If his itinerant childhood made it difficult to find a place to call his own at home or at school, rap music provided a refuge. But his move across America's racial tracks was not easy or always welcomed. He was a slight, unimposing white boy embracing what is vigorously touted as a black art form. In those early and harrowing years, he learned that being white and poor was a dreadful combination. Despite the large numbers of poor whites in America, their image barely dots our media culture or public consciousness. White poverty, unlike black poverty, violates the nation's myths about race and class and can produce a striking sense of shame. Years later the stain of Eminem's impoverished life would establish a deep sense of anger and provide ample ammunition to launch an avalanche of lyrical bombs that would gain him widespread notoriety and scrutiny.

As a kid growing up in and around Detroit there was no reason, other than perhaps desperation and youthful innocence, to believe that he actually had a future in a musical genre so closely associated with young African Americans. But Mathers's beleaguered background eventually served him well in a musical genre that derives much of its power from an outsider and outlaw status. By reaching into the depths of what he characterized as a miserable experience, he managed to establish a connection to hip hop's aggrieved spirit. Mathers found fuel to light his creative fire and, along the way, fashioned one of the most arresting personalities in American pop culture. Like the character he would play in the movie *8 Mile* years later, he wielded his pain and subordinated social status like a mighty sword, fighting off would-be attacks while also earning his hip-hop stripes as a casualty of America's preference for the privileged.

Eminem's emphasis on his demoralizing past and the anger he harbored toward society played well because these were also pivotal themes in hip hop. It was as if Eminem were saying to the hip-hop nation, "I too am young, poor, and despised." In short, "Look past my whiteness and you will see that I am one of you."

Deeply rooted in Eminem's appeal to the disadvantaged and the poor, irrespective of race or color, is a powerful message: that despite their real and perceived racial differences impoverished communities share important interests. In a nation long divided by race, the message is revolutionary at its core. It was, after all, the lethal combination of his whiteness and working-class situation that made Elvis Presley's momentary jaunt across the nation's racial boundaries such a latently dangerous act. The idea that poor whites and poor blacks might come together, in fun or in fury, remains radical. But racial boundaries have often divided the poor against each other thus helping, in the end, to sustain society's racial and economic distinctions. When those boundaries are violated, if only symbolically, so too are the powerful myths and power relations that sustain the status quo.

That a poor white high school dropout could find hope and inspiration from a musical genre so closely associated with ghetto youths is, without question, the most fascinating aspect of Eminem's spectacular rise. And yet, a substantial part of hip hop's currency is derived from the fact that dispossessed youth around the world have claimed it as theirs: their voice, their identity, and their opportunity to make a mark on a world that renders them useless and easily disposable. In the end, young Mathers's embrace of hip-hop culture was not that unusual. That he believed in hip hop is precisely its magic: the ability to connect so emphatically with the powerless and give them a voice—a sense of purpose and worth—even as the world sees little, if any, value in them.

•••

Eminem's superstar status brings to light hip hop's greatest paradox: the rise of young white consumers as the most lucrative and preferred market in the movement's expansive economy. The voracious appetite for rap by young whites fortified hip hop's status. And yet, white youth's embrace of hip hop also exacted a costly, albeit seldom acknowledged toll on the movement. Eminem, as his dispute with *The Source* clearly suggested, became a visible symbol of that toll and the struggle for hip hop. But white youth's fascination with rap and the debate that it sparked began long before a young white kid named Marshall Mathers mattered.

That Eminem and Interscope Records labored so hard to deal with his whiteness in hip hop was notable considering that white consumers drive the production and consumption of rap music. This particular fact became vividly clear on June 15, 1991. That day was a defining one in hip hop's history. Though no one knew it at the time, the reverberations that week also began paving the way for Eminem's breakthrough eight years later. To the surprise of nearly everyone watching the *Billboard* music charts that week, the top-selling album in the country was the N.W.A. (Niggaz With Attitude) gangsta rap album, *Efil4zaggiN* (Niggaz4life spelled backward). In just the fourth week of *Billboard*'s adoption of the SoundScan point-of-sales reporting system, the music industry and all of the conventional wisdom about it up to that point was slowly being turned on its head.

The week before, N.W.A. had entered the *Billboard* 200 as the second-best-selling album in the nation. It fell a mere two thousand units shy of Paula Abdul's album *Spellbound*. The group's debut position was the highest-charting entry by any album since Michael Jackson's *Bad* entered at number one in 1987. Even before it reached number one on *Billboard*, it was the highest-charting album on an independent label since the late 1970s. In his "Chart Beat" section of *Billboard* that week, Paul Grein wrote "N.W.A.'s solid but unspectacular track record didn't prepare us for this roof-raising debut." Bryan Turner, the founder of the label that distributed N.W.A., noted that three weeks after its release Priority Records had shipped close to 900,000 units. As he beamed with unmistakable glee, Turner admitted, "We're speechless. The euphoria of the chart position is one thing; the relative sales are another."

Despite or maybe because of the album's brutal lyrics and shocking imagery, the sales figures were astounding. The pace at which the album was moving units even led the vice president of Memphis-based distributor Select-O-Hits, Johnny Phillips, to assert: "Priority could be the lifesaver of the independents this summer." Dismissing the concerns about the album's foul content, Phillips added, "This is something we need. Any business is better than no business and this is real good business."

And while the group's unexpected success sent tremors throughout the music industry, no one was more surprised than N.W.A. Eazy-E, the group's founder, said, "We thought it was gonna be like Number Fifty." Another group member, MC Ren, concurred, "I thought it was gonna be a hundred and fifty, to tell you the truth."

N.W.A. was well aware that SoundScan had given them a commercial legitimacy and visibility that would have been virtually impossible to attain otherwise. "We're just thanking that new system," Eazy-E told *Rolling Stone* in 1991. Even though their debut album went double-platinum, it only peaked at thirty-seven on the *Billboard* Pop charts. N.W.A. knew that their actual record sales were never accurately reflected in their chart position. "We got fucked around on the last record," says Ren. "It should have been Top

Twenty at least. But it was all politics. If you wasn't on rotation on MTV, they wouldn't have nothing to do with your ass. Now it's all sales."

Even more telling than the white-hot sales numbers were who was buying the album, white suburban teenage males. As industry insiders began to sift through the SoundScan data, it was clear that N.W.A.'s album sales were propelled by one of the entertainment industry's most sought after demographics. A store manager from an affluent suburban California Tower Records store told *Time* magazine, "T.B.W.A.S. [teenage boys with attitude], that's who's buying N.W.A.'s album," exclaiming, "these boys are looking for something to relate to, to rebel with. They're rebels without a clue." Music chain retailers described *Efi14zaggiN* as a "monster," referring to its ferocious appeal.

N.W.A.'s top-charting position defied conventional wisdom. The brutal misogyny found in titles like "One Less Bitch" and "Findum, Fuckum & Flee" coupled with the vividly detailed but mostly fantasy-driven stories of life in America's ghetto streets assured that the album would be disregarded by radio. Whereas most platinum-selling albums are released with either a lead single, music video, or marketing campaign, *Efi14zaggiN* had none of those attributes. In fact, the album's success was based on word-of-mouth advertising, street-savvy marketing, and a voracious appetite for hard core rap that few people knew existed before that June.

N.W.A.'s rise atop the pop charts and appeal with white teens did not go unnoticed by a press that did nothing to conceal its dismay. The *New York Times* wrote that even though N.W.A. struck the pose of ghetto outlaws fighting against an oppressive system, "they're selling boxloads of records—many of them to thrill-seeking white teenagers—by reducing themselves to self-parody and playing up the stereotypes of rappers as sex-starved buffoons." Despite the claim that the group was simply reporting the grim realities of ghetto life their music was, as the *Times* pointed out, "a situation thick with irony but N.W.A. are probably too busy counting their earnings to care." *Time* magazine maintained that "*Efi14zaggin* is an entire open season for negative stereotyping," adding, "rappers like N.W.A. and Public Enemy want to scare the living hell out of white America—and sell it a whole mess of records—by making its worst racist nightmares come true."

A few years after N.W.A.'s success, Eazy-E reflected on hard core's mainstream breakthrough. "When N.W.A. was together we were talking directly to our homies on the street, in our language, about what was happening to us; and they were buying it," he said, referring to young whites. "But the big secret before SoundScan was there were some white kids picking up the records too. Now everybody knows the secret."

The unveiling of that secret left a profound mark on the selling of hip hop. After 1991, the year SoundScan was introduced, there was growing recognition that hip hop's market was much wider and whiter than previously understood. The revelation altered the very character of hip hop, or at least its commercial identity. For the first time in the movement's commercial history young white consumers, a crucial demographic in the cultural and economic mainstream, emerged as a primary consideration rather than an afterthought in the making and marketing of hip-hop-related merchandise.

After that June in 1991, corporate hip hop, though few would admit it, was manufactured first and foremost with young white consumers in mind.

• • •

The attraction of affluent white youths to hip hop's hard core ghetto narratives was one of the great cultural mysteries of the 1990s and a complete enigma to music insiders and observers. Several theories have endeavored to explain the inexplicable. Surprised by the huge sales numbers of *Efi14zaggiN* at some of his rock and heavy-metal stores, one vice president of a regional distributor said, "I guess it's because rap is the rebellious music of the 90's." The idea that whites enjoyed hip hop because it was a source of rebellion was a widely shared view though certainly not unique to the moment, or the music of hip hop. For decades pop music has been a clarion call to arms in young people's uprising against parental and adult authority. Still, the degree to which white youth immersed themselves in hip hop was different, both quantitatively (music, film, magazines, videos, apparel) and qualitatively (lifestyle, attitude, language). Other commentators argued that white youth's fascination with rap was a sign of waning racial hostilities, a closing of a once great and seemingly intractable racial divide. The fact that young whites were willing to welcome ghetto-derived narratives and images into their bedrooms, peer groups, and spaces of leisure—in a way that was simply unlikely a generation ago—highlighted, some contended, the erasure of longstanding racial repulsions.

But the reverse claim that white youth's fascination with hip hop did not reflect the declining significance of race but, rather, a more complex expression of racism was just as compelling and, in the end, more likely. Rap's crossover appeal represented a strange form of cultural tourism for many young whites. William "Upski" Wimsatt, a long-time admirer of ghetto youth culture, believes white youth gravitate to hip hop because it offers a way to vicariously experience the resilience of ghetto youth. White youth, he argues, "suspect they wouldn't make it through what inner-city blacks do, so there's an embedded admiration that's almost visceral." Hip hop was their fantasy island, a place to travel largely through the pleasures of consumption—rather than actual contact into a foreign world—where they could live out some of their wildest desires. Hard core rap's disdainful attitude and unabashed pursuit of pleasure allowed white youth to do what generations of whites have done for years: revel in the alleged den of black iniquity.

Whatever the reasons, the producers of rap music did not stop to dissect N.W.A.'s appeal among white consumers, they simply imitated the group's hard-core demeanor, profane lyrics, and woman-hating tendencies. Soon, other industries figured out ways to exploit hard core rap's commercial triumph. Throughout the remainder of the decade, America's silver screens, prime-time television line-up, music videos, radio airwaves, sports franchises, video games, and youth fashion trends would bear the marks of N.W.A.'s unflinching embrace of "ghetto realness." The world—or at least prominent parts of the pop culture landscape white youth inhabited—had become, of all things, a ghetto.

•••

As a youngster Eminem looked at N.W.A. with real reverence. The group's "rage against the machine" spoke a dialect he understood. Unlike the relatively privileged and middle-class white youths who found great pleasure and safe distance in their consumption of N.W.A.'s ghettocentric narratives, Mathers identified closely with their outcast status. In his mind N.W.A. spoke for people like him, who had been left to fend for themselves on society's margins. When Eminem met Dr. Dre, the architect behind the sonic mayhem and lethal lyrics that pulsated throughout N.W.A.'s hard-driving beats, he openly acknowledged his awe and appreciation for the hard-core trendsetter. "It was an honor to hear the words out of Dre's mouth that he liked my shit," Eminem acknowledged years later. "Growing up, I was one of the biggest fans of N.W.A., from putting on the sunglasses and looking in the mirror and lipsinking [sic] to wanting to be Dr. Dre, to be Ice Cube. This is the biggest hip-hop producer ever."

Eminem's single-minded quest to carve out his place in hip hop began by honing his lyrical skills in one of the culture's most fabled traditions: the battle. As far back as the pioneering days in the Bronx, battles between aspiring MCs, DJs, graffiti writers, and break dancers were how reputations, respect, and even rewards were earned. The rugged culture of battling produced a Darwinian-like world in hip hop, a place where only the "illest" survive. Part of Eminem's success can be attributed to the dues he paid in Detroit's hip-hop underground milieu, proving himself in clubs like the Palladium, Ebony Forum, and The Shelter.

For Eminem the battle rap competitions were more than an opportunity to display his skills as an MC. Just as important, it was an opportunity to earn hip hop's respect. His willingness to get down and dirty in hip hop's trenches established a connection to the culture that would later help blunt charges that he was simply a tourist out to exploit its commercial value. Eminem not only survived the rough-and-tumble world of battling, but also learned how to use the constant racial put-downs he faced as part of his own arsenal. Battling became a crucial, life-defining experience in his efforts to navigate the treacherous racial fault lines that run beneath hip hop's surface. In many of the interviews he conducted for 8 Mile he discussed the significance of battling. "I remember if I lost a battle, it would be like my entire world was crumbling," he told reporters. "A lot of people would say 'What's the big deal? Get over it. You lost, try again.' But I would feel like my whole life was over. It may look silly to a lot of people, but to a lot of us, it's our world."

Slowly, Eminem achieved a reputation as a formidable battle rapper. He spent pivotal years of his young life making the rounds in the underground circuit trying desperately as they say in the rap game, "to get on," that is, sign a recording contract and ride the successful wave that buoyed hip-hop music to great heights. Most people who heard him conceded that he had style and skills. Nonetheless, his desire to sign a major deal was undermined by one obvious obstacle: his whiteness. Becoming a respected and successful rapper was the only thing he really cared about in the world. Consistent with his lifelong string of bad luck Eminem's career aspiration may have been the only legitimate profession in America where being white was a liability. Despite the constant hustling, battling, and deal-shopping, he could not persuade a label with national-distribution clout to sign him.

His first album, *Infinite,* was produced in 1996 by Jeff and Mark Bass in their Oak Park, Michigan, basement studio that resembled a shack. The album was barely noticed and even provoked charges that Eminem was imitating black MCs. Reflecting on that first recording, Eminem says: "*Infinite* was me trying to figure out how I wanted my rap style to be, how I wanted to sound on the mic and present myself. It was a growing stage. I felt like *Infinite* was like a demo that just got pressed up."

The questioning of his skills and the failure of the album drove him into an even more intense state of rage and depression. His sense of rejection worsened. Desperate and fearing that his dreams were on the verge of slipping away, he created an alter ego, "Slim Shady." As Slim Shady he fired back at his critics with lyrics that were both clever minded and cold hearted. The character provided the creative spark and voice to fashion an identity that was bizarre and beguiling. The new identity separated him from virtually every other rapper and allowed him to play with various sides of his temperament, which included among other attributes, a demeanor that could be vicious and dark or humorous and colorful—but always entertaining.

Throughout the late 1990s Eminem continued to compete in rap contests bringing home several first-place prizes. *The Source*, his future nemesis, even recognized him in the magazine's "Unsigned Hype" column in March 1998. Despite all of this, he had no money or recording contract to show for his hard work and dedication. Struggling to pay his bills, he managed to scrape up enough money in 1997 to enter *Rap Sheet* magazine's annual freestyle rap competition in Los Angeles called the Rap Olympics. He wanted the prize money bad and also realized this may have been his last best chance to "get on." Though his skills were on fire that night, he ended up placing second. With no prize money or the chance to leverage a victory into a recording contract, he returned home not really sure what the future held. But then for one of the few times in his life, Eminem was struck with good luck.

A copy of his *Slim Shady LP* made its way into the hands of some of the key players from Interscope Records. It just so happened that

Interscope was home of one of rap music's most successful and re-spected producers, Dr. Dre. The various accounts explaining how Dr. Dre discovered the bleached-blond kid from Detroit have become part of the Eminem myth. In his biography of Eminem, Anthony Bozza asserts that assistants brought the demo to Interscope execu-tive Jimmy Iovine, who asked Dre to listen to it. Bozza quotes Dre saying, "I thought the tape was incredible," adding, "in my entire ca-reer in the music industry, I've never found anything from a demo tape." Initially, Dre did not even know Eminem was white, but once he discovered that he was, it likely only heightened his curiosity. Whereas the major labels feared that signing a white rapper would be rejected as a gimmick, Dr. Dre sensed an opportunity to make music history again. He had recently started his own label and was eager to try something different. Nothing could be more different than an outrageously badass white rapper from Detroit, who had a great flow and a greater sense of theater. Not even Hollywood, the ultimate fan-tasy factory, could have created a wackier idea.

• • •

Since his arrival on the pop culture stage in 1999, Eminem has been compared most often to one figure, Elvis Presley. As irresistible as the comparison is the parallels between the men who engineered their successful launch—Sam Phillips and Dr. Dre—are equally telling.

Phillips's story is one of the great ones in American pop music history. In the middle 1950s he was one of the few white men who was willing to record what was then derisively labeled "nigger music." Phillips believed that the beauty and emotional power of black pop-ular music would one day take the world by storm. But his enthusi-asm for the music was tempered by the racially segregated customs of his day. By law in the South and by custom in the North, blacks and whites lived in separate neighborhoods, attended separate schools, and even gravitated toward separate entertainment venues. So, when

Phillips heard a young white Memphis crooner named Elvis sing for the first time in his studio, the unthinkable had come true: a white singer who could ride the beat and sound like a black singer. Phillips understood the implications immediately. Here, he thought, was the perfect opportunity to carry the music he enjoyed to a larger and much more lucrative market, young white music buyers.

Dre's discovery of Eminem is reminiscent of the find Phillips made more than forty years earlier—but with several important twists. It was Dre, a black music producer, who recognized the opportunity to carry a black musical style to white consumers. Whereas Elvis's whiteness made rock 'n' roll palatable to whites, it was Dre's blackness that made Eminem believable to young white music buyers. Dre certainly recognized Eminem's rap skills, but he also recognized the lucrative opportunities that existed if the right sound, style, and image could be crafted. Based on his experiences with N.W.A. and Death Row, he knew that the big money in rap, despite the genre's intimacy with ghetto America, was in selling music to young whites. The hard knock realities of the music business had a sobering effect on Dre's views about rap, race, and commerce.

Earlier in his career, the thought of producing a white rapper would have seemed outrageous, even treasonous given the racial authenticity claims so pervasive in hip hop. But by the time he met Eminem, Dre was more than a little contemptuous of the music business and hip hop's racial assertions. Dre believed that he had been burned not once, but twice in the industry by shady types who used his creative talents to sell millions of records and then cheat him out of what he believed were his just desserts. That both of these instances involved black businessmen made it all the more painful and any claims of racial loyalty, from his vantage point, superficial.

Dre was the musical mastermind behind N.W.A., but he controlled neither the financial nor business affairs of the group. Those duties rested with fellow rapper Eazy-E (Eric Wright) and his business associate Jerry Heller. Over the course of a brief but bodacious career, N.W.A. sold millions of records and helped make hard core rap a lucrative entertainment franchise. The lessons Dre learned while with N.W.A. were, in all probability, the most important ones he would gain about life in the music business. What mattered in the end was not how good your music was but rather how well you were compensated for it.

After fleeing N.W.A., Dre teamed up with the notorious Marion "Suge" Knight to launch Death Row Records. Driven by Knight's heavy-arm tactics and Dre's musical wizardry, the first slate of albums released by Death Row went platinum or better, an unprecedented achievement. In an entertainment culture always looking for new faces, the label "broke" new talent like Snoop Doggy Dogg and a reinvented, thugged-out Tupac Shakur. Despite or maybe because of their dizzying success, the partnership between Knight and Dre soon began showing signs of stress. Dre wanted to expand his creative wings by experimenting with various musical styles and genres. But Knight insisted that the label maintain a strict focus on the ghetto-tough anthems that made it an instant hit factory. Knight took on anybody and everybody—the music industry, critics, politicians, black spokespersons, and perhaps most significantly, rival rap labels. The same attitude that propelled Death Row atop the music world eventually led to its demise.

Gangsta rap took the "keeping it real" mantra, so central in hip hop, to the extreme. At the height of the genre's appeal, record labels had even resorted to marketing the criminal background of rappers as a way to ensure "street cred." Eventually, the line between performing gangsta and living gangsta became blurred. Dre was in the rap game for the music and the money, but not for the mayhem that had become commonplace at Death Row. He believed the environment, at the label he helped build, was changing and no longer conducive either to his musical interests or, as time passed, his personal safety. As Knight, and others around him, plunged deeper into personal and professional chaos, Dre decided he wanted out.

In 1996 the producer extraordinaire told *Vibe* magazine that after some deep soul-searching he called up Iovine and told him, "I'm ready to bounce. Make me a deal, and I'll make you some hit records." Dre's track record as an industry rainmaker spoke for itself. The people at Interscope realized the potential benefits in maintaining their relationship with him. After all, they thought, Dre was among a small elite class of media producers who possessed the unique ability to package ghetto culture, now a golden goose, for mainstream consumption.

In the new deal Dre received his own label, Aftermath Entertainment. "Now I'ma be able to do whatever I wanna do," he told that same *Vibe* reporter. "If it works, it's on me. If it fails, it's on me. But I'm an innovator. I like trying things." Clearly confident about his place in the industry, he added, "I'm gonna make a lot of superstars. That's my business. I take people that have a talent, mold it, make it presentable to the public, put 'em out there, and have their back 110 percent."

Two short years later Dre's desire to try new things would bring him and an unknown white rapper from Detroit's underground scene together. From the beginning of their relationship several press accounts understood that Dre provided Eminem the cover and credibility he needed to thrive in hip hop. But virtually no one recognized that Dre also needed Eminem. His deal with Interscope was predicated on being able to continue producing the kind of hits that brought Death Row, Interscope, and hard core rap commercial success. Two years after launching his label Dre still had not produced a hit. Inevitably, talk began to surface that he was no longer relevant. In 1999 Dre acknowledged, "For the last couple of years, there's been a lot of talk out on the streets about whether or not I can still hold my own, whether or not I'm still good at producing."

Eminem, Dre realized, was a golden opportunity to reinvent himself once again and deliver on his promise to make hit records and superstars.

• • •

Around the same time that Dre and Eminem hunkered down in the studio to cut the tracks that would define the latter's commercial identity, MTV, one of the world's most prominent youth brands, was busy remaking its own identity. In 1998 MTV conducted a music study that focused on trendsetters. The network's ratings—as well as its status among young people—had slipped in recent years and now the executive brass was looking to revive the MTV mystique as a hip media franchise and lifestyle choice in the worlds of teens and young adults. MTV general manager Van Toffler, explained, "It had been quite a while since we had gone in-depth and went to our viewers' homes and said, 'What CDs are in heavy rotation in your home, and what else do you do?' Because the generational shifts are so tremendous... we wanted to be more in touch with what they're doing, especially around music."

The study produced some findings that informed MTV's own strategic planning and programming philosophy. According to Toffler, the study showed that young people "are yearning for an emotional connection" with their music. Further, he noted, there is "[m]ore of an interest in lyrics, in information around the artist, in the genesis of a song, and the album, and what went into making it." The study concluded that trendsetters "feel as if music today has no depth and no meaning" and "want music and musicians they can believe in, not prepackaged performances and vocal dummies. They feel the heart has fallen out of the music business, and they want it back."

It was this burning desire for music that was real rather than redundant, passionate and not pokerfaced, meaningful instead of meaningless that bolstered rap's appeal. Throughout the nineties the perception that rap was urgent, uncensored, and uncompromising made it a genre that youth found refreshing. It explained why MTV, by 1998, was featuring hip hop throughout its entire programming schedule. MTV's interpretation of the trendsetter profile also explained the network's emphatic embrace of Eminem within a year of the study. The rapper's in-your-face demeanor and shockingly personal lyrics certainly achieved what MTV believed its viewers were looking for in the modern pop star. Here was someone, in the study's words, who was "not fake, phony, and superficial." Through his songs and videos Eminem established the kind of emotional connection to young music lovers that, according to MTV's trendsetter study, had become an essential but mostly missing part of their music media experience.

MTV, in general, and the music video, in particular, were the perfect stage for Eminem's antics and his politics. Eminem's precarious racial presence in hip hop required an adroit handling of his image; music video was crucial in his bid for hip-hop authenticity. Ironically, music video was the place where Eminem, as much by necessity as by choice, took on his status as a racial outsider in hip hop.

• • •

Eminem's 1999 breakthrough video for his breakout single, "My Name Is," begins with him in self-deprecatory disguise. Throughout the video Eminem plays what is arguably his most distinguishing role—the great cultural prankster and provocateur. In the role he simultaneously laughs at himself, winks at his audience, and thumbs his nose at institutions of tradition and power. In the "My Name Is" video, Eminem plays with some of the most enduring images of whiteness in American culture: the overly moralistic and idealized family situation-comedies like *Leave It to Beaver* and *The Brady Bunch*, as well as figures of white masculine performance and power in the forms of Johnny Carson and Bill Clinton. Eminem's whiteness and, more specifically, the need to address it gives him a degree of artistic freedom that eludes his black counterparts.

Music video, a medium increasingly predicated on craft, story, image, and performance, provides an ideal venue to act out the outlandish personalities and politics Eminem weaves into the fabric of his music. Thus, Eminem can dress in drag, play a comic book superhero, fast food service worker, assume various aliases, or spoof other cultural icons (Clinton, Britney Spears, or Elvis Presley) with little or no fear of being labeled a counterfeit MC. The more politically robust aspects of his antics also shore up his reputation as a true rebel, willing and able to assault the power elite (Dick Cheney for one) and even find humor, when few others dared to, in America's post-9/11 obsession with Osama Bin Laden. It is all part of a larger arsenal that makes him both a villain and a victor in America's pop culture economy. The image he crafts in music video is both corny and cool, bombastic and believable, and allows him to carve out a distinct niche in hip hop and beyond.

In the end, Eminem is nothing if not the master of the art of disguise. His greatest act of concealment is the ability to mask his own whiteness and the potential threat it poses to hip hop. Significantly, Eminem does not ignore his whiteness or the legacy of white theft of black cultural art forms. He is savvy enough to know that neither hip hop's racial realities nor America's racial history will allow him to do that. Still, the manner in which he makes his whiteness an issue also makes it a nonissue. This is never more evident than in the climactic scene of the film *8 Mile*. In that final scene Eminem's character, Rabbit, defeats his rap rival by acknowledging his own whiteness, destitute class status, and other personal frailties. Doing so means that Rabbit's status in hip hop as a racial outsider cannot be attacked. He effectively takes away his opponent's mic and silences him.

Eminem's ability to make his whiteness both matter and not matter is a true Houdini act. Like the movement to which he gives added color and controversy, Eminem is nothing if not a constellation of contradictions. Music critic Kelefa Sanneh understands the complex manners and maneuvers that make Eminem a true sociological phenomenon. Sanneh writes: "Eminem is an extremist by inclination, but he also has a knack for triangulation, an ability to find a midpoint between seemingly contradictory impulses. His style is all hip-hop swagger and hard-rock self-loathing (can we call him the original angsta?)...." Eminem's music, flow, disguises, uproarious music video, and celebrity persona fall somewhere between a bizarre form of twenty-first-century blackface minstrelsy (he's acting black) and beguiling political commentary (he's debunking black myth). Perhaps more than anything, Eminem's rise atop the world of rap and pop music suggests that he navigates the very real and zealously guarded racial boundaries in hip hop with an aplomb that is second to none. And that makes the Eminem Show, like it or not, one of hip hop's most stirring spectacles.

•••

Eminem's ability to navigate hip hop's racial fault lines has not gone unnoticed by those in the movement. Though most of hip hop's elite are measured in their criticism of Eminem, the fact that a white performer is touted as the game's best rapper fuels a growing concern about the impact of whites on the movement. Even if the attempt to discredit Eminem by *The Source*'s Benzino and Mays does little to erode the rapper's popularity, their larger concern—the outside forces muscling in on hip hop—have more than a little merit. But this issue does not start or stop with Eminem.

Since the introduction of SoundScan in 1991, a new logic has dominated hip hop's corporate identity. Though the movement's creative and entrepreneurial elite will never admit it, their efforts since the early nineties have focused primarily on the young white consumers who make hip hop a lucrative culture industry. Eminem, like every other successful figure in hip hop, wants black kids' respect and white kids' money. "In the suburbs," Eminem told *Rolling Stone* in 2002, "the white kids have to see black people liking you or they won't like you." That is the peculiar logic of corporate hip hop. Even as the "keeping it real" mantra pays homage to hip hop's urban roots, the effort to "get paid" hones in on suburban spenders.

The focus on Eminem's whiteness is, in actual fact, an expressed anxiety about blackness—particularly the perception that black street culture is spreading into spheres of white domestic comfort, privilege, and consumer culture. As songs like "White America" and "Sing for the Moment" attest, Eminem is well aware that his affinity for hip hop likely expands an already substantial population of white youths who find themselves, for a dizzying set of reasons, identifying with black youth culture and style. The surging popularity of hip hop among young whites explains why Eminem matters in hip hop. But it also explains why he does not matter. Scholar and writer William Jelani Cobb maintains that "in the race to imbue Eminem with some enduring significance... the fact that he is not all that significant to hip hop has gone almost completely unnoticed." In other words, it does not matter if black kids—long considered hip hop's core—really like Eminem or not because their young white counterparts clearly do. In their own way, white youth, largely as consumers, have become just as important to hip hop as black or Latino youth.

Many hip-hop heads openly speculate about the growing influence of outside forces on the movement. Big media, with its control over corporate hip hop, shapes how most of the world views the movement. White youth, with their deep pockets, shape how most of the world consumes the movement. Take for example, the popularization of hard core rap music. It was whites, consumers and radio programmers, not black program directors who first embraced hard core rap for radio. Doing so pushed a style of rap music that left some in the movement uneasy about the proliferation of gangstas, playas, and pimps in hip-hop culture. In truth, white program directors are not constrained by the responsibility or the burden carried by black programmers. The latter have to contend with the legacy of racism and concerns within the black community about the black image.

Eventually, the popularity of hard core rap on pop radio and MTV forced black radio and even BET to adopt an aspect of hip hop that, deep down, left them feeling uneasy and in some instances even terrified. It is another example of how the struggle for hip hop is driven, in part, by forces that the movement does not control. In his assessment of corporate radio, and what it means for the movement, Chuck D, one of hip hop's biggest champions, lays it on the line. "I think corporate radio—I call it white-owned black radio—has no accountability to the neighborhoods it's programming for. Therefore they can get away with saying and doing anything. I believe it's the biggest cancer to black America, because it doesn't inform, it just sells product."

The forces that drive the selling and buying of that product heighten long-standing concerns about who and what control hip hop. The growing presence of big media and young thrill-seeking white consumers generates serious anxiety within the movement and intensifies the struggle to promote what its most devoted defenders find especially endearing and hopefully enduring about hip hop.

# CHAPTER FOUR

# The Digital Underground

*Technology will beat technology each and every time. And the whole paradigm of the music business is changing because there is another parallel music world to the one that has been dominated by the former rules. The new rules of music-sharing, music distribution, music exposure are now globalized.*
—CHUCK D

On May 24, 2000, the U.S. Congress Committee on Small Business held a hearing to learn more about the potential economic impact of downloadable music. Peer-to-peer (P2P) file sharing, or what was more commonly known as music swapping, was steadily growing and now Congress was preparing to weigh in on the technology and the rapidly expanding community of file sharers it produced. Lawmakers knew where the major record companies stood on the issue of music file sharing. Officials from that industry had recently enlisted the authority of Congress and the courts to initiate a crackdown on what they characterized as rampant piracy. The May hearing was designed to learn what the smaller labels and upstart Internet companies thought about the new technologies that were radically remaking the music world. The hearing room was packed with interested onlookers, including young people who were deeply devoted to the online music experience. The size of the crowd indicated how intensely debated the issue was and the level of curiosity.

Among those called to testify before the committee were Tom Silverman, founder and CEO of Tommy Boy Records, and Peter Harter, vice president of Emusic.com, at the time the nation's largest retailer of online music. Many industry observers believed that selling music on the Internet represented the future. The major record groups had been slow, even somewhat resistant, to accept online music as a reality. As a result, an outside band of entrepreneurs, artists, and techno-geeks beat them to the punch and were now laying the foundation upon which the industry's future rested.

Also called to testify before the committee was hip-hop icon, Chuck D. He had recently emerged as a forceful advocate for Internet music ventures, digital music, file sharing, and anything else that threatened to loosen the major record groups' grip on the production, distribution, and consumption of pop music. During his appearance he combined searing testimony, humorous anecdotes, and luscious sound bites with an intense intellect. Chuck D, like many other new media advocates, championed the rise of Internet-based labels that ran parallel to the traditional record companies.

With his typical candor, Chuck D told the committee that he thought the current structure of the music business "had to be eradicated for everybody to participate and start from scratch." Additionally, he said, "A business model will come up out of this new century. It won't destroy the old companies, but it will reconfigure their ways." He went on to use an arresting analogy to explain the Internet's impact on the business-as-usual ways of the music industry. The Internet, he noted, was like a shower of meteors and the major labels were dinosaurs soon to be made extinct by the forces of technological change—if they did not adapt.

Chuck's high regard for the Internet placed him at odds with the music industry establishment. But that was nothing new. He thrived on being an instigator. In addition to appearing before Congress that year, he also found himself in a high-profile debate with Metallica's Lars Ulrich over the rise of Napster and the spread of music file sharing.

In May 2000 Metallica became the first well-known group to legally challenge Napster and peer-to-peer file sharing. By contrast,

Public Enemy was one of the first well-known groups to stand up for Napster and file sharing. When Metallica discovered that a song still in progress was circulating on the Internet, the band took notice and then decided to take on Napster. Metallica forced the network to block access to more than 300,000 fans who had downloaded their music through the site. Speaking on behalf of the group, Lars maintained that file sharing was about control and copyright protection. "It really is about this whole perception about if it's intellectual [property] do I have a right to it for free because technology allows," Lars proclaimed.

Like Lars, Chuck D thought the issue was about control. Unlike Lars, he was not concerned about who should control copyrighted works. Rather, he believed that the media giants' ownership of intellectual property allowed them to dominate the most important resource in the modern world, the media airwaves. He argued that the real issue was about the creation of an information landscape in which the many—not the few—could circulate their worldviews. From Chuck D's perspective of the music world, Napster was "the new radio of the millennium" and the Internet represented "power going back to the people."

By supporting Napster, Chuck D was also defending what he viewed as a much larger and more important cause: the ability to produce and distribute music that stood for something. Throughout his career as a rapper and provocateur, Chuck D inspired the group he created, Public Enemy, to reach legendary pop status. Their music sparked the spirit of protest, while reveling in its anti-establishment manner. Chuck D's booming baritone voice, hard rhyming lyrics, and visionary approach to pop art helped to revolutionize the hip-hop imagination. Once he was a voluble and visible force in hip hop, but the unforgiving winds of cultural, musical, and generational change had pushed him aside. A younger roster of rappers and a new set of priorities favored hip hop's commercial identity over its political identity.

Chuck D had evolved over the years speaking passionately about rap, race, and reality. Certain that hip hop was surrendering much of its value to corporate America, he had added technology to his critical repertoire in the late 1990s. The Internet, he believed, was hip hop's greatest hope for counterbalancing the economic and ideological hegemony of the major record groups. Though his elder statesman's status symbolized the culture's past, his grasp of technology —and the impact it was likely to have on the movement—suggested he also understood hip hop's future. His spirited testimony before Congress, lively debates with Lars, and emergence as a nationally recognized enthusiast of online music demonstrated that after nearly two decades of raising hell the self-proclaimed "rebel without a pause" was still "louder than a bomb." Chuck D had spent his entire career as a performer hyping revolution. But the adoption of the Internet to challenge the corporate takeover of hip hop was, without question, his most radical attempt to "fight the power."

• • •

In the late 1980s and early 1990s no group or artist influenced hip hop more than Public Enemy. The group's flair for pop theater and racial drama broadened the aesthetic and thematic possibilities of rap music. As chief architect of the sound and fury that defined a turning point in hip hop, Chuck D enlarged the language of pop by creating a space for music that was stimulating, boldly original, and unflinchingly political.

Despite the group's image as a forceful voice for Ghetto USA, the idea for Public Enemy formed at Adelphi University, a Long Island liberal arts school. After deciding to major in graphic design, Chuck D, born Carleton Ridenhour, entered Adelphi in the fall of 1979. That was the same year that rap music's first commercial hit, "Rapper's Delight," broke. Soon after enrolling in college, Chuck D found himself gravitating toward a musical culture that was molding its identity and cultivating a distinct voice. Unfocused as a student he demonstrated great precision while working with his friend and future collaborator Hank Shocklee to hone their music-making talents, build important professional networks, and establish their place in hip hop. The infusion of black nationalist politics in Public Enemy's music and style was in tune with the times. The eighties and the rise of Reaganism ushered in a period of intense racial and political discord. Many black collegians found themselves in the eye of controversial storms about affirmative action, diversity, and the degree to which race mattered—nearly a decade and a half after the civil rights movement's most important victories.

In 1982 Chuck D moved a step closer to launching Public Enemy when he got his own radio show on Adelphi's WBAU. A DJ crew he had joined a few years earlier inspired the show's name, *The Super Spectrum Mix Hour*. In response to the show's popularity, the station manager expanded it to an hour and a half. In those days WBAU's audience consisted of black listeners from Queens and Long Island, in addition to young whites who enjoyed the garage music and indie rock that was featured on the station. When the show first began, there was not enough recorded rap music to feature on the regularly scheduled program. In order to fill the time slot, Chuck D and the small crew he worked with began making original tapes of local talent to air during their broadcast.

Chuck D started experimenting with his own vocals, honing the MC skills that would leave an indelible mark on hip hop. Though he was drawn to hip hop, Chuck D was not eager to sign a recording deal. His activities as a radio personality, party promoter, mix tape producer, and MC had introduced him to a number of individuals who had been exploited by rap music's first wave of recording labels.

From the very beginning of his rap career, Chuck D was different from most MCs. When he made his first commercial recording in 1987, he was twenty-six, ancient in hip-hop years. But he believed his age gave him added perspective, a more mature worldview about the realities of race, which shaped his approach to and purpose for rhyming. "Rappers," he wrote in 1997, "only rap about what they know," noting, "I didn't want to rap about 'I'm this or I'm that' all the time." Instead of boasting about himself, or battling other rappers, he wanted "to rap about battling institutions, and bringing the conditions of Black people worldwide to a respectable level." Ultimately, the fact that Chuck D was modestly middle class, college educated, and older than most MCs did not diminish his voice in hip hop; it simply produced a different cadence.

Chuck D and Public Enemy seized pop culture as a stage to act out a daring yet mostly symbolic revolution. The group's politically charged symbolism was its main source of currency in the world of pop culture. Once Chuck D and Hank agreed on a name for the group every aspect of Public Enemy's image was carefully choreographed for maximum effect. Chuck D's public persona—bold, serious-minded, and keenly intellectual—was a calculated play on the legacies and images of strong black leaders. His pensive stare and fearless voice personified Malcolm's "by any means necessary" expression of unassailable black masculinity and power. His forceful, though at times disjointed, message about economic freedom evoked Marcus Garvey and Louis Farrakhan. And his valiant plea for black freedom mimicked the spiritual legacy of Martin Luther King, Jr.

Contrasting with the steely image of Chuck D was the jesterlike character of Flavor Flav (William Drayton). Flav was comic relief to Chuck D's tenacious hard-rhyming style. If Chuck D was shrewd and serious, Flav was ludicrous and lightweight. But underneath Flav's clownlike caricature was an edge that remained faithful to Public Enemy's incendiary theater.

Chuck D used his graphic design skills to create the famous Public Enemy logo of a defiant silhouetted figure caught in the scope of a firearm. The logo, like the group, was rich with symbolism. It suggested that strong-minded blacks were "public enemy number one" and, thus, one of society's most visible targets. As a whole, the group's eclectic mix of characters and iconography were nothing if not a critique of the very pop culture landscape it, ironically, became a part of.

If Public Enemy understood the fine line between pop art and revolution, they also comprehended and grooved to the politics of pleasure. The group's production team, appropriately named the Bomb Squad, adopted a genuinely fresh and radical approach to making popular music. The manner in which their music incorporated sounds from everyday life—conversational dialogue, police sirens, TV news, street noise, ambulances, and political speeches—was essential to Public Enemy's efforts to capture the tone and texture of young America's urban milieus.

Shocklee, one of the principal figures in the Bomb Squad's sonic experiments, characterized his approach to making music this way: "The sound has a look to me, and Public Enemy was all about having a sound that had its own distinct vision." According to Shocklee, "We didn't want to use anything we considered traditional R&B stuff— bass lines and melodies and chord structures and things of that nature." Their style was anything but traditional and exuded a mood that was frenzied, furious, and funky. The Bomb Squad created their music by using thousands of sound fragments to build what Chuck D called a sonic wall. "If you separated the sounds, they wouldn't have been anything—they were unrecognizable," Chuck D says. They called their music "organized noise."

But as hip hop grew more popular the collagelike compositions that Public Enemy meticulously crafted ran into legal problems, specifically, copyright infringement. Public Enemy's most innovative and important album, *It Takes a Nation of Millions to Hold Us Back,* was made before labels distributing hip-hop music had to get clearances for the samples producers used in their recordings. By the early 1990s the densely packed musical productions that Public Enemy pioneered were simply too cost prohibitive to continue making. The copyright clearances produced a disincentive to keep creating the complex musical soundscapes Public Enemy preferred. Like other aspects of the movement, Public Enemy's musical style became a casualty of hip hop's wider appeal and increasingly corporate demeanor.

What was truly revolutionary about the group was its sense of theater, its understanding of the power of the image, and how they mined America's tragic, but equally dramatic, racial past to make a mark in American pop culture.

By choosing to move beyond the traditional thematic fare in pop culture, Public Enemy thrust itself in the dangerous crossfire of America's contentious culture war. When Professor Griff (Richard Griffin), leader of SW1s, a pseudo-security force for Public Enemy, told a *Washington Times* reporter in May 1989 that "Jews are wicked" and responsible for "the majority of wickedness that goes on across the globe," his comments exposed the ugly racial chauvinism and ideological zealotry that colored Public Enemy's more madcap moments. As the leader of the group, Chuck D came under tremendous pressure—the comments setting off a firestorm of criticism as well as charges of anti-Semitism that threatened the group's future. Hip hop's biggest act had fought fire with fire, and now they were getting burned.

Determined to save hip hop's boldest voice, the entire Public Enemy camp went into damage-control mode. At a press conference Chuck D delivered a public apology: "Offensive remarks by Professor Griff are not in line with Public Enemy's program. We are not anti-Jewish. We are not anti-anyone. We are pro-black, pro–black culture, and pro–human race." He added, "We apologize to anyone who might have been offended by Griff's remarks. We're offended, too." The group's distributor, CBS Records, and label, Def Jam, moved to put out the fire. Shortly after the debacle, Public Enemy announced its retirement. In August the group released a statement simply proclaiming, "we're back in action." All of the activity for and against Public Enemy indicated that hip hop, once a social nuisance at best, touched some of the most urgent issues of its time. Hip hop mattered.

Along with its contributions and controversies, Public Enemy defined hip hop by redefining its political possibilities. Rap music's commercial life was still forming when the group began dropping lyrical bombs that targeted racism, miseducation, incarceration, and media misrepresentation. Chuck D's now legendary claim that "rap music is the CNN of black America" is audacious and cleverly recognizes that pop culture can be, and often is, political. Though not entirely accurate, the claim highlights the degree to which Public Enemy's innovations make it possible to talk about the real world issues that frustrate the hip-hop nation. Drawing rap's stories and images from the harsh terrain of everyday life pushed the genre toward what was later packaged and marketed as "reality rap." The shift to reality rap encouraged MCs to be grittier, franker speaking, and even journalistic in their rhymes. In the end, Public Enemy's belief that rap could be relevant and socially conscious not only shook up hip hop, it also gave the pop landscape a serious jolt. Their style of music was revealing, if not revolutionary, and established the conditions for a notable change in rap's tone.

Ironically, Public Enemy's gift to hip hop, the idea of making music real and relevant, also became a curse. The same traits that enhanced reality rap's commercial vitality—raw lyrics, aggressive style, and disdain for the establishment—also created space for a translation that was much coarser and less politically sophisticated. By the early 1990s a new crop of "reality rappers" directed their gaze toward the ghetto underworld of crime, crack, and street hustling. This particular interpretation of reality rap outdueled Public Enemy in pop music's ultimate arena, the commercial marketplace. As hard core styles like gangsta moved more toward shock reality, rap became more about marketing than the message, more sensational than cerebral.

Throughout the 1990s, as rap grew more corporate, the persona and politics of Public Enemy wore down commercially. Like every other group in the world of pop music, Public Enemy's market value rested not on the integrity or political efficacy of its message but rather on the commercial appeal of its image and music. Predictably, Public Enemy's "too black, too strong" politics, once all the rage, became vulnerable to the volatile and viciously short attention span of the youth marketplace. The issues that Public Enemy addressed in their music were never temporary or trendy. Still, while the concerns

Chuck D continued to express about the state of hip hop remained perceptive, they were also increasingly peripheral in the glamorous world hip hop was becoming.

• • •

By the middle nineties, the genre that Chuck D helped define and establish commercially was moving far away from his vision of rap music as a fountain of politically provocative discourse. In 1998, though no longer part of the mainstream mix, Public Enemy was preparing to deliver their latest album, a collection of previously unreleased remixes titled, *Bring the Noise 2000*. Their sales had dropped off over the years, and they were no longer a prominent act for Def Jam Records, one of the premier labels in the music industry. Together, Def Jam and Public Enemy had fought some of hip hop's greatest battles over the years, but their relationship became increasingly strained in the nineties. The turning point came in 1994 when Polygram Records purchased Def Jam.

Chuck D thought that because Public Enemy had played such a crucial role in establishing Def Jam's cultural and commercial credibility that they deserved a small cut of the deal. When it became clear that Public Enemy would not receive anything from the multi-million dollar transaction, their relationship with Def Jam turned increasingly sour. According to Chuck, "[All] that talk about us being family was just bullshit. I said 'fuck that, I'm outta here. Find me a taxi and execute this contract.' "

Unsure when or how Def Jam planned to release *Bring the Noise 2000*, Chuck decided to make some of the songs available as free downloads on Public Enemy's website. Within two weeks of uploading the songs, according to several news reports, the group got a letter from Polygram lawyers threatening a lawsuit if they did not remove the music from the website. Under the terms of the group's recording contract Def Jam, not Public Enemy, owned the masters. Legally, that meant Def Jam controlled where, when, and how the music could be distributed. Chuck D, despite his wishes, relented and removed the songs. But he also used the group's website to strike back at the industry that was about to become the focus of his anti-establishment fury. He even cut a new song, "Swindler's Lust," a scathing critique of the label he helped put on the map. In the song he compared corporate ownership of master recordings with the ownership of slaves.

Before downloading the song, visitors were invited to read the following statement: "It seems like the weasels have stepped into the fire," he wrote. "The execs, lawyers and accountants who lately have made most of the money in the music biz are now running scared from the technology that evens out the creative field and makes artists harder to pimp. Let 'em all die...I'm glad to be a contributor to the bomb." Throughout the college lecture circuit, and media interviews he conducted, Chuck D continued his hard-hitting assessment of the music business and repeatedly stated that he was determined to "murder his contract with Def Jam."

In January of 1999, after a twelve-year historic run together, Public Enemy and Def Jam severed ties. Public Enemy and Def Jam drove each other to new heights and helped to make rap music a relevant genre around the world. Their breakup symbolized the profound conversion hip hop was undergoing.

• • •

Rick Rubin and Russell Simmons, the two men that created Def Jam Records, were an unlikely duo. The chemistry between them set Def Jam on fire. In the end, however, their distinctive backgrounds ultimately drove them apart. When they met, Rubin, a Jewish kid from a Long Island upper-middle-class family, was studying at New York University. Simmons, who came from a modestly middle-class Hollis, Queens, family, was an upstart—yet still largely unproven—promoter and manager hoping to establish himself during hip hop's humble beginnings. As a student at NYU in 1981, Rubin was going to rap shows every week but felt as though the lively character that defined the music he was experiencing in clubs was missing in the few recordings being made at the time. Convinced that he could capture that energy on vinyl, Rubin asked one of his favorite club DJs, Jazzy J, if he wanted to make a record. That collaboration, "It's Yours" by T. La Rock & Jazzy J, formally introduced Rubin to the world of music production. Soon thereafter Rubin and Simmons met.

According to Rubin, he suggested the idea of starting a record label together. Rubin was playing in a punk rock band and running Def Jam, then a small independent label, out of his NYU dorm. Though Rubin was smart, visionary, and hard working, Simmons had two things that he lacked. First, Simmons had a stable of rap performers through his artists' management company, Rush Entertainment. Speaking about the decision to enter into a partnership with Simmons, Rubin recalls: "He's a great promotion man. The reason our partnership worked was that he made it real. He was an established person in the rap community, and I was a kid in a dorm. He gave me credibility." Second, Simmons was black and that was crucial. Rightly or wrongly race has always been synonymous with credibility in hip hop. Among other things it conveys a connection to the culture's urban origins and its struggle to create an outlet of expression for youth relegated to society's margins.

The irony was that Rubin's musical sensibilities were far more innovative than Simmons'. The production instincts and vision of Rubin inspired the early and essential Def Jam recordings including the Beastie Boys, LL Cool J, and Public Enemy, which put the label on the music map. Though their sounds and images were thoroughly different, they all possessed the rock energy Rubin believed made hip hop, in his words, "the black punk." By that he meant music that was born to be loud, abrasive, and seditious at heart. Rubin saw rap music's future and understood its diverse potential before most did. He insisted on fusing hip hop's resilient personality with the thunder of hard-nosed rock to produce earth-shattering music.

It was Rubin who made the case for signing Def Jam's most influential group, Public Enemy. When he first heard Chuck D on tape, he knew instantly that he had to sign him. Relentless in his efforts, Rubin pursued Chuck D for several months trying to persuade the hard rhymester to sign with Def Jam. Initially, Simmons was not impressed with the group because their sound, style, and philosophy was completely unlike anything he or anyone else had ever heard. Though he would later grow to appreciate Public Enemy's firebrand interpretation of hip-hop music, Simmons's more middle class and R&B inclinations led him to question Rubin's enthusiasm for the group early on. After hearing Public Enemy's first album Simmons told Rubin: "I don't know why you're wasting your time with this garbage. This is like black punk rock. You make hit records; you made pop records with the Bangles. How can you waste your time on this garbage?"

While he could never be accused of being born with a silver spoon in his mouth, Simmons's bourgeois instincts did not subscribe to the angry antics and anti-establishment tone that characterized Public Enemy's sound. Still, he eventually learned that the essence of Public Enemy's appeal—assertive and confrontational black cultural politics—made for great theater and even greater profits. Simmons, in his 2001 autobiography, *Life and Def,* wrote that his life "has largely been about promoting the anger, style, aggression, attitude, and aspirations of urban America to a worldwide audience." Public Enemy's raucous rhymes and belligerent beats showed him the light and the way to pop fortune and influence.

Rubin was a rare species in the big-media, big-money world rap was evolving into. He made hit records but did not seem to worship celebrity. Soon after launching Def Jam, Rubin and Simmons began to clash over the creative direction of the label. From the start of their joint venture, they knew that their musical tastes were different, but they also shared a passion for rap. Rubin wanted to be more open and experimental, so he pushed the creative envelope, signing hard-core-rock act Slayer and, later, controversial comedian Andrew Dice Clay. Simmons believed that Rubin's efforts strayed from building the company's equity as a hip-hop brand. Even as Def Jam was enjoying some early recognition and success, Rubin got a glimpse of rap music's future—the reduction of the genre to product and constant corporate manipulation—and was turned off by what he saw. He began to lose interest in rap sometime between the first and second Public Enemy records. That was 1988. The frequent disagreements with Simmons became so frustrating that Rubin left Def Jam.

Years later, he explained, "I felt like rap had left me more than I had left rap." He believed that when rap's money-making potential was established it opened the way for a different set of interests. He believed the changes fostered a climate in which those responsible for selling hip hop stopped caring about the music. "When I started," he told *Rolling Stone* in 1995, "nobody had really made any money doing it, so that wasn't the goal. As it got bigger, it got less interesting. The new stuff began to sound like people capitalizing on what someone else had done. The intentions seemed wrong." Rap, he believed, "became a way to make money."

And making money certainly became the unabashed goal of Def Jam in the post-Rubin era. As hip hop's fortunes grew so did Def Jam. The label became one of the premier "shops" in the music-recording industry. When the French water and utility company Vivendi purchased Seagram-Universal, Def Jam's parent company, in 2000, one of hip hop's oldest labels was poised to become its most dominant brand. Vivendi/Universal was the bold idea of Jean-Marie Messier, a forty-four-year-old charismatic and controversial French tycoon who dreamed of creating a world media empire that rivaled America media titans like AOL/Time Warner and Disney. The transformation of Vivendi, a 147-year-old French water, energy, and utility company, into a global media giant was quick and spectacular.

According to one news account, in his pursuit of glamour and power, Messier became "a serial acquirer." In the span of eighteen

months, he spent more than $50 billion buying up stalwart proper-
ties like Universal Studios and theme parks as well as the largest
music company in the world, the Universal Music Group (UMG). He
banked the acquisition on the belief that wireless technologies like
phones and hand-held devices—another chief Vivendi investment—
would become the new delivery system for music and video. His
vision outpaced the technology.

Like many of its global media and entertainment conglomerate
rivals, bigger did not prove to be better for Vivendi/Universal. In
June of 2002 the company reported that it was more than $34 billion
in debt. The losses Vivendi suffered after building its massive media
empire were the biggest in French corporate history. Desperate for
debt relief, Jean-Rene Fourtou, the company's new CEO, began shopping Vivendi's glitzy media and entertainment properties. But early
on, the company decided it would retain its music holdings. UMG
had the largest share of both the global and U.S. markets. Vivendi
concluded that due to the depressed state of the music industry and
the uncertainties about online music, it would sell the world's biggest
music-recording company when it could get its true value.

Though it was home to a number of music labels and divisions,
UMG's dominance in the U.S. and global markets could be traced directly to rap's rise. The two most important assets in Universal music
holdings were Island Def Jam Music Group and Interscope/Geffen/
A&M. Both Def Jam and Interscope began as small, free-spirited independents. Both companies made their name selling rap music the
majors refused to touch. And now they were two of the most powerful music labels in the world. In a media and entertainment economy
enchanted with size, no pop music genre had a bigger buzz around
the world than rap music. Still, the idea that rap's two most influential labels were owned by a century-and-a-half-old French water and
utility company highlighted the astonishing changes that accompanied hip hop's cultural and commercial ascendancy. It was an indication of how far hip hop's appeal reached and how mainstream it was.

• • •

Throughout its early history, hip hop amassed most of its appeal by maintaining an aura and edge that placed it in opposition to the cultural mainstream. But hip hop's status as a lucrative industry, and fixture in the mainstream establishment it once stood in direct contrast to, put its creative class of artists, entrepreneurs, and executives in an odd position: defending the movement's success. Many of hip hop's notable figures and staunchest proponents understood that the journey from the margins to the mainstream contradicted some of the prominent truisms in hip hop about street cred and authenticity. Seeking to explain and even justify hip hop's obsession with mainstream success, a new claim emerged.

"Hip hop," the assertion declares, "did not cross over to the mainstream but rather the mainstream crossed over to hip hop." The claim is carefully designed to insulate hip hop's entrepreneurial elite from charges that it "sold out" the movement for the accoutrements of the mainstream—money, celebrity, and pop prestige. But even as the movers and shakers within the hip-hop industry exclaim they are "staying true to the streets" they do so from well-appointed corporate suites. In the end, the claim is as deceptive as it is preemptive.

More than anything, the assertion that hip hop did not cross over to the mainstream fails to appreciate the complex genius of the movement's creative class. It implies that they had no sense of hip hop's cultural and economic potential nor the changing world around them. Just as the cultural mainstream actively pursued hip hop, many of the movers and shakers within hip hop sought out the mainstream. In the end, hip hop did not simply join the mainstream; in effect, it redefined the very meaning and experience of the mainstream.

Hip hop's entrepreneurial elite as much as any other community of pop culture producers, executives, and artists understood the mainstream marketplace—its impulses, its desires, its habits of the heart—and how to manipulate it for commercial gain. The man-

ufacturers of rap rose atop the pop music world not because they ignored the mainstream but precisely because they understood it.
Rap's rise occurred because the producers of the genre adapted
quickly and effectively to a music industry in the midst of extraordinary change. The multiplatinum albums, blockbuster opening-week
sales, frequent radio spins and music video rotations—and impact of
hip hop in the rise of hip youth brands like Nike and Sprite—indicated that some of the movement's most dynamic creators and executives had their fingers on the mainstream's pulse.

Chuck D knew that in its pursuit of the mainstream hip hop
began dancing to the beat of a very different drummer—the rhythmic patterns of the mainstream marketplace. "[I]n the first ten to
twelve years of rap recordings," Chuck says, "rappers rapped for the
people, and they rapped against the elite establishment. In the last
[ten] or so years, rappers rap for their companies and their contracts,
and they're part of the establishment now. It's two diametrically op-
posed ideas."

The corporate takeover of the movement explained why Public
Enemy, despite its legacy as one of hip hop's most important groups,
was expendable. The corporate pursuit of mainstream props and
profits muted the sonic shouts of Public Enemy. Chuck D, convinced
that hip hop had sold its soul for mainstream access and financial
success but determined to keep hip hop's social conscience alive,
looked for other ways to "bring the noise."

• • •

Before the breakup with Def Jam became official, Chuck D knew that
Public Enemy would have to take a different course if it wanted to
continue to matter in the world of hip hop music. Just as Chuck D
began looking for new ways to broadcast Public Enemy's politically
charged music in the face of an increasingly indifferent industry, a
new information technology was penetrating American households.
Chuck D was first introduced to the Internet in 1991. Along with

Public Enemy he used it occasionally to conduct interviews more efficiently. The group had always been proponents of technology. Their groundbreaking sonic experiments involved innovative uses of technology and helped them build a reputation for thinking outside the box. In the beginning Public Enemy used technology to craft an aesthetic assault that redefined how young people experienced music. In the wake of their commercial decline, Public Enemy mined new developments in technology simply to create and distribute their music.

After making history with Def Jam, Public Enemy made history again when they became the first platinum-selling music artists in the United States to release a new album through the Internet. In April of 1999 the group negotiated a deal with Atomic Pop, an upstart online music and entertainment company, to distribute *There's a Poison Goin' On*. The deal pushed many of the issues that fueled Chuck D's fire—artistic freedom, corporate domination of pop media culture, and the struggle for hip hop—into the new frontiers of digital technology and new media.

Atomic Pop was the invention of former CBS music president Al Teller. While still an executive at MCA Music Entertainment Group, Teller wrote a brief *Billboard* editorial assessing the state of the music industry in 1994. Anticipating some of the major challenges the industry was certain to face, Teller wrote: "The industry's No. 1 priority as a whole is to emerge from the new technology fray with an improved ability to deliver software to each and every consumer across the globe." Five years later he attempted to do just that. Both Teller and Chuck shared the view that digital distribution was the next big thing in the music industry. They hailed Atomic Pop as a first step toward the reinvention of the industry. "Change is inevitable, and everything is about to change," Chuck D told the *New York Times* that April. He predicted that once an established act like Public Enemy tried online distribution others would follow.

The arrangement with Atomic Pop, according to Chuck, was

"utopia for an artist." If the album sold well, Public Enemy stood to benefit from a larger than usual royalty share. Most importantly, Public Enemy owned the master recordings, which meant that it controlled the songs as well as any ancillary revenue they generated. "At its core," Teller noted, "this label is embracing the power of the Internet in addition to traditional music practices." The prospects for Internet commerce were still largely illusory at the time.

Most of the media's focus on the Public Enemy-Atomic Pop partnership aimed at the unique aspects of the deal—the financial split and the curiosity about the Internet as a new mode of music distribution. But the album also broke new ground topically for Public Enemy. Specifically, *There's a Poison Goin' On* represented a new direction in Chuck D's politics. His concerns about corporate media, democracy, and technology were more populist than black nationalist. In many ways, his new crusade had more in common with Ralph Nader than Louis Farrakhan. It was a sign of his own ideological and political evolution, indeed, an expansion of his critical repertoire and worldview.

On the album Public Enemy set its critical sights on corporate radio, record labels, and the executive brass that, according to Chuck D, ruled the big media behemoths. Pop music, he argued, was less about artistry and more about industry. That had been true for decades. Nevertheless, in the new conglomerate corporate structure, the pressure for hits was even greater, the pursuit of blockbuster profits more intense, and tolerance for a diverse menu of pop music virtually nonexistent. Chuck D's anti-corporate stance played well with online enthusiasts frustrated by what they believed was a lack of creativity in pop music caused largely by the emphasis on radio and retail. Still, the populist tilt in his message did not mean that it would resonate with the young music masses or move more units.

Like other online music advocates, Chuck D and Teller embraced the Internet as an alternative industry and ideology that could subdue the power of the traditional record labels. Their effort to harness the power of the Internet to challenge the major music groups' dominance in the pop music world reflected a larger sentiment regarding the potential impact of the new technology.

In the initial years of the Internet's arrival as a home-based technology, there was great optimism that it would be a democratizing force in the rapidly evolving world of communication and information technology. Advocates of the Internet proclaimed it could empower the many, instead of the few, to use media to circulate their voices and views to a wider public. But even as Internet junkies, geeks, and gurus were extolling the democratic virtues of new media, another reality was also forming.

The promise of the burgeoning online culture and community as a formidable challenge to the hegemony of the global media giants was seriously dampened by the latter's aggressive efforts to preserve its dominance. The most powerful media and software companies responded swiftly to the Internet's growing appeal by buying out upstart online ventures, litigating services like Napster into submission, and using their vast holdings in media and other properties to develop and promote their online enterprises. In a relatively short period of time the Internet, once perceived as a tool for activism, education, and civic engagement, was turned into a tool for consumption, leisure, and entertainment. In the high stakes competition among big media, high tech, and software giants for global economic supremacy, the Internet became the new battleground.

Roughly nineteen months after Atomic Pop's highly publicized launch, the Internet's economic bubble burst—bringing the company and many other online enterprises to a sudden halt. It was a real blow to those who fashioned the Internet as a viable alternative to the major record groups. Though the digital distribution of music was the future, the vision shared by Teller and Chuck D was still a few years from being fully realized. Still, for Chuck D the future was now.

• • •

Soon after the online release of *There's a Poison Goin' On*, Chuck D directed his experience and energy toward developing an arsenal of Web-based music initiatives. In addition to Publicenemy.com he started Rapstation.com, Slamjamz.com, and Bringthenoise.com. While his various Internet endeavors took on the mighty music machine's three R's—record labels, radio, and retail—his most immediate and intimate concern was the corporate takeover of hip hop. Public Enemy's decision to make its case for hip hop via the Internet underscored a growing concern in hip hop that rap and, by extension, the movement was yielding to the persuasive powers and profit motives of corporate interests. Because rap music was hip hop's most visible and viable art form and commodity it was, by default, the movement's most important symbol. That made rap, for better or worse, ground zero in the struggle for hip hop. It also made the Internet—a growing force in the world of music—a key, albeit unanticipated, resource in the struggle for hip hop.

The idea that hip hop should have a strong Internet presence is striking, given some of the pivotal debates about race and technology. In the late 1990s the digital divide, the growing gap between the "information haves" and "information have-nots," generated considerable discussion. Early data suggested that those who had access to the Internet were more likely to come from affluent or well-educated households. But as the debate about digital media became more refined, it acknowledged that the issue was not only about access but also the skills people acquired to enhance their experience with technology. The focus on the digital divide overlooked the fact that many blacks and Latinos were, despite the conventional wisdom, wired. Chuck D, looking past the data and the debates, believed hip hop's future rested with the new technology. At the height of the debate about the digital divide, in 1999, he told *Billboard:* "There's a lot of misconception out there that the rap and hip-hop community isn't online, but the development of this music community has always run parallel to technological advances."

Hip hop has a big presence on the Internet. Within the movement the technology is regarded as a source of power and pleasure, commerce and community. For many hip-hop heads the technology has become a way to advocate for a more lively social consciousness in hip hop. More than radio, corporate rap, or music video the Internet has become the new town square in hip hop, a vital public sphere for building an imagined community, organizing political initiatives, and conducting provocative debate about the state of hip hop. Chuck D's adoption of the Internet reflects a wider optimism within the movement about the role technology can play as a counterbalance to the corporate interests that are driving the movement toward an obsession with money and celebrity, seemingly at all costs. The idea that the Internet is a rapidly rising component of hip hop should not come as a total surprise; hip hop has always been a technology-savvy movement. "This community," Chuck D told *Billboard*, "was the first to embrace emulators and DAT machines in the creation of music. The Internet is no different."

Like many hip-hop heads, Chuck knew that there was a rich and incredibly deep reservoir of rap music that existed well beyond the radars of the corporate-financed television networks and radio stations, which featured only a tiny fraction of hip hop's music. He cringed at the fact that so few people experienced the genuine eclecticism and diverse worldviews that drive the more complex tonalities of the music he devoted his life to. By his estimation the major record labels back about 15 percent of the artistry in hip-hop music. He believed it was the job of people like him to promote the other 85 percent.

Slamjamz.com, Chuck D's Internet-based label, was designed to accommodate the arrival of digital music media. It also reflected Chuck D's approach to making music in the new millennium. Speaking about his philosophy, Chuck D says, "I made up my mind in 1999 that I was gonna change how I recorded and how I approached the concept of a whole album." He asserted that the traditional album format, the industry's biggest moneymaker, was dead and that digitally compressed music files, MP3s, were the new 45s in what was rapidly turning into a singles-driven industry. Based on his online experiences and the troubles that besieged the major labels, he believed that the music audience, especially the younger segments, preferred singles to albums as well as the ability to customize their own music-listening experience. The philosophy of slamjamz.com was tailored to make music in a world in which file sharing, downloading, and CD burning were common practices. Public Enemy's embrace of the Internet was consistent with a career that thrived on cutting against the cultural and musical grain.

In their heyday Public Enemy developed a reputation for innovation. Their politically charged style, lyrics, and brand of pop theatrics stood out in the cluttered terrain of pop culture. But rap music, once known for its stylistic and thematic innovations, had become more formulaic, predictable, and astoundingly boring. There was widespread belief among many in hip hop that as rap crossed over into the pop world it settled for the catchy hooks that usually generated radio spins and cushy paychecks. Meanwhile Public Enemy, cast aside by the rap and pop music industries, had no choice but to continue its innovative ways. It was, quite frankly, their only means of survival.

In August of 2002 Public Enemy broke new ground again by producing what was widely touted as one of the world's first truly interactive albums. For the *Revolverlution* project, Public Enemy placed four a cappella versions of previously recorded songs on slamjamz .com. Next, they invited visitors to the website to download the songs and produce their own remix versions. Speaking about the experiment, Chuck D says, "My thing was just looking at the community and being able to say, 'Can we actually make them involved in the creative process?' Why not see if we can connect all these bedroom and basement studios, and the ocean of producers, and expand the Bomb Squad to a worldwide concept?" The songs were downloaded 11,000 times and more than 400 mixes were submitted. The four winners selected came from all over the world including Argentina and Austria.

Despite their fading status on the U.S. pop charts, Public Enemy remained popular and respected around the world. From the very beginning of the group's career, Chuck D saw the bigger picture and developed an appreciation for the wider world that existed beyond the U.S. pop market. In 1987, while still seeking to find their voice and place in the U.S., Public Enemy took its riotous stage show to Europe where the group's apocalyptic rhetoric garnered great press and even greater fan interest. They "did" London, Amsterdam, Norway, Sweden, Denmark, and Germany. Recalling Public Enemy's first world tour Chuck D wrote in *Fight the Power:* "It was a great experience. That's when we realized that if we never dominated the U.S. market we would take the markets that nobody else wanted—the rest of the world." The Internet was a way for the group to stay connected to their global audience.

Armed simply with digital and new media technologies, Chuck D had taken on one of the music industry's most powerful players, the big record groups. But he did not stop there. Also in his sights was another powerful pillar in the pop music establishment: big radio.

• • •

"The thing that got me into the MP3 technology was necessity," says Chuck D. He was forced to find other avenues to continue making and distributing music after he went to his label with a new song and was told by executives, "Chuck, it is going to cost you about $750,000 in order to get the record played on radio." Public Enemy's emphasis on complex rather than club-oriented beats, thought-provoking rather than strictly hummable lyrics made them of little use to the programming priorities of big radio. The dilemma Public Enemy faced was not unique to the group; it characterized a more chilling reality that was wreaking havoc in the music industry. Ten years after

Public Enemy first entered the fray, the business of pop music was driven by a different set of rules, costs, and new commercial realities.

The high cost scenario that Chuck D described to the House Committee was emblematic of the increasingly high-stakes industry pop music had become. By 2000, artists, music labels, media activists, legislators, and even some radio programmers began expressing concerns about the "pay-for-play" arrangements that determined which songs most radio listeners were exposed to. In his investigation of the changes that reshaped the face of commercial radio, Salon.com senior writer Eric Boehlert concluded that "virtually all the songs played on a typical commercial radio station—known as 'adds' in the trade—are paid for." The rise of pay-for-play was disheartening for artists, costly to record companies, and detrimental to listeners. Songs made it on the radio, not because they were necessarily good or genuinely preferred by listeners but, because the record labels paid out huge sums of money to gain the spins necessary to put a song in position to be a radio and commercial hit. It was that kind of corporate money game that rendered groups who did not fit into the proven formulas of the day virtually obsolete in the new world order of pop music.

Most disturbing, it was not simply a widespread practice but also accepted as a legitimate means for determining playlists. Pay-for-play suggested that for all of the talk about greater consumer choice and diversity of media content, pop music tastes, trends, and charts were still being manipulated. Only this time the controlling force was a new and even more powerful radio establishment.

Radio's power to determine pop hits is a sign of how much and how little has changed in the music industry. While MTV may be the glamorous face of music promotion, radio is still the real backbone. Despite the visual magic of the music video in crafting and selling an image, radio is still the most important medium in selling records. Radio maintains an intimacy with music audiences that music video can never achieve. The medium, despite its problems, is personal, portable, and, in its unique way, still powerful. Those and other factors make pop radio an indispensable part of young people's everyday lives. For decades radio has been the lifeline of the pop music industry. However, the medium's impact on pop music changed dramatically in the aftermath of the most sweeping piece of U.S. telecommunications policy in more than sixty years.

On February 8, 1996, President Bill Clinton signed the 1996 Telecommunications Act from inside the Library of Congress. The event was staged to highlight the main claim of the legislation, that passage of the act symbolized the passing from the old media economy to the new media economy. "This law is truly revolutionary legislation that will bring the future to our doorstep," Clinton pronounced. "It will provide for more information and more entertainment to virtually every American home." It was true that American households had access to more media than at any other time in the nation's history. However, critics complained, and rightfully so, in the face of subsequent consolidation more, strangely enough, seemed like less.

The overhaul of American telecommunication policy produced its most immediate impact on broadcast radio. When the act was passed, proponents and opponents alike knew the effects on everyday American life would be dramatic. One of the least discussed features of the 1996 telecommunications legislation was the relaxation of media ownership rules, particularly, in broadcast media such as radio and television. The exact implications of the legislation, however, remained a mystery. Before the act, no one company could own more than two radio stations in a single market. After the act, a company could own as many as seven or eight commercial stations in a single market.

The speed at which mergers and acquisitions took place was nothing less than stunning. In the first year of the act, 20 percent of the commercial radio stations in the country experienced ownership change. A year and a half after the passage of the Telecommunications Act, the Department of Justice reported that *more than a thou-*

*sand* mergers took place. The Federal Communications Commission reported that between 1996 and 2001 there had been more than a 7 percent increase in the number of radio stations in the U.S. During that same time the number of radio owners fell by 25 percent.

One of the biggest critics of the merger and acquisition frenzy that remade America's radio airwaves was the Future of Music Coalition, an organization that seeks to educate the media and policy makers about music and technology issues. In its assessment of the after-shocks of the 1996 act, the group produced its own report, noting that ten companies controlled two-thirds of both radio listeners and revenue nationwide. Ownership consolidation also led to format consolidation and shorter playlists, which, according to the Coali-tion, "deprives citizens the opportunity to hear a wide range of music." Like Chuck D and other critics of big media's spread and dominance, the Coalition believed that rather than encourage com-petition and diversity of viewpoints putting ownership of the na-tion's radio airwaves in the hands of a few "led to less competition, fewer viewpoints, and less diversity in programming." The group concluded that "deregulation has damaged radio as a public resource."

The symbol of big radio was San Antonio–based Clear Channel Communications. Between 1996 and 2000, Clear Channel rose from obscurity to become the dominant player in broadcast radio and an undeniable force in pop music. In 1996, Clear Channel owned thirty-six radio stations. By 2002 it owned more than 1,200 commercial stations or more than thirty times the previous ownership caps. That total far outpaced its closest rivals, Cumulus Media and Infinity Broadcasting, which owned 250 and 180 radio stations, respectively. In addition to the radio stations, the company Boehlert called "the big bully of radio" also owned SFX Entertainment, the nation's dom-inant owner of concert venues and promotion. If a label or band did not play by Clear Channel's rules, it had the means and some believed the will to strike back by limiting the number of radio spins or out-lets for promoting concerts and tours.

Concern about Clear Channel's alleged heavy-handed ways and

influence in pop music was so strong that a few years after it passed the 1996 act, Congress openly pondered the consequences of its decision. Of all the legislators who weighed in on big radio, none was more forceful than Wisconsin senator Russ Feingold. Speaking from the floor of the U.S. Senate in January of 2003, Feingold explained why he had introduced new legislation intended to curb the anticompetitive practices in big radio. "People should have choices, listeners should have a diversity of options, and Americans should be able to hear new and different voices. Radio allows us to connect to our communities, to our culture, and to our democracy. It is one of the most vibrant mediums we have for the exchange of ideas, and for artistic expression," he said. Feingold's concerns about radio resembled the concerns in a hip-hop movement that experienced shocking decline in the range of voices, perspectives, and viewpoints found in the music that big radio vigorously promoted.

The 1996 Telecommunications Act had a profound impact on the hip-hop movement. The emergence of big radio, as much as any other factor, hastened the rise of corporate rap. Because they were committed to securing a place in the pop mainstream, many of hip hop's top producers learned to play by the new rules that governed big radio: pay-for-play, testing, call-outs, and corporate-controlled playlists. Whereas saying and doing something original in rap was once a main goal, in the era of big radio the mimicking of already established styles and trends meant more. Its image of rebelliousness notwithstanding, rap grew remarkably conservative in style, tone, and musical structure.

As a whole, rap's many regional accents—East Coast, West Coast, the Dirty South—made the genre a lively mix of different styles, communities, and voices. But corporate rap, the hip-hop music heard by most of the world, developed a national dialect that gravitated toward a standard pop vocabulary that consisted of catchy hooks, hummable lyrics, and uptempo R&B style arrangements. This trend avoided the complex, multilayered rhymes and rhythms that defined the aesthetic and sonic achievements of Public Enemy.

Dominated by a handful of powerful labels and radio owners, corporate rap was also defined by a shrinking cadre of celebrity producers—Timbaland, The Neptunes, P. Diddy—whose main charge was to keep the nation's pop and urban radio airwaves bouncing. Rap was no different from the other genres it competed against for market share and status in the corporate-controlled milieu of broadcast radio. The genre's elite players focused on gaining access to commercial radio and music video, the two essential gateways to America's pop consciousness.

All of this explained why the hip-hop movement's most voluble voice—rap music—had surrendered much of its ambition and originality for music that cared more about servicing rather than subverting the status quo. It explained why Public Enemy had become essentially obsolete and disposable and, like so many others longing for fresh voices and perspectives in hip hop, sought refuge in the digital underground.

• • •

Public Enemy's flair for political drama and socially conscious rap took place mainly among the bright lights and hype of pop culture. That fact alone established both obstacles and opportunities for its message of protest. When the pop culture stage shifted its appetite away from the group's hyper-political stage show, Public Enemy found itself looking for new ways to keep hip hop's social consciousness alive and well.

Hip hop's digital underground—websites and webzines, chat rooms, Internet-based radio programs and music labels, and digitally enabled activism—fought to reinvigorate hip hop's legacy of social and political struggle. The digital underground was a resilient rejection of the media consolidation and conglomeration that dominated the nation's media airwaves and severely restricted hip hop's creative spirit.

Hip hop's digital underground embodies a growing cascade of

concern within the movement—about the movement— producing a more introspective mood. Despite the euphoria about hip hop's commercial success and trendsetting ways, the movement's ability to have an empowering and enduring impact in the lives of ordinary youths remains largely unrealized. So after thirty years of hypnotic beats, pop success, and the creation of its very own star system, some in the movement dare to ask: Does hip hop deserve more? Can its impact reach beyond the pop sphere and into the political sphere? The notion that hip hop can have real political clout was pondered as far back as the eighties. Twenty years later the idea that hip hop can develop a more dynamic political identity is an idea whose time has come...again.

# PART TWO

# POLITICS and the STRUGGLE for HIP HOP

CHAPTER FIVE

# *Move the Crowd*

*The most important thing we gotta do
is make it cool to show up at rallies,
make it in style to pay attention.*

—RUSSELL SIMMONS

Two days before the close of New York State's 226th annual legislative session several major bills remained trapped in political gridlock. Lawmakers were working feverishly to hammer out deals that they could take back to their various constituencies as proof that they were doing the people's business. One of the most highly publicized pieces of legislation was the attempt to repeal what had become known in the state as the Nelson Rockefeller drug statutes. Though most lawmakers agreed that the law was too severe, striking a deal to repeal had eluded them the previous two years. Now, just days before summer recess, the state's three most powerful elected officials, Governor George E. Pataki; Joseph L. Bruno, the Republican senate majority leader; and Sheldon Silver, the Democratic speaker of the state assembly, met in a closed-door session in Pataki's state capitol office.

It was typical backdoor politicking but with one atypical twist. To the dismay of veteran state politicos and a press that was covering the legislative session, New York's three most powerful elected officials were joined by hip-hop mogul Russell Simmons. Pataki believed that Simmons could help bridge some of the gaps that had precluded a deal from being made in years past. Simmons's presence, needless to say, added double the intrigue and irritation to the politics-as-usual norms of state government.

In the months leading up to the June 2003 state legislative session, Simmons had helped spearhead a high-profile campaign to repeal the drug laws. Achieving the repeal in 2003 would be an important symbolic and political victory for proponents of the effort. Thirty years earlier, the drug laws had been passed with the support of then governor Nelson Rockefeller in response to a crime wave linked to the drug trade. Among other things the state statutes imposed a mandatory minimum of fifteen to twenty-five years for selling two ounces or possessing four ounces of an illegal drug. Critics charged that petty dealers and small-time drug addicts were hit hardest.

The arrival of crack in the mid-eighties unleashed a wrath of hell that devastated many poor and working-class communities. In the ensuing years of the drug laws, the vigorous and equally vicious underground drug economy that took root in some of the nation's poorest urban communities provided a fast track to long-term prison sentences. The racial implications of New York's drug laws were severe. According to New York State's Department of Correctional Services, more than 90 percent of the 18,300 drug inmates in 2002 were black or Latino.

Because of its impact on New York's black and Latino communities, supporters of the repeal thought Simmons was a natural fit for the campaign. He had developed a reputation as an urban market guru, someone who understood the tastes, tempo, and temperament of urban life and, especially, its most dominant force, hip hop. That was the reason Andrew Cuomo, a former gubernatorial candidate, asked him to join a broad-based coalition that called itself "Countdown to Fairness."

Simmons was eager to make a deal. Sources familiar with the proceedings noted that is why Pataki invited him to join the eleventh-hour negotiations. The governor believed that the hip-hop mogul was willing to make concessions on some of the terms Democrats had proven unwilling to compromise on. Hopeful that a deal could be struck, Pataki stated that he was prepared to make sentences more proportionate for the lower-level drug crimes that were receiving fifteen- to twenty-five-year sentences. But standing firm with his more conservative Republican mates, he added, "I also want to see tougher sentences for people who use children or sell drugs near schoolyards or who have a weapon, use a gun, or drug kingpins, and I think we're seeing some progress toward that." New York Republicans also wanted prosecutors, rather than judges, to maintain final say regarding sentencing. These were some of the main points of disagreement that kept the Republican senate and the Democrat-controlled assembly from reaching an agreement.

Simmons came from a place, the world of business, that was far apart from the planet professional politicians inhabited. Thus, he was less concerned with political quibbling than he was with clear-cut results. Two weeks before his late-night session in the governor's office, he told reporters, "Repeal or reform, I think, are semantics, but there will be dramatic change," adding, "we know it is going to get done." Supporters of a full repeal had expressed concerns that Simmons, a political novice, was too eager to compromise. Simmons was no stranger to deal making. He built his entire hip-hop empire on the ability to cut deals, and now he was trying to wield that same magic in a different and much more significant arena, state legislative politics.

A few days before the end of the legislative session he told the *New York Times*, "I negotiate deals every day and I don't care about people being upset. This law has been there for 30 years and it needs changing now. If there is a deal at all, it will be a compromise." Sounding like a political pragmatist who believed that something was better than nothing, he noted, "In this session, there will not be a full repeal. I want a deal. I want people to get home. What we want is for nonviolent, first-time offenders never to be subject to these harsh laws."

With Simmons and his star-power model of politicking, "Countdown to Fairness" was able to generate more attention for the repeal than any other previous effort. It was one of the things that opened the door for Simmons to become a player in the high stakes world of politics. In his effort to mount greater pressure on lawmakers, Simmons rallied support from the world he was most familiar with, hip hop. As one of the most successful entrepreneurs in hip hop's thriving culture and economy, Simmons had access to the movement's elite creative and celebrity classes. A few well-placed phone calls from him could turn out some of the biggest names in hip hop and entertainment—Jay-Z, Sean "P. Diddy" Combs, Alicia Keyes, Mariah Carey, LL Cool J—to support whatever cause he promoted and that sparked big crowds and even more important, free media publicity.

In the weeks leading up to the close of the legislative session Simmons used his ties to hip hop to stage an all-out campaign blitz that included high-profile public rallies at City Hall Park and the Public Theater on Lafayette Street in the East Village. Simmons also worked to run spots on some of New York's most popular urban radio stations. It was a calculated effort to use his clout with the street and the hip-hop elite to apply public pressure on lawmakers.

Famous for his success in selling hip hop to the mainstream Simmons was slowly establishing a foot in the political arena. It was an unlikely move from a man who, by his own admission, had never been involved in politics and had only recently bothered to vote. Already a major cultural and economic force, hip hop had created its own small power elite that had access to the things politics and politicians are drawn to most: money, celebrity, and the influence both generate. That was certainly the case four years earlier when Simmons held a $1,000-a-plate fundraiser at his SoHo apartment for the then would-be junior senator from New York, First Lady Hillary Clinton. That gathering was his first official bid to be what one newsweekly called, "the President of hip hop." Simmons was clearly positioning himself as the man who could not only deliver a constituency—the hip-hop generation—but more important a group of young, hip leaders in business and entertainment who could bolster any politician's bid for office.

It was that kind of influence that drew considerable fire from critics who asserted that Simmons's unprecedented access to state lawmakers was an example of the kind of influence peddling that has muddied the political waters. Some Republican and Democratic lawmakers complained that Simmons's participation in the down-to-the-wire negotiations was inappropriate and demonstrated once again how money and power can buy the kind of access simply not available to most citizens. Blair Horner, a New York Public Interest Research Group lobbyist said, "It is the clearest example of how the wealthy and the famous have unbelievable access to the state's top officials. Albany is increasingly becoming a world of the political elite, the big donors, celebrities and the politically powerful, like trade associations and unions, while everyone else is left scrambling around for scraps."

The parties emerged from the governor's office at one o'clock in the morning after an unprecedented seven-hour session. The meeting was later described as tense and tough toned. According to staff members, on several occasions, Simmons managed to keep the meeting alive when everyone else was ready to give up. Throughout the marathon negotiations he urged them on, declaring, "we have to close this, we have to close this." At one point in the meeting Bruno reportedly announced, "I'm out of here," which provoked a rather heated exchange between him and Simmons that involved shouting and threats.

As he boarded a private helicopter waiting to fly him home, Simmons was under the impression that a deal had been reached. Though compromises had been made, he believed the forthcoming repeal was much better than the previous condition. The nuts and bolts of the deal would have to be worked out in conference with state assembly staff. However, once the elected officials convened the conference later that day, the framework for the deal collapsed. Political insiders described the breakdown as politics as usual. Once again, and despite a massive publicity effort and rising public pressure, lawmakers failed to agree on a repeal of the state's drug statutes.

A few days after the marathon session, obviously disappointed that a deal was not secured, Simmons expressed his regrets: "I feel it is a disservice to the people of New York that 85 percent of the people want this law changed and that it is these guys' job to live up to the people's will."

Simmons's crusade for what he called social and political justice did not start or stop with the repeal effort. A few years earlier, inspired by what he saw as a newfound spirituality from his appreciation of hatha yoga, Simmons began devoting more time to social issues and charitable causes. Like the hip-hop movement, Simmons was full of contradictions. While he vehemently defended corporate hip hop—the misogyny, violence, and ghetto-fabulous excesses— as artists simply staying true to themselves and their hard knock experiences, he also readily acknowledged that he was packaging urban style and culture for mainstream consumption. Simmons told a reporter once, "I have never targeted any of my products to African-Americans. . . . What I do is for cool Americans."

Maybe it was age or simply the realization that the indulgent lifestyle he was living as a result of his ability to package "ghetto culture" for more upscale markets smacked of hypocrisy. Or maybe it was simply time to give back to a movement that had given him so much. In 2001 Simmons launched what he hoped would be his boldest and most important initiative ever, The Hip Hop Summit Action Network (HSAN). The organization, in his words, was dedicated to "helping provide a voice for those who did not have a voice."

Though the HSAN would receive considerable press and publicity, it was, in truth, just one of a number of efforts under way to make hip hop matter in the realm of politics.

• • •

Whatever social or political impact hip hop has had on young people has come primarily in the world of popular culture. Hip hop's evolution launched a revolution in youth culture. All the things that traditionally matter to young people—style, music, fashion, and a sense of generational purpose—have come under the spell of hip hop.

Whether it has been the incendiary theater of Public Enemy, the pro-woman statements of Queen Latifah, or the millennial musings of Kayne West, hip hop's oppositional ethos has led to some of the most memorable moments and images in recent American pop culture history.

Hip hop's mostly symbolic moves against establishment authority illustrated how politics can often reach beyond familiar methods and venues. Nevertheless, because hip hop's grandest political moves have taken place on the stages of pop culture, they have not been able to directly engage or affect the institutions that impact young people's lives. The movement's political identity has played a subordinate role to the power and popularity of hip hop's commercial identity. But efforts to realize its political potential have re-emerged with renewed vigor.

The idea that hip hop can be a political resource is not unique. Afrika Bambaataa, one of the movement's pioneers, experimented with the notion that hip hop could and should use its sway to inspire young people to be agents of social change. Despite the corporate takeover of hip hop, the movement's die-hard troops have continued to maintain that hip hop still belongs to the people and communities that inspired its formation. That romantic sentiment notwithstanding, the hip-hop world has changed dramatically since the days it served mainly as a creative and recreational outlet for marginal youths.

With competing interests and ambitions in full swing, the effort to tap and cultivate hip hop's political potential is sparking an intense debate within the movement. Hip hop, despite the images of a youth-based and exuberant culture, is made up of several factions. The movement is comprised of various age groups ranging from a forty-something member like Chuck D to bright-eyed teenagers who have never known a world without hip hop. Hip hop is also marked by regional, racial, and ethnic divisions. The clash between those who see hip hop as a source of profit versus those who view it as a source of politics is also intense. The challenge of devising a real political program in the midst of these and other divisions is immense.

There is general agreement on some themes regarding hip hop's impending bid to become a political force. Because hip hop is so closely associated with black and Latino youths, there is widespread agreement that racial politics will be a major part of the mix. There is also reasonable consensus that hip hop will be an urban-based movement. But the prospects for sustaining consensus regarding hip hop's political future quickly diminish after that. The issues that confront the hip-hop movement, inevitably, are intertwined with some of the larger and more vexing challenges facing millennial America.

Developing an urban-based political agenda is increasingly difficult work because of the racial and ethnic flux that characterizes America's cities. For decades the term *urban youth* has been synonymous with black youth. Likewise, for most of its history hip hop has been made synonymous with black culture. But both logics have become essentially obsolete as the presence of Latino and even Asian American youths redefine America's urban landscape and the timbre of hip hop.

Efforts to mobilize a political base in hip hop typically start with the false premise that the movement is essentially black. Not only does the premise disregard hip hop's rich history and cultural legacy; it also limits its reach and potential impact. Even during its humble beginnings hip hop was never strictly a black thing. It has always been multiracial, multicultural, and multilingual. Those qualities formed a movement that has defied all attempts to impose the strict racial definitions and caricatures that endeavor to limit its potential reach and influence. By insisting on borrowing from various cultural, musical, aesthetic, and political traditions, hip hop became an incredibly rich fountainhead of youth creativity and expression. While black youth play a central role in hip hop, white, Latino, and Asian youths continue to make their mark on the movement, too. The idea of a national hip-hop political agenda, while enticing, faces enormous difficulty due to the sheer complexity of the movement and its ever-evolving constituency.

In addition to coming to terms with the changing racial makeup of hip hop, the movement's would-be movers and shakers must also grapple with the messy and contentious work of forming a political agenda. Unlike the issue that defined the generational mission of civil rights—de jure segregation—there is no single great issue around which the hip-hop movement can rally. After the civil rights movement won its most important legislative and constitutional victory, the defeat of legalized racial discrimination, racial politics became considerably more complex and, as it turns out, difficult to wage.

Not only have the issues multiplied—public health, segregation, education, and incarceration just to name a few—but finding common ground can also be elusive. The cleavages within black and Latino America are decisive and incredibly divisive. In addition to the generational tensions within these communities, conflict also appears along the lines of class, gender, color, and sexuality. The idea that blacks and Latinos in America can and should share similar interests within their respective communities baffles any effort to establish a modern-day civil rights movement.

The desire to develop a more urbane political sensibility within the hip-hop movement is growing more robust and reflects a certain degree of maturity and introspection. The idea that hip hop can—and even should be—a political force has compelled many in the movement to begin thinking more seriously about how best to realize such a vision. This all comes at a critical juncture in hip hop's history; a time when many in the movement believe that if hip hop does not harness its political energy soon, the chance or the desire to do so will evaporate. This sense of urgency, the idea that hip hop is ready to make a bigger mark on the world, sets the stage for the movement's most important struggle—a struggle within its ranks to define its political calling.

At its core the struggle for hip hop is a debate about how the movement can regain a sense of responsibility and commitment to its overwhelmingly, though admittedly diverse, youth-based constituency. The will to translate hip hop's momentum into a catalyst for social change represents a noteworthy moment in the movement. Even so, it offers no guarantees about its future political identity or efficacy.

•••

According to the HSAN's mission statement, it is "a non-profit, non-partisan national coalition of Hip-Hop artists, entertainment industry leaders, education advocates, civil rights proponents, and youth leaders united in the belief that Hip-Hop is an enormously influential agent for social change which must be responsibly and proactively utilized to fight the war on poverty and injustice." The group promotes itself as the biggest organization of its kind and frequently implies that it is best suited to realize hip hop's political potential. While naming himself chairman, Simmons, in a surprising move, chose Dr. Benjamin Chavis Muhammad as CEO and president of the HSAN.

Chavis Muhammad was a forty-year veteran of the civil rights struggle in America. His baptism into politics began at the early age of twelve, when he became a member of the National Association for the Advancement of Colored People (NAACP). Chavis Muhammad was part of the Wilmington 10, a group of African Americans who were wrongly convicted of setting a white-owned grocery store on fire in Wilmington, North Carolina, in 1971 during a period of local racial unrest. They were later found innocent of the charges, and a judge released them from prison after they had served four and a half years.

The experience reinforced Chavis Muhammad's steely commitment to racial justice and equality. He went on to become a full-time activist and one of the civil rights movement's young lions, immersing himself in grassroots activism. When he was chosen as CEO and executive director of the NAACP in 1993, he called it a logical progression: the culmination of a life's effort devoted to the struggle for racial equality. Aware of the dwindling influence of the NAACP at the time, Chavis Muhammad announced that two of his goals were to modernize the organization and infuse it with energy, excitement, and a younger membership. He took great pride in the fact that he appreciated the need to reach out to young street gangs and generation "next." "I'm not a stranger in the 'hood," he proclaimed at his first press conference as CEO. "I know we need to reach out and embrace our young people."

Soon after what he believed was his crowning achievement Chavis Muhammad found himself in the center of a public debacle when the NAACP Board of Directors alleged that, without its knowledge or approval, he used $332,400 from the organization's funds to settle a sexual harassment and discrimination lawsuit a former employee of the organization had filed against him. On August 20, 1994, just sixteen months after being named to the organization's top post, the Board voted to dismiss him. Three years later Chavis Muhammad joined the Nation of Islam, changed his name, and hitched his political future to Louis Farrakhan.

• • •

Even as hip hop struggles to define what it is politically, it has always professed to know what it is not—the civil rights movement. Like most youth-based cultures, generation hip hop believed that previous generations simply did not understand the world it inherited or why the movement was so important to them. Thus, it was striking that a member of the old black political guard was selected to lead what was widely considered a much younger and future-oriented political enterprise. But the choice of Chavis Muhammad made perfectly good sense to Simmons. "He is not judgmental," Simmons explains. "He sees the goodness of kids and makes the kids see the beauty in their ideas. To have Ben on my team is the most credible stamp of approval."

By choosing Chavis Muhammad to run the HSAN, Simmons gave a strong indication about the direction of the organization's political work. Simmons's affection for Chavis Muhammad and his religious and political ally, Minister Farrakhan, tilted the HSAN toward the Nation of Islam, an organization whose political program and philosophy is notably conservative when it comes to the politics of race, gender, and the family. Despite the desire to break new political ground that distinguishes hip hop's political program from others, the HSAN, at least early on in its career, has invested the bulk of its energy and resources in rallies, threatened boycotts, and massive voter registration drives—all staple activities in the struggle for civil rights.

The HSAN is best known for the various rallies held in some of the nation's biggest urban markets, including New York, Philadelphia, Chicago, Houston, Detroit, Los Angeles, and Miami. In 2003 and 2004 the HSAN focused its efforts on Hip-Hop Team Vote, a massive youth voter-registration campaign. The goal was to impact the 2004 presidential elections. In January 2004, the HSAN looked to register 10,000 new voters. Later, in May, the Detroit Hip Hop Summit, with the help of Eminem's scheduled appearance, had a turnout of more than 4,800 at the Fox Theater downtown. At that summit Chavis Muhammad announced that since the Detroit summit the previous April, the organization had registered more than 40,000 young people in the Motor City. He noted that statewide another 35,000 had been registered. HSAN representatives declared they also registered 40,000 in Chicago and 60,000 during its Los Angeles event. The HSAN boasted that its Philadelphia summit registered the most voters ever, 80,000, by a hip-hop-related event.

But most political analysts agree that the biggest challenge to impacting election outcomes is not necessarily registering voters but getting them to turn out at the polls. That is a different and, ultimately, much more difficult effort. When it comes to turning out the *youth* vote, the challenge is even steeper. Moreover, there were no real signs that the HSAN had developed the local networks necessary to actually turn out young voters to the polls in the cities the organization visited. According to the U.S. Census Bureau, in the 2000 elections the lowest voting rate, 36 percent, belonged to eighteen- to twenty-four-year-old Americans. This group was half as likely to vote as persons ages sixty-four to seventy-two. The focus on registration and the difficulty getting young people to the polls on Election Day suggests that the HSAN's biggest effort, as noble as it is, is unlikely to have much of an impact.

Though the summits have generated considerable buzz, some have questioned their relevance in hip hop's future as a political force. After observing the 2004 Detroit Summit, Brian McCollum, the *Detroit Free Press* music and pop culture critic, offered some keen observations. He noted that efforts to register young voters are essentially flawed because they work from the assumption that young people share the same goals. "Apparently, if you're 23, you're against oil companies, gun rights and tax cuts. Critical thinking is abandoned for the insulting notion of 'youth' as some like-minded bloc." Ultimately, McCollum came away from the summit unconvinced that it would have an enduring impact on Detroit-area youths.

"Simmons and his summit," McCollum writes, "storm in and slip away leaving a big paradox: Hip-hop is a potent catalyst for transforming the world, but hip-hop is merely entertainment." Rather than engage in substantive debate, he thought, the summit relied too heavily on the appearances of hip-hop celebrities like Eminem and catchy slogans: "Mobilization. Empowerment. Involvement." that possessed very little meaning. In the end, he rated the summit's ability to inspire young people to get involved in politics somewhere between slight and ineffectual.

After the Houston summit in January of 2004, City Council member Ada Edwards came away with a similar observation. Like the thousands of hip-hop fans in other cities, the 20,000 people who filled the campus of Texas Southern University attended the event for various reasons. Some came to catch a glimpse of some of hip hop's finest celebrities. Others came hoping to get a foot inside hip hop's industry door. Still others came hoping to learn more about how hip hop could enhance their involvement in important social and political issues.

In anticipation of the event, one eighteen-year-old Houston woman captured the sentiment of many young people: "I'm hoping that we get to see another side of them [the celebrities] as people and hear their thoughts about how involved we should be in the community." Council member Edwards helped to bring many of the one hundred fifty high school kids she works with in a local youth-initiative organization. When the event was over, she recalls, "Many of them left the event feeling disappointed. They felt like it was essentially old people talking to themselves." Once again the HSAN put on a good show, but the net effect of the results was minimal at best. "You don't use episodic rallies to motivate people or at least sustain real political momentum," Edwards believes.

One of the biggest dilemmas facing the HSAN has been its inability to speak to the local issues that might actually captivate young people's interest in politics. Critics believe that by reaching for broad themes, instead of local and specific issues, the HSAN fumbles away a great opportunity to make politics real, salient, and tangible for young people. Not singling out the HSAN specifically, Edwards laments, "I wish that we would stop selling our young people short. This generation is smart and has access to unprecedented technology and other means of self-empowerment. To play them like a rap song is inexcusable."

In his bid for the political spotlight Simmons, like the seasoned politician he professes not to be, has learned to stay on message. "I have no aspirations [to seek political office]. To move young people to a higher consciousness is my greatest aspiration, to make a difference in terms of young people." Many people, including his critics, believe that his heart is in the right place. But they also believe that Simmons recognizes the power and financial gain in his newfound political calling. The *Village Voice*'s Ta-Nehisi Coates calls Simmons's political philosophy "Compa$$ionate Capitali$m," noting that for hip hop's would-be political king, "business is politics and politics is business, so it's essential that while he hawks voter registration he also hawks his latest product."

More than a few people have speculated whether or not Simmons's political efforts are simply another way to promote himself, his hustle, and his branding of hip hop for widespread consumption. One can only wonder if Simmons is talking about the hip-hop community or himself when he boasts, "The hip-hop community takes pride in growth. They love big. Not cool, small, and alternative. Hip-hop aspires to own the mainstream."

The use of celebrity as a catalyst to generate youth interest and media attention for the causes he champions is Simmons's modus operandi. "The most important thing we gotta do is make it cool to show up at rallies, make it in style to pay attention," he says, waxing his own brand of political acumen. But the aura of power that celebrity confers is where his political juice, his power, comes from. Simmons's access to money endears him to politicians who otherwise maintain a safe distance from anything that smacks of hip hop. However, his use of celebrity and strong ties to corporate America also ignite the ire of his critics.

Inside the hip-hop movement is a growing segment of hard-core subscribers who believe that the idea that Simmons, a figure they associate with the hostile corporate takeover and subsequent demise of hip hop, can realize hip hop's political destiny lacks credibility. No position articulates this sentiment more forcefully than New York–based hip-hop and grassroots activist Rosa Clemente. In an open letter that generated quite a stir on the Internet, Clemente challenged Simmons's self-appointment as hip hop's political leader.

"Dear Russell: Here is a news flash, as quiet as its been kept YOU ARE NOT HIP HOP!," Clemente roars in the opening line of her letter. "Many of us have this conversation about you and others in the industry like you every day. The industry who has pimped hip-hop culture" by promoting images "that allow law enforcement to criminalize the Hip-Hop generation" and "allow for ten year old children to use the word Nigga, Bitch, [and] Ho, as frequently as they say 'What's up?' " The letter berates Simmons for claiming to speak for the streets while socializing with the likes of Donald Trump and Martha Stewart and holding fundraisers for politicians like Hillary Clinton. Clemente asks Simmons, "How many fundraisers have you held for the numerous grassroots organizations?" The letter represents a view that is widely held among hip-hop activists—that Simmons is out of touch with the movement's grass roots and fails to appreciate, assist, or even acknowledge their efforts. In several media interviews he seems to equate access to big name rappers with access to hip hop's pulse. Thus he can easily dismiss activists who in his words, "don't know no rappers."

Though Clemente's letter strikes a seemingly personal chord, it was consciously political and purposefully polemical. Deep down it reflects a growing anxiety within the movement about Simmons's bid to control all things hip hop. Influencing how hip hop is packaged for global consumption is one thing. Influencing how it serves as a resource for political empowerment is another one. The concern about Simmons is a recognition that in a capitalist culture money equals power. Over the years Simmons has used his access to wealthy investors to establish a firm niche in hip hop's widening commercial empire. Thus, Simmons's vision of hip-hop politics will likely hold a seat at whatever political table or party the movement is invited to join.

In an effort to outmaneuver the HSAN, Clemente and a group of young community activists organized the National Hip Hop Political Convention. The group convened hip hop's first ever political convention five months before the 2004 presidential election. Reportedly more than two thousand delegates attended the affair. Like Simmons, the organizers realize that there is untapped political power in hip hop's widening and maturing constituency. Unlike Simmons, the convention sought to gain its political prestige and influence from below, opting to be an organization comprised of the people rather than personalities.

The convention focused on a five-point agenda: education, economic justice, criminal justice, health care, and human rights. Predictably, there were several organizational and administrative glitches that provoked a reality check about the business of organizing on a national level. After realizing how difficult it was organizers apparently decided against an earlier decision to hammer out a party platform that could be delivered to the two major political parties. Jeff Chang, author and one of the organizers of the event, noted that while the event was historic it was also chaotic. He reported that "subgenerational conflict threatened to flare between hip-hop activists under 25 and those over 25."

Though some came away unsure about the convention, others went back to their communities confident that a new movement had been launched. Perhaps the most significant achievement of the convention was serving notice that hip hop's political future would not be left in the hands of the very corporate interests that blunted its political edge. While they never acknowledged Simmons directly, the national convention was a clear salvo in the emerging struggle for the soul of the hip-hop movement. That message, more than anything, is likely to resonate for years as hip hop's true believers move to both imagine and realize an actionable political agenda.

$$\bullet \ \bullet \ \bullet$$

For all of the insistence that it represents a dramatic break from past political efforts, the political discourse in hip hop remains mesmerized by the legacy of civil rights. Even as the National Hip Hop Political Convention set out to carve out a new era in American politics the organization, like the HSAN, looked backwards to move its agenda forward. Inspiration for the convention was drawn from the 1972 effort to organize a black political party. During that historical meeting in Gary, Indiana, blacks came face to face with the harsh realities that accompanied the changing class structure and widening ideological and political gulf in black America. At that meeting the divisions between capitalists and Marxists, humanists and econo-mists, radical and establishment ideologues, Democrats and Repub-licans were too severe to put aside. The disagreements that erupted on the floor of that convention shattered the notion that blacks could easily come together under one tent, forge a united front, and form a national political agenda. It was a bruising defeat and one that also signaled just how complex racial politics would be in the aftermath of the civil rights struggle.

Similarly, Simmons and the HSAN are also seduced by the legacy of civil rights. Chavis Muhammad's selection suggests that Simmons envisions hip-hop politics as black politics. But that vision fails to understand the steadily changing character of hip hop or black America. From the very beginning the movement has struggled with questions like "who is hip hop?" and "what is hip hop?" Now, as it be-gins to move its political agenda forward, it will have to grapple with another challenging and equally contentious question: "What causes will hip hop fight for and on whose behalf?"

The rallies and threatened boycotts staged by the HSAN are at-tempts to reenact one of the grandest political dramas in American history. On a more personal note Simmons has used the power that celebrity confers to fortify his own celebrity and bid to become hip hop's chief political power broker. His high-profile efforts to repeal New York State's drug laws, to help in the fight against Mayor Mi-chael Bloomberg's proposed cut to New York City public education, and to organize the various Hip Hop summits have elevated his status as a political player. Simmons has used his savvy instincts and media contacts to engineer a buzz that suggests he is the figure and the force that can best realize hip hop's political future. In 2003 *Newsweek* reported that because of his ties in business, media, and politics, Simmons "is now emerging as potentially the most credible and effective leader of the post-civil-rights generation." It is certainly a position that Simmons, his denials notwithstanding, covets. But there is one slight problem in his bid to become hip hop's premier political player: Hip hop is a movement that neither needs nor wants a lone spokesperson. Simmons's move is similar to the dilemma that has baffled the black political establishment ever since the passing of the civil rights movement.

In a highly provocative piece Mark Bowden, a correspondent for *The Atlantic Monthly,* argues that the job of the Negro spokesperson no longer exists. Bowden writes: "Civil-rights progress has desimplified black politics. African-American voters no longer come in one flavor. Today they find common cause in a yearning for continued racial progress, but they increasingly disagree—just as white voters disagree—over how to achieve it." In spite of this, the legacies of Martin and Malcolm and the idea of a galvanizing figure continue to capture the imagination of black leaders and their grandiose though largely unrealizable visions of modern-day political leadership. Despite the Herculean effort by Simmons, no one person can represent the phenomenally diverse world hip hop has become.

Seeking to find its place in the political arena, the HSAN has formed into a top-down organization proposing to lead what has always been a bottom-up cultural movement. And though the organization claims to be nonpartisan, its political philosophy and ideology lean decisively left and liberal in the traditional sense. Early on in their stewardship of the HSAN, Simmons and Chavis Muhammad used what little political capital they had to influence national election outcomes by visiting the nation's largest urban constituencies. Simmons and Chavis Muhammad measure their impact largely in terms of voter registration. Their notion of politics is, in some ways, purely a numbers game: in essence assessing their political relevance in terms of number of registered voters. And while the drive to register young voters is a noteworthy effort, it remains unlikely to produce the kinds of political change the two men are pursuing.

Ironically, the HSAN can enlarge its impact on politics by downsizing its current vision. In terms of electoral politics, a focus on turning out the hip-hop vote in key battleground states could be highly effective and, most importantly, manageable and measurable. While such an effort may not be as grand or conspicuous as the celebrity-driven summits the HSAN sponsored, it would likely have a more meaningful impact. A hip-hop political agenda that *matters* needs to be more strategically focused and requires people willing to do the messy work that emphasizes substantive change over publicity-seeking media events. Up to this point, the HSAN has generated huge crowds of young people and media attention, but the power of celebrity cannot sustain a movement or deliver important political victories by itself. At its heart the HSAN reflects a surprising degree of naiveté regarding hip hop's political potential. As noble as their intentions may be, Simmons and Chavis Muhammad represent a brand of politics that, ultimately, is of little use to hip hop.

These and other criticisms notwithstanding the HSAN's idea of organizing hip hop's political potential remains viable. As hip hop imagines and works toward the day it can genuinely impact the conditions and institutions that shape the life chances of young people, the political career of the movement becomes even more uncertain. The HSAN's goal of realizing and cultivating hip hop's budding political future would be served well by adhering to a principle that Chavis Muhammad professed to hold as he poised himself to revive the NAACP by making it more relevant to a younger constituency. "You don't get young people back by just making speeches. You've gotta get out there in the 'hood."

# CHAPTER SIX

# Young Voices in the Hood

*Ain't no power like the power of the youth,*
*'cause the power of youth don't change!*
—BOOKS NOT BARS

The West Coast hip-hop scene exploded onto the pop culture stage with a bang, literally and figuratively, in the late 1980s, powered by the melodic grooves, gangsta rhymes, and thug-life theatrics of some of the era's most colorful pop personalities. Ice-T, Ice-Cube, Dr. Dre, Snoop Dogg, Tupac Shakur, and Suge Knight represented the West Coast to the fullest. Whether it was the G-funk beats, pimp narratives, or a shrewdly calculated outlaw image, the indelible mark they left on America's pop ethos put West Coast hip hop on the map. By the middle nineties the styles and trends developed in California were undeniable forces in a hip-hop movement that was making waves far beyond its New York epicenter. But commercial success and notoriety also subjected West Coast hip hop to the scrutinizing gaze of politicians, law enforcement officials, and culture pundits who lambasted gangsta rap, in particular, for its alleged corrupting influence on America's youth. Still, even as it found itself in the middle of a controversial debate about hip hop, censorship, and the moral health of America's young, California was also where the movement, far away from the glare of the media spotlight, was struggling to form a viable political voice and constituency.

In the mountainous terrain, vast highways, and eclectic bed of urban and suburban communities that make up California's Bay Area, young people of different colors, creeds, and cultural ancestry have made hip hop an incredibly vital fountain of identity and creativity, expression and exploration, pleasure and politics. It is not unusual to see a Chinese American dropping some clever lyrics at a local venue, a Mexican-American break dancer rocking some acrobatic moves, or a white DJ doing work on the turntables.

"In the Bay Area," Andreana Clay says, "there is no way hip hop can be simply a black or white thing. There are so many other groups." For two and a half years Clay, who holds a Ph.D. from the University of California at Davis, studied the Bay Area hip-hop scene, visiting the many places—youth centers, community organizations, political rallies, and performance venues—where hip hop has managed to thrive as a very tangible part of young people's everyday lives. There is no debate or discernible tension regarding hip hop's multiracial face; it is simply accepted as a matter of fact. Maybe it is endemic to a region where racial and ethnic diversity is a fact of life.

In addition to its complex racial and ethnic character, the Bay Area has also become home to one of the liveliest political scenes in hip hop. Those immersed in or familiar with the Bay Area's hip-hop movement view it as more than a consumer culture. Hip hop does not simply determine the music young people listen to or the clothes they wear; it has, in many instances, become a significant way of life. Though often blamed for sullying youth values and promoting antisocial behavior, hip hop remains a fountain of inspiration and hope, a prominent vehicle used by young people to find their voice and place in the world. This is especially the case in many local communities that bear witness to grassroots activism around critical issues in the lives of America's youth. The intersection between hip hop and politics has empowered a generation of youth to believe that they not only have a right but maybe even an obligation to make a difference in their world. The effort to revive hip hop's sense of urgency as well as its voice of insurgency is strikingly foreign in a movement dominated by big money, big media, and big pimping.

While the activist impulse in the Bay Area's hip-hop scene can be partially attributed to the rich history and culture of social movements in the region, it also comes at a time when many young Californians have been pushed to the brink. Perhaps it is only fitting that the Bay Area has produced one of the most politically active hip-hop communities in the world because California has become ground zero for some of the most serious issues facing young people.

California is known as a national trendsetter. For years the University of California (UC) system was considered *the* model in public higher education. Hollywood has long been considered the capital of a global entertainment economy, the place where media-made fantasies and heroes loom bigger than anywhere else in the world. California's climate and location have made it a crucial player in the nation and the world's agricultural heartland. And in the 1990s California was the epicenter of the dot.com boom and the promise of the digital age. But California also developed a more dubious distinction in the nineties. It became the state with the nation's biggest prison population and corrections system. Just how California became the symbol of the United States' "punishment industry" is a story several years in the making.

Critics of America's rising prison population argue that the sharp racial disparities in the criminal justice system were the new civil rights issue of the millennium. That was certainly true for California's black and Latino youths who were filling up the state's correctional facilities in record numbers. California's emphatic embrace of "tough on crime" politics meant that many poor and working-class youths would end up spending some part of their lives under the supervision of the criminal justice system. That tragic reality, more than anything else, planted the seeds and the inspiration for the rise of the most politically robust constituency in the hip-hop movement.

• • •

California's harsh turn toward juvenile justice became official on March 7, 2000. That day 62 percent of those who participated in the state's primaries voted yes for the Gang Violence and Juvenile Crime

Prevention Act of 1998 or what was more commonly referred to as Proposition 21. The measures approved by Californians were by far the nation's toughest on juvenile offenders. Among other things Proposition 21 allowed prosecutors rather than judges to decide whether a young person would be tried as an adult, reduced confidentiality protections for juvenile offenders, increased penalties for gang-related crimes, allowed police to wire-tap suspected gang members, and deemed $400 worth of property damage a felony—essentially making some youthful pranks and indiscretions a more serious offense.

The changes mandated by Prop 21 were not simply sweeping, they were radical. At its core Prop 21 represented a stunning philosophical break from longstanding ideas and approaches to dealing with wayward youth, many of whom suffered as much from poverty, broken families, inadequate education, and mental health problems as they did any personal or moral defect.

For more than a century and a half the nation's juvenile justice system was based on the idea that if properly cared for, instructed, and treated, young offenders could be rescued from a life of crime and self-destructive behavior. What clearly distinguished juvenile justice was the idea that young people should be treated differently from adult offenders. Most juvenile justice operations emphasized education, job training, and counseling as ways to rehabilitate and prepare youth for an eventual return to their community. But throughout the 1980s and 1990s that philosophy came under increasing attack as media portrayals of juvenile crime became more graphic and sensational, and politicians realized that by standing up against crime, they could gain support from an electorate that tended to be older, whiter, and more affluent than the youth often targeted by tougher crime laws. Proponents of a harsher juvenile justice system asserted that previous models were outdated and needed serious upgrading to deal with the modern youth offender.

Amazingly, even as politicians and the state District Attorney's association rallied support for Prop 21, California's statistics from the state's Department of Justice confirmed that juvenile crime decreased steadily throughout the 1990s. In 1991 the state made 93,655 juvenile felony arrests. By 2000 that number was down to 63,880. Violent offenses committed by the state's youth reached 21,000 in 1991 but fell to 16,000 by 2000. Likewise, youth crimes against property declined during the same period, from 54,952 to 31, 139. In 1959, the state made 4,059 first commitments to youth correctional facilities. In 2001, the state's first commitments were significantly lower: 1,592. *Instead of* being praised for their decreasing crime rate, California's youth were being punished. The perception that youth crime was more rampant, more violent, and more menacing to law-abiding citizens than ever before was simply out of touch with reality. Prop 21, according to one *San Francisco Chronicle* editorial, "seems a solution in search of a problem."

The push for a tougher juvenile justice system in California had been years in the making but was ignited by the personal and political ambitions of Pete Wilson. During his tenure as governor of California, Wilson, with an eye on the Oval Office, helped launch a number of ballot initiatives relating to immigration, affirmative action, and crime, which touched off the state's deeply rooted racial fault lines. Wilson tried, unsuccessfully, to persuade the Democrat-run state legislature to approve tougher measures regarding juvenile delinquency. He eventually bypassed the legislature and, along with the state District Attorney's Association, successfully placed a youth crime measure on the state's ballot. Even after Californians voted him out of office, Wilson pressed hard for Prop 21. His Democratic replacement, Gray Davis, also supported the measure. Davis's critics charged that he was beholden to the political influence of one of California's most powerful lobbies, prison guards.

In his enthusiasm for Prop 21 Wilson relied heavily on nostalgia, the symbolic power of language, and what amounted to carefully coded race-speak. In an editorial that appeared in several newspapers throughout the state and in *USA Today* Wilson charged, "Today's juvenile justice system was designed in the 1940s, when 'serious' youth offenses included truancy, curfew violations and fistfights, and was intended to deal with 'juvenile delinquents' whose most serious offenses were petty theft and vandalism. It was never intended or designed to handle gang murderers with semi-automatic weapons or rapists preying upon innocent women."

But Wilson saved his most hyperbolic sales pitch for the various rallies, public meetings, and television appearances he participated in throughout the state claiming that Prop 21 was tailor made for "young super-predators." The concept of the super-predator was developed by criminologists who projected that an oncoming surge in the youth population would also trigger a subsequent explosion in youth-related crime. The notion that future generations of youths—at a time when many were likely to be brown, black, or red—represented a new species of criminal was one of the many ways in which the discourse about juvenile justice was cloaked in race-speak. Despite the careful coding, the racial undertones rang loud and clear. The super-predator image presented an unfair caricature of typical youth offenses that were overwhelming property related. According to California's Office of the Attorney General, 696 youth arrests for homicide were made in 1991. In 1998 the number of such arrests was less than half of that, 308.

Proponents and opponents of Prop 21 fought one another vigorously. However, both sides did agree on one thing. If the measure passed, it would dramatically increase the state's youth prison population and trigger the need for more beds and correctional facilities to house what was sure to be an upsurge in youths committed to the state's juvenile justice system.

California's own legislative analyst reported that Proposition 21 would cost hundreds of millions of dollars in prison construction costs, in addition to annual costs in the tens of millions for implementation. The financial and human costs Prop 21 was poised to tally were staggering. Richard Shumsky, chief probation officer for Los Angeles County, proclaimed that Prop 21 "has the potential to be overwhelming. How it plays out depends on what prosecutors and juries do, but if we're going to put many more juveniles behind bars, we're going to have to find the space and the money to do that."

If it achieved nothing else, Prop 21 promised to continue making the state's corrections budget and system, already the largest in the nation, an even bigger enterprise and that spelled big trouble for California's black and Latino youth population.

• • •

On October 28, 1994, the Bureau of Justice Statistics, a division of the U.S. Department of Justice, reported that for the first time in its history the U.S. state and federal prison population passed the one million inmates mark. It was a watershed moment in a furious trend that ushered in the rise of America's prison industrial complex, a corrections-based culture and economy. In their analysis of the prison industrial complex the Report of the National Criminal Justice Commission said, "Like the military-industrial complex that dominated defense policy during the Cold War, this crucible of private companies and government exercises a powerful influence on crime policy."

In 1980, according to the Bureau of Justice Statistics 329,821 inmates filled the nation's state and federal prisons. By 1994 that number had more than tripled to 1,053,738. The 1994 prison population, including county jails, represented a 212 percent increase since 1980. The explosive growth in America's prison population did not stop there. One year later, 1995, the U.S. experienced its second highest prisoner increase ever, surpassing the 1994 figures by nearly 41,000. The nation's greatest one-year growth occurred in 1989, roughly three years after the U.S. government declared war on drugs.

Relative to other parts of the world, the U.S. prison population was in super-growth mode between 1980 and 2000 as the nation's concerns about street crime, criminals, and public safety reached a feverish pitch. According to the Report of the National Criminal Justice Commission, between 1980 and 1996, more than six hundred new prisons were built in America at a cost of several billion dollars. In 1994 Congress and President Bill Clinton passed the most expensive crime bill in the nation's history, allocating billions of dollars to hire more police and build more prisons. Many called the prison boom the era's greatest public works program, a sad commentary on the state of national affairs and just how influential and lucrative the politics of crime had become.

The nation's prison population reached yet another milestone on June 30, 2002, when it topped two million. Malcolm Young, the director of The Sentencing Project, a Washington, D.C.–based criminal justice policy organization, called the push past two million "the legacy of an infrastructure of punishment which has been embedded in the criminal justice system over the past 30 years." That same organization reported that one of every one hundred forty Americans was in jail or prison by June 2003. Just as alarming as the number of persons filling America's prisons and jails was who were filling them: black and Latino men.

Blacks and Latinos combined made up roughly 25 percent of the general population, but they represented more than 60 percent of the prison population. The Bureau of Justice Statistics reported that more than 12 percent of all black men ages twenty-five to twenty-nine were in prison at the end of 2002. Comparatively, 2 percent of Latino men and 1 percent of white men in the same age range were in prison. At every stage in the criminal justice system—arrests, convictions, and sentencing—blacks were subjected to disproportionate representation and considerably harsher treatment. By the time the prison boom had run its more than twenty year course, the U.S. 2003 rate of 715 inmates per 100,000 residents was the highest the world had ever seen; it established the U.S. as the global leader in per capita incarceration.

If the U.S. was the world's prison nation, then California was its undisputed capital. The California Department of Corrections reported that the state's jail and prison population grew from 54,300 in 1980 to 248,516 in 2000. That was an average annual growth rate of about 14 percent. In the 1980s alone the population quadrupled. Like the general U.S. prison population, California continued record growth throughout the nineties despite steep declines in violent crime. The state's census concluded that between 1990 and 2000 the number of people incarcerated in federal and state prisons and county jails expanded by nearly 40 percent. By the late 1990s California's prison population was greater than France's and Germany's prisoner counts—combined. It was nearly ten times the level of the early 1970s. The growth was fueled by several factors: increase drug-related arrests and convictions, mandatory sentencing, passage of the "three strikes" law, and an unusually high rate of parole violators being returned to the corrections system.

Criminal justice activists in the state wondered out loud if California's "race to incarcerate" was a response to the dramatic demographic shifts that are remaking the state's population and personality. As recently as 1970 whites accounted for nearly 80 percent of California's total population. By 2000 that number had fallen to just below 60 percent. And as population projections have maintained for at least the last fifteen years, California is well on its way to becoming a state where whites will soon be a numerical minority. By 2000 nearly one-third, 32 percent, of California's population was Latino. Asian Americans, growing annually, made up 11 percent of the state's population. Blacks made up 9 percent of California's population.

In addition to its changing racial composition, California was trending younger by 2000. Thirty-seven percent of California's population is under the age of twenty-five, and a growing percentage of that demographic is made up of Latino, Asian, and black youths. California's seismic racial shifts have stirred paranoia, a sense that a once great state is being overrun and even undermined by the onset of a major racial makeover.

As they surveyed the statistics confirming the state's surge of prisoners, many in the criminal justice activist community argued that the increasing investment in incarceration and the decreasing investment in education created a situation in which California's most disadvantaged youth "were being set up to be locked up." The claim is not nearly as alarmist when you break the state's incarceration of youth down by race. In California's twelve largest counties, which make up 75 percent of the state's population, Latinos make up 43 percent of the youth population, followed by whites at 35 percent, Other (most notably Asian) at 13 percent and African Americans at 9 percent. In those same counties blacks made up 43 percent of youth arrested. Twenty-five and 19 percent of youth arrested were, respectively, white and Latino. The overwhelming majority of youth incarcerated in California are either black or Latino men.

California's tough response to young offenders did not exempt young women. For much of their history, America's prisons have been a place where the number of male inmates far outnumbered female inmates. While men continue to represent a substantial majority of America's record-high prison population, the number of women prisoners between 1980 and 2000 actually increased at a rate greater than their male counterparts. In 1980, in America, 12,331 women were behind bars. Fifteen years later, the number of women in U.S. prisons had risen to 64,403.

In California between 1987 and 1997, the female population increased by 31 percent and has continued rising at a pace greater than the male population. In their analysis of juveniles and the criminal justice system, the Center on Juvenile and Criminal Justice (CJCJ) found that black women make up the state's fastest growing segment of the prison population. In 2000 about 25 percent of the state's misdemeanors and 17 percent of the felony arrests were young women.

Rachel Bolden-Kramer, a young Bay Area activist, now attending Harvard, remembers that shortly after the passage of Prop 21 a number of young women she worked with in the San Francisco–based Center for Young Women's Development began to disappear. That organization worked closely with a wide range of young women, including the homeless, victims of abuse, single mothers, and prostitutes. "We were simply losing young women who could have either been released or put on probation," recalls Bolden-Kramer. She witnessed up close how the state's incarceration of youth led to the loss of young friends and crucial relationships.

Concerned about the rising presence of girls and young women in the state's corrections system, San Francisco's Commission on the Status of Women authorized a study in 1996. Titled *Out of Sight, Out of Mind: The Plight of Adolescent Girls in the San Francisco Juvenile Justice System,* the report found that the situation facing girls in the criminal justice system was "grim, unfair, and continued to be in a crisis." The report offered several sobering facts. Throughout the nineties arrests of girls increased by more than 50 percent. Nationally, arrests of girls made up a quarter of all juvenile arrests. In San Francisco, girls' offense bookings for all offenses jumped 121 percent from 1990 to 1994. The report also found that because there are fewer correctional facilities for girls they spend longer periods of time at juvenile hall than boys. Girls were also more likely to be arrested for status offenses like running away or breaking curfew laws. But state crime statistics also show that arrest rates for girl felons remained relatively unchanged compared to boys. Throughout the 1990s the felony arrest rates for juvenile boys—82,387 in 1991 and 63,889 in 2000—showed steady declines. The felony arrest rates for girls did not show a similar decline—11, 278 in 1991 versus 10, 893 in 2000—according to the California Department of Justice statistics on juvenile felony arrests.

As in many states around the country, California was forced to modify and expand its approach to corrections in the face of a growing female population. Many corrections officials and administrators discovered that girls come into the system with an array of gender-specific medical and psychological needs. Many girls and young women who end up in the state's correction system are often victims of some combination of emotional, physical, and sexual abuse. In the most extreme cases many have endured homelessness, drug addiction, prostitution, or the enormous stress associated with teenage pregnancy.

The 1980s and 1990s defined what some termed *the punishment decade*, a whirlwind of political, legislative, and legal maneuvering that subscribed to the idea that the best way to deal with young offenders was to lock them up for extended periods of time. Whether blacks or Latinos, young men or women, hip hop's youth found themselves—or someone close—chained to a correctional system and culture determined to mete out severe punishment. The harsh turn in the juvenile justice system added up to more than the raw number of youths sentenced to lockup. For some of hip hop's most disenfranchised and disempowered youth, the rise of the prison industrial complex was all too real and that was all too tragic.

• • •

At the center of the state's youth incarceration crisis was the California Youth Authority (CYA). Created by law in 1941 the CYA began providing educational training and parole supervision for juvenile and young adult offenders two years later. According to its own mission, as described in Section 1700 of the State Welfare and Institutions Code, the CYA was created to protect the public from criminal activity. Among other things, the law mandates that the nation's largest youthful offender agency provide a range of educational, treatment, and training services for young offenders and also aid in the development of crime prevention programs and services.

Like many of the earliest juvenile justice programs in the U.S., the CYA was created to reform and improve the lives of young people who had presumably lost their way. That idea dated back to the early nineteenth century when a series of reform measures were created to deal specifically with young offenders. The first facility created for children was the House of Refuge in New York in 1825. Several states followed suit and began creating facilities and services for errant youth. Though some of the institutions may not have been ideal, many of them did abide by an important philosophy. For more than a century and a half the U.S. juvenile justice system was based on the idea that young offenders, if properly cared for, instructed, and treated, could be salvaged and returned to their communities as healthy and productive citizens. What clearly distinguished juvenile justice was the idea that young people should be treated differently than adult offenders. But in the 1980s and 1990s that philosophy came under increasing attack, as the image of juvenile crime became more graphic and sensational.

In response to the perception that youth offenders were more violent and dangerous, a much more aggressive approach was adopted by the juvenile justice apparatus. Throughout the nineties management of the agency California's young wards simply called "the YA" reflected the shift toward punishment in the U.S. criminal justice system. By 2000 the CYA was a $427 million a year operation whose eleven institutions and four fire-fighting camps housed 7,563 wards. But its approach to dealing with young offenders generated statewide conflict and controversy. Several prisoners' rights and youth advocacy organizations began to document what they called systematic abuses and a poorly run state department that was wasting the public's money and, most significantly, causing juveniles more harm than good.

As an assortment of first-hand accounts and outside reviews began to shed light on life inside the CYA, the concerns and scrutiny intensified. Many wards of the CYA shared stories that were often haunting. Discussing his experience, one former ward said, "When they put me in YA, they didn't sit down with me and say, 'We're feeling what you're going through, we want to help you.' It wasn't like that. What they did was lock me up, throw me in the cage, take me to the psychologist, he diagnosed me as crazy, and they gave me drugs. That was the solution." Like many other wards, he described the CYA as a place where rehabilitation was an afterthought and staff abuses were common.

In addition, family members had to face the growing likelihood that life in the CYA for their children would be full of harsh treatment and inadequate care. One mother, discussing the CYA experience of her son, expressed the fears of many parents in an editorial that appeared in the *San Francisco Chronicle.* "Before he was incarcerated," Laura Talkington wrote, "my son was a happy and goofy kid, full of energy." As a first-grader her son was diagnosed with a hyperactive disorder. The medications he received made his behavior aggressive and unpredictable. Like a lot of poor and working-class parents, she could not afford the treatments that might have provided him better care. Eventually, his aggressive behavior led to a series of arrests that ended up placing him with the CYA at the age of fifteen. Privately, she may have believed that in the care of the CYA he would finally receive proper treatment. That was, after all, part of their stated mission.

Four years later, however, her hopes came face to face with the harsh realities of a youth corrections ethos that had hardened toward the young people it was designed to help. Instead of helping her son, the CYA appeared only to make life more perilous for the youngster. During her visits Ms. Talkington noticed the cuts, choke marks, and bruises from the constant attacks he faced. "I have seen him lose confidence in himself, become cold and depressed and fearful for his life," she said, adding that "California fulfills its obligation to rehabilitate troubled youth by putting them in large warehouses that are no different from prison." She called for the elimination of the CYA and a new approach to dealing with young offenders like her son.

First-hand accounts like these were not the exception; sadly, they represented the rule as many young people and family members found themselves caught up in the CYA's unique form of juvenile justice. For years advocacy groups had been calling for an overhaul of the CYA. Those calls had gone largely unheard, with the exception of a few minor responses here and there. But in the early part of 2004 the abuses within the CYA and its stunning failure, marked by a 90 percent recidivism rate, became too overwhelming to ignore.

On January 19, CYA authorities found Durrell Feaster, 18, and Deon Whitfield, 17, hanged from a top bunk in their cell at the Preston Youth Correctional Facility. Durrell was committed to the CYA in 2001 for crimes that included stealing a car and receiving stolen property. Still, his parents, who had adopted him as a toddler, said that he was a good kid at heart. Allen Feaster, Durrell's father, told reporters that the CYA took away his son's joy. "They killed my son," he said. "They treated him like an animal. He was not a hardcore criminal. He was a child."

Located forty miles southeast of Sacramento in the town of Ione, the Preston facility was eighteen years old and included fourteen living units, five with individual rooms and nine in open dormitories. The facility was home to seventeen- to nineteen-year-old males committed by the juvenile courts. In theory Preston offered a number of health and educational programs, but many people familiar with the unit said it was a haven for violence. One eighteen-year-old gang member and ward of the Preston facility told the *San Francisco Chronicle*, "You're going to get tested when you get here, and if you fail you're going to be a victim." Life at Preston as described by wards, staff, and outside observers resembled the kind of hardened prison culture one might expect to see in a gritty film about life inside a facility for adult offenders. Rampant violence, a survival-of-the-fittest way of behaving that subjected the mild mannered to physical and even sexual abuse, and corruption defined typical life in the CYA.

The CYA was a world apart from what most people imagine life should be like for young offenders. Barry Krisberg, president of the National Council on Crime and Delinquency, says, "When I came to California in the early '70s, the California Youth Authority was regarded as the pinnacle of enlightened and progressive corrections in this country. It was the place you went to find out what the best, cutting-edge practices were." Like many, he wondered, what had happened: "How did we (the state of California and the CYA) get here?"

The CYA took another hit in early 2004 as a series of outside independent reviews began to paint a dreadful picture of mismanagement and abuse. In response to a 2000 lawsuit filed by the Prison Law Office, a nonprofit organization that provides help to prisoners, California Attorney General, Bill Lockyer, commissioned a series of outside independent reviews of the CYA's structure, management, and culture. Each of the groups concluded that the CYA was failing miserably in its approach to juvenile justice. Among other things the outside investigations revealed that many wards are subject to: twenty-three-hour-a-day lock-up and solitary confinement for extended periods of time (up to three months); a level of violence that is unlike any other youth corrections agency in the U.S.; the misuse of medication; a lack of appropriate mental and medical health care; and little to no access to educational instruction. It was a stunning set of revelations that even the CYA, fiercely committed to its brand of juvenile justice, could neither dismiss nor defend.

While the report may have come as news to some, it did not surprise the community activists and organizations that had been campaigning against the CYA. Many of the organizers were either based in, or had close contact with, the communities that were shouldering the brunt of the youth incarceration crisis. These groups were more than familiar with the grim conditions that characterized life inside the CYA. A few years before these revelations, they had been pushing for a total overhaul of the CYA, claiming that it was part of the problem and not the solution to juvenile crime. When officials from Alameda County announced plans to build a new facility for young offenders, Bay Area activists took notice and then took action. The plan to use millions of dollars of state funds to build more space to house young people, even as juvenile crime was steadily declining, catalyzed a movement that had been simmering.

Now, with the call for more beds, a catastrophic state budget deficit, and Prop 21 going into effect, hip-hop activism was poised to make some noise.

• • •

One hundred days after the suicide deaths of Durrell Feaster and Deon Whitfield, Books Not Bars and Let's Get Free, two Bay Area grassroots organizations, held a candlelight vigil across the Golden State. More than a thousand people turned out for what was described by organizers as a time to come together for "healing, justice, and hope." For three years the two groups, along with a growing network of other organizations, had been campaigning against the abuse and neglect of the CYA, calling it "a factory of misery and child abuse." The vigil was the latest in a series of planned events that had gained the group's campaign against the incarceration of California's youths local, statewide, and even national attention.

The Bay Area campaign against the youth incarceration crisis was officially set off in the spring of 2001. That was when Alameda County Board of Supervisors' plans to build a new $176 million, 540-bed youth correctional facility in Dublin, a suburban outpost about an hour's drive from Alameda's largest city, Oakland, became public. If it was built, the new project would be one of the largest juvenile halls in the nation per capita. It seemed like overkill and a misplacement of priorities in a state where youth crime was declining and the budget deficit was growing. But the proposal was consistent with a statewide mentality and political ideology that fueled the world's biggest prison buildup in history. Most of the young people locked up in the Alameda facility were black and Latino, many of them from east Oakland, the city's poorest district.

That same spring the Ella Baker Center for Human Rights, the umbrella unit to groups like Books Not Bars and Let's Get Free, launched the "Stop the Super-Jail" campaign. It would be one of the longest and most intense political campaigns involving youth in the state.

The campaign had to confront the triple bind of race, class, and youth that made life a real challenge for many young Californians. To be young, black or Latino, and poor in California was almost a crime itself during the punishment decade. Proposition 21 had gone so far as to declare that three young people hanging out together and dressed the same could be classified as a gang. The criminalization of a generation made incarceration a reality for many young people and, like the prison industrial complex, set the stage for what some call America's new civil rights movement. It was a unique situation that defined a unique period in America's ongoing, but steadily evolving, racial saga. It was also what distinguished the hip-hop generation's struggle against social and economic injustice from the civil rights generation.

Van Jones, founder of the Ella Baker Center (EBC), offers a poignant assessment of the historical challenges that confronted California's youth in general and any effort to translate hip hop's pop-culture capital into genuine political capital. "Politics of liberation in the new century that [exists] in terms of integration vs. segregation is anachronistic. It has little to do with what's happening today. So we raise new slogans: 'schools, not jails'; 'books, not bars'; 'jobs, not jails,'" Jones explains. "The people we see on a daily basis, when they go to high school the police cars are already there, because they are stationed there. If they get into a push-and-shove match in the hallway, they don't go to the principal's office, they go to the precinct in handcuffs. That's the reality we're dealing with: over-policing, over-incarceration." Drawing an important distinction from the civil rights movement, Jones adds, "It's a very different fight. At the same time it's a continuation of the fight that started years ago."

The lead organizers of the move against the state's mighty prison industrial complex understood that their efforts to improve the lives of young people would be better served by getting young people energized and involved. And that is where hip hop entered the political mix. Coordinators at the EBC turned to hip hop as a way to get access to and inside the world of young people. The organizers understood hip hop's larger resonance and everyday relevance in the lives of young people. Many of the twenty- and thirty-something organizers at the EBC grew up with hip hop as part of their own cultural experience.

David Kahn, a coordinator of the Oakland-based group, Let's Get Free, says, "All of our staff, my co-workers and co-organizers, we all grew up on hip hop. So, aside from using it tactically or strategically as a culture hip hop informs the language we use, how we dress, and even our worldview." Hip hop has become a central component in the EBC's youth-organizing principles.

"For us," Kahn maintains, "hip hop is not some exotic thing, or something that scary kids do. It's part of who we are. And that is attractive to young people." Many of the events coordinated by the EBC use local hip-hop artists, both established and aspiring, to perform. At rallies, forums, teach-ins, and other planned events, hip hop serves as the all-important drawing card energizing young people as it strives to enlist their support in local and state causes.

But hip hop is more than a magnet that attracts young people to local campaign-related events. It is also the medium through which they articulate a vision of their world that is insightful, optimistic, and tenaciously critical of the institutions and circumstances that restrict their ability to impact the world around them. "Young people are amazing because they can take hip hop and do anything with it," says Andreana Clay, a professor who has studied the Bay area hip-hop scene. In their efforts to make hip hop matter some young people have insisted on mining the movement's political potential. This was especially evident as the campaign against the "Super-Jail" unfolded.

Organizers ratcheted up their fight against the juvenile hall by attending the Alameda County Commissioners meetings to make their case. They even made the journey up Interstate 80 to Sacramento to take their case to the California Board of Corrections, the body that made all of the final decisions about corrections in the state. Campaign organizers made it a point to bring dozens of teens with them to the meetings they attended. The goal was to let the community most affected by the state's corrections system—teens and twenty-somethings—share their thoughts, concerns, and experiences regarding the state's approach to juvenile justice. The move proved to be both powerful and persuasive.

The young people who attended the board meetings used a variety of methods to deliver their message to those in power, drawing their political inspiration and imagination from hip hop's deep creative well. If young activists were refused the opportunity to address the board, they demanded to speak until permission was granted or the meeting was shut down. When they did address city and state officials, they did so in the style, vernacular, and character of hip hop. Rachel Jackson, one of the campaign's key coordinators, noted that the young people "represent all of the stereotypes of people of color —the baggy pants, hats backward—they're the ones that are getting up in front of the Board of Corrections and speaking 'truth' to power whether that be through poetry, personal testimony, policy analysis, or hip-hop rap."

It was one of the silent achievements of the hip-hop movement. For all of the hype about hip hop's grandiose presence in pop culture, or its presumed negative impact on youth behavior and values, few people acknowledged the extent to which it has enhanced, enlarged, and empowered the views and voices of young people. With that comes confidence, a greater sense of self-worth, and the kind of political efficacy young people generally lack.

Jones thought that the young people recruited to participate in the campaign were extraordinary and just what the effort needed to succeed. "Young people have a lot of energy and a lot of passion," he says. "They're smart, funny, charismatic, great on TV, impossible to ignore." That was more than apparent in the outcome of the meetings the community organizers attended. Slowly, but surely, the grassroots effort was having an impact. First, the Board of Corrections decided to reduce the number of beds by four hundred fifty. A few weeks later they lowered the number even further. It was clear that pressure from the Bay Area community was influencing the process, and that motivated activists all the more.

Something changed in the aftermath of the clash between county and state officials and the young activists. Many young Californians had been awakened in the aftermath of Proposition 21. That measure essentially singled out young people precisely for being who they were, young people. In response, many Bay Area youths became actively involved in the fight against the juvenile justice system. At the age of thirteen, young Bay Area activist Bolden-Kramer found herself attending educational workshops and rallies that tapped into young people's fierce reactions to Prop 21. Those workshops provided a space to learn about the politics of crime, race, and the justice system. Young people also had a chance to explore questions like "What is hip hop?" and "What are the key elements of hip hop?"

Bolden-Kramer says, "We [her young peers] staged walkouts at school, helped organize rallies, and supported our friends who were being locked up in increasing numbers." Hip hop, along with the Super-Jail campaign, gave them an opportunity to engage the officials and institutions that made the decisions affecting their lives. Many young people described attending those meetings as a life-altering and empowering experience. They stood up to the powerful corrections board, demanded, and even won, important concessions that reversed earlier board positions. They realized there was strength in numbers, and that in a democracy, power really can belong to the people.

When plans for the Dublin correctional complex began, in the spring of 2001, young people were nowhere near the discussions that propelled the project forward. But that changed once they got involved. According to Rachel Jackson, of Books Not Bars, "These youth came out of nowhere, won at the state level and are now driving the process at the county level. At first young voices were no factor in discussions about building this massive juvenile hall. Now they are the main factor. Their success is proving that young people today do care, and that their activism can make a tremendous difference on issues central to their own lives."

• • •

The California Board of Corrections met in San Diego County's Marine Village Conference Center on May 17, 2001, to make a final decision about the Dublin complex. The meeting was originally scheduled for Sacramento, located several hundred miles north of

San Diego. Some observers of the unfolding showdown between the community activists and the board believed that the meeting was moved in order to get it away from the throng of Bay Area activists, who had demanded to make their voices and views heard at earlier meetings. But early that morning a number of Bay Area activists boarded a flight for San Diego. By the time the board's meeting began, more than forty community activists were in attendance.

Holding up signs that read "Schools Not Jails" and "Education Not Incarceration," their presence and intent were unmistakable. There were at least five other items on the board's itinerary, but the major issue was Alameda County's request for an additional $2.3 million to expand its youth correctional facility. This moment had been building for several months. It was now time to make an official decision on the project. Twenty-four people signed up to speak during the meeting. Most of them came to oppose the project.

As much as they hoped for a positive outcome, the community activists knew that the prospects of the board overturning the allocation of funds for the project was unlikely. After listening to the speakers, the board held a discussion among themselves. Then it announced its vote, a resounding 10-1 tally (along with one abstention) in favor of rescinding the $2.3 million. Shocked by the vote the organizers broke out into a celebratory chant, "Ain't no power like the power of the youth, 'cause the power of youth don't change!" Their hard work had paid off.

After the meeting board member Zev Yaroslavsky, a Los Angeles County supervisor, acknowledged that the impassioned pleas from the young activists helped persuade him to overrule the subcommittee's recommendation. "I wouldn't have given them ten cents for their odds to change the minds of the Board of Corrections, but they did it," he said. "After hearing them speak, the board decided, 'Let's take a second look at this.' I was a protester when I was young, and I never got those results."

But it was only a partial victory. Though the board decided not to allocate more money to the Dublin complex, they did announce plans to use the funds to build more beds in other counties. Suddenly, campaign organizers realized that they had successfully impacted the local debate in Alameda but not the larger debate throughout the state. On the one hand, their efforts represented a breakthrough in hip hop's career as protest politics but, on the other hand, their efforts also demonstrated the limitations of protest politics. Protest politics are reactive rather than proactive.

In the aftermath of the Super-Jail campaign, the Bay Area hip-hop activists had to ponder the inevitable question: what next? In addition to fighting the power, how could hip hop accumulate more power? As effective as the activists had been on the outside of the political and policy-making apparatus, some began to wonder if they could also be effective on the inside.

While the press played up the teens that attended the board meetings and rallies, the Stop the Super-Jail campaign was made up of an interesting cast of players. Alongside the energetic and bright-eyed teens who believed they could change the world were twenty- and thirty-somethings who also believed they could make a difference. Consisting of lawyers, organizers, educators, and nonprofit professionals, they provided the guidance, leadership, and organization that supported their younger partners' zeal for change.

More than anything, hip hop's older demographic is coming face to face with the burden that every generation must confront: assuming the reins of leadership and political power. Hip hop's political life will come in various forms and on various fronts. Protest politics are one form but so is moving into those positions that influence some of the most vital services (education and health care) and institutions (the criminal justice system, for one) in the lives of generation hip hop. Some in hip hop are even calling for entry into the unpredictable but all-important world of electoral politics.

The burden of leadership is real and immense but—as hip hop grows older and presumably sager in its ways—these are the kinds of issues it must grapple with. Thus, in order to have a greater impact in the lives of ordinary youths, the hip-hop movement must make a move on the positions and institutions that not only bring hip hop the aura of power, which it already possesses, but the authority of power, which, for the most part, it has never possessed.

# CHAPTER SEVEN

# "Our Future...Right Here, Right Now!"

*Our day is coming. It's inevitable that the president
in another five years will be a hip-hopper. The mayor
of Chicago will be somebody who has grown up on
N.W.A., Chuck D, even Lil' Kim and Foxy Brown.
All of it will make sense then.*

—KRS-ONE

For two straight nights in the summer of 2003 more than 45,000 fans
filed into brand-spanking-new Ford Field, the home of the Detroit
Lions. The fierce buzz that filled the downtown Detroit evening air
was palpable. The exhilaration that pounded throughout the sta-
dium was not for the hapless Lions; instead, it was for the city's latest
and biggest hometown hero, rapper Eminem. Not only was he king
of the music charts; he was also coming off a stunning Oscar win for
best original song in a movie. Earlier in the year he had announced
that while he would not be headlining any tours in North America,
he would hold two live sets in the city he called home. Just hours
after going on sale, Ticketmaster, the giant concert ticket retailer, reported that the more than 90,000 seats for the July 12 and 13 concert
dates had been sold. Local media coverage reported that fans from all
over the U.S. and the world had flocked to Detroit to see the "Real
Slim Shady."

To no one's surprise the Eminem Show was its characteristic self:
big, loud, and carnivalesque. Featuring guest performances from 50

Cent and Missy Elliott, the show was also magnified by the latest inventions in concert theatrics—computer technology, pyrotechnics, high-powered speakers, and a giant screen. In search of perfection, Eminem had spent the last few nights obsessing over the final cut of the video that was to kick off the show. The video opened with a light-hearted skit that included another local favorite, Detroit mayor Kwame Kilpatrick. Playing himself in the skit, the mayor telephones Eminem and makes a pitch for the rapper to perform in his hometown. "What about Detroit? What about the city that put you on the map?" the mayor implores. "For you and the city?" Eminem replies, "I'll do two [concerts]."

It was, in all likelihood, the first and last time that admiration for Eminem would reach as far as the offices of a big-city mayor. Three years before, Eminem had actually run into trouble with the city when Mayor Dennis Archer's office expressed concern that his concert video was too violent and inappropriate.

But Kilpatrick was no ordinary elected official. He was the youngest big-city mayor in the country and the youngest ever to hold the position in Detroit's three-hundred-year history. After winning the office, he became known as America's first "hip hop mayor." The dual claim to Eminem and Kilpatrick distinguished Detroit, once an outpost in the hip-hop nation, as a prime location in hip hop's widening empire. Kilpatrick's vault into the city's main elected office signaled yet another important moment in hip hop's young but intriguing career: the arrival of a new vanguard of political leaders and elected officials who promised to convert hip hop's increasing desire for political power, influence, and responsibility into something real.

• • •

Kwame M. Kilpatrick was born in 1972 and raised in middle-class Detroit. A product of the city's public school system, he graduated near the top of his senior class from Cass Technical High School. Rather than attend one of the major state universities, Michigan or Michigan State, Kilpatrick migrated south to attend the historically black Florida A&M University. A high school football star, the six-foot-four Kilpatrick went on to become a pro prospect at A&M, but a back injury in his senior season ended his chances of pursuing a career in the NFL. Fortunately for Kilpatrick he had always taken his studies seriously and graduated from A&M with honors and a degree in political science.

After graduating from A&M, he returned home and earned a degree from Detroit Law School before taking a job as teacher, mentor, and basketball coach at Marcus Garvey Academy. But Kilpatrick always dreamed big. At the tender age of twenty-five, he decided to run for a seat in the Michigan House of Representatives. His mother, Carolyn Cheeks Kilpatrick, had vacated the seat in her bid to join the U.S. Congress. The younger Kilpatrick's decision to keep his mother's state house seat in the family was not a surprise to anyone who knew the Kilpatricks. Kwame's decision to enter politics seemed predestined.

In addition to his mother's career in politics, his father, Bernard Kilpatrick, had once been Wayne County commissioner. During his campaign the mayoral candidate often joked with reporters and voters that his parents baptized him in the fiery waters of electoral politics at an early age. He recalled being sent out as young as five years old to knock on neighborhood doors and stump for votes. If the arena of big-time politics, with its endless handshaking and back-slapping, demands big personalities and even bigger ambition, then Kilpatrick was a natural.

After winning the state seat, he quickly climbed the Democratic party ranks making a name for himself as a bridge builder and consensus maker. Kilpatrick also became the first African-American leader of one of the state's major political parties, when he became the House Democratic leader in the Michigan legislature. He cut his political teeth on some key initiatives. In a 2002 interview he noted that one of his proudest accomplishments as a state legislator was gaining "remediation for children with low MEAP [Michigan Educational Assessment Program] scores." At the time, he noted, a low test score simply led to labeling a kid, which brought stigma and continued low achievement. "What I did was change it so that when they didn't pass the first time, the state had to go in and do some remediation—help these children understand, help them read, [do] math, whatever part they were failing in."

Having an impact on the state's youth would continue as a signature feature of his political ambitions in his home state. His rapid rise made him an immediate player and rising star in the Democratic party. Term limits prohibited the young state representative from running again. Kilpatrick, much as he had all of his life, took aim at another challenge, this time the pursuit of the mayor's office in the nation's tenth largest city. He was thirty-one years old.

• • •

In spite of the outward demonstration of confidence and youthful exuberance, Kilpatrick experienced some private doubts about his age and the challenges that were certain to confront the next mayor of Detroit. Many local observers were surprised when Dennis Archer, the city's two-term mayor, announced that he would not seek a third term. His decision opened up the door for a long and even zany cast of hopefuls, pretenders, and would-be mayors. As late as May 2001, and with the citywide primaries just five months away, Kilpatrick still had not officially announced his plans.

One day, as he was weighing the decision to run or not at his mother's home on Detroit's west side, Kilpatrick sought momentary refuge in the basement. There he picked up a Bible, hoping to find guidance and wisdom during a moment of great uncertainty and trepidation. He would later describe what happened next as an omen. According to Kilpatrick, he inadvertently opened the Bible to the book of Samuel and the verses that describe how thirty-year-old David became king. "That day," Kilpatrick told reporters, "I decided to do what God wants me to do, instead of making excuses." His decision to run was not simply a bid for the mayor's office; it was also an attempt to make history.

Despite the entry of more than fifteen candidates for mayor, the race quickly became a contest between Kilpatrick and Gil Hill. At age seventy, Hill was more than twice the age of his opponent. A long-time fixture in local Detroit affairs, he was coming off a twelve-year stretch as city council member, having spent the last four as council president. Prior to that he had devoted thirty years to the city's police department, at one point heading the unit's homicide division. Hill is best recognized for his role as Eddie Murphy's tart-tongued boss in the popular *Beverly Hills Cop* films. In Detroit, Hill represented the established old guard and entered the race with a commanding lead due mainly to name recognition and his lengthy tenure as a public servant.

When it became clear that Kilpatrick would be his main adversary, and a formidable one at that, Hill moved to make their age difference a campaign issue. The older candidate warned voters, "You want an experienced driver behind the wheel, not someone with a learner's permit, not someone who needs a coach in the passenger seat to provide directions." It was a note he struck throughout the campaign. In essence, Hill looked to make Kilpatrick's youth a liability by associating it with a lack of experience, wisdom, and preparation for the task of tough decision making. Hill's campaign slogan, "Experience Counts," embodied his old-guard status.

But team Kilpatrick was nothing if not savvy in the ways of electoral politics. They understood that while their candidate's youth could be portrayed as a liability, it could also be made a defining strength. To emphasize the positive attributes of Kilpatrick's youth, they developed the campaign slogan "Our Future...Right Here, Right Now!"

It was the right counter to Hill's initial attack. It conveyed strength and a sense of the future without disrespecting his older challenger and the city's older base. The slogan, however, was more than just a slick counterpunch; it also indicated that the Kilpatrick team would make change and the transition to a new generation of leadership a resounding theme in the campaign.

On May 17 Kilpatrick officially announced his candidacy for mayor on the front porch of the home he grew up in. Standing behind him that day were his parents and key figures from Detroit's business, religious, and political communities. Kilpatrick, a son of the city, made an appeal that showed his connections to Detroit's past and future. "I'm your grandson. I'm your great nephew," the young state rep proclaimed before a small crowd of supporters and local television news cameras. "I'm that little boy you told to get off your grass. I'm also that little boy you told to stay in school, make something out of yourself and come back to this community and serve this community."

His speech that day and the arrival of his candidacy signaled a generational battle that had been twenty-five years in the making.

• • •

Like a few other campaigns around the nation, the Detroit mayoral race developed a historic story line: the civil rights generation versus the hip-hop generation. For more than half a century, African American politics have been dominated by the civil rights generation. But hip hop, now nearly thirty years old, has spawned a generation who are growing older, more mature, and ready to move into the positions of power and leadership previously dominated by civil righters. The various campaigns unfolding around the nation reveal that the gulf between the two generations is growing wider, more apparent, and, in some cases, more rancorous.

Generational divides are nothing new. But the divide around hip hop takes on some truly disturbing patterns. According to author and cultural critic Michael Eric Dyson, "What is new and particularly troublesome is the sheer hostility that bruises relations between older and younger blacks." Dyson adds, "For perhaps the first time in our history, blacks over thirty have a fear and disdain for black youth." That divide and the hostile sentiments it sparks have far-reaching implications that are even touching the worlds of pop culture and electoral politics.

That was especially the case in Newark, a city that like Detroit, found itself choosing between an old guard candidate, Sharpe James, and a younger candidate, Corey Booker. Though Booker was not a hip-hop-identified candidate, his age, thirty-four, signaled the coming of urban America's next wave of leadership and the difficulty it faced convincing older black Americans that it was ready to assume the responsibilities of political leadership.

James's campaign slogan, "The Real Deal" was emblematic of the divisive racial and class motifs that emerged from his campaign. Throughout the contest James and his team implied that Booker, a light-skinned African American who grew up in an affluent New Jersey suburb and attended elite schools, was not "sufficiently black." James's attack suggested that his younger rival was unable to relate to and truly represent a Newark constituency that was more than 50 percent black. The sixty-six-year-old James was a local hero. His political persona and philosophy were greatly influenced by the racial unrest that gripped the city and the nation in the late 1960s. Along with others, he ushered in Newark's first generation of black elected officials in 1970. Many longtime Newark residents associated him with the protracted struggle blacks waged to gain respect and a foothold in city politics and government. James was seeking his fourth term.

Booker's candidacy, by contrast, represented a real break from the previous regime, both in terms of agenda and political perspective. Booker came to national prominence by staging a hunger strike in one of Newark's poorest housing projects. Garnering attention from venerable news outlets, such as *60 Minutes* and *Time,* he agitated for more police to come in and help wipe out the drugs that infiltrated the complex. Booker accused the incumbent mayor of complacency and charged that his older opponent was committed to a political machine that favored some Newark interests over others. His campaign theme, "A Renaissance for the Rest of Us," suggested that the politics of old—cronyism and racial patronage—were ill-suited for moving the city forward. Booker's campaign was also notable because, while a Democrat, he supported ideas typically associated with conservative Republicans. For instance, he favored vouchers for public schools, a stance that stood in direct contrast to that of the Democratic party.

Throughout the campaign Booker tried to make the case that Newark, like urban America in general, was overdue for a new vision, a new brand of leadership. His willingness to think beyond traditional liberal political thought put him at odds with the civil rights establishment that colored him as a wolf in sheep's clothing. James and members of the old guard who supported him, Jesse Jackson and Al Sharpton, argued that Booker's political agenda represented a threat to the half-century struggle for black civil and equal rights. The voucher issue was one symptom of a larger tension that emerged in the standoff between the civil rights establishment and the next wave of urban leaders. The younger generation believed that blind commitment to traditional liberal politics, and the Democratic Party establishment, worked mainly to handcuff rather than free black political aspirations and agendas.

While questions about Booker's political stripes and intentions swirled throughout the bitterly contested campaign, his candidacy also pointed to the sea shifts that were remaking urban politics. James was clearly the choice of Newark's old black vanguard and citizenry. Newark residents who remembered the struggles of the sixties and the seventies remained steadfast in their support of the man they believed stood by them when the city's race relations reached catastrophic dimensions. James, they believed, understood their hopes and their dreams. He was one of them.

By contrast, Booker was the choice of the city's younger population, the twenty- and thirty-somethings who were generally college educated and working professionals. He also ran strong among the city's growing Latino population, a number of immigrant communities from places as diverse as Brazil, Puerto Rico, and the Dominican Republic. Realizing the demographic shifts that were remapping the city, Booker refined his Spanish-language skills as a way to communicate more effectively with a constituency that in 2002 represented nearly a third of the city's population.

The Newark contest, like others around the nation, was an indication of just how dramatically the theater of urban politics was changing. The customary battle lines, white versus black, were no longer viable. Newark, like urban America as a whole, was in flux and that necessitated a shift in political philosophy and policy.

The contest between James and Booker was marked by contradiction as well as controversy. It was more than a little strange that James attacked Booker for possessing the very things—a highly educated and middle class pedigree—he presumably fought for blacks to have access to. Even Booker acknowledged that his achievements—Stanford graduate, Oxford Rhodes Scholar, and Yale Law—owed a huge debt to the efforts of James's generation.

When all of the votes were tallied, James prevailed with 53 percent versus 47 percent for his younger opponent. *Washington Post* writer Dale Russakoff, discussing the historic clash embodied in the Newark mayoral race wrote, "The question embedded in Booker's candidacy is here to stay, as it is nationally: What defines urban leaders in a post-riot, post-movement generation?" Even though he lost, Booker's ability to mount a serious campaign gave evidence that the political waters in urban America were shifting course. But like the sea shifts that transformed urban pop culture, the oncoming shifts in urban politics were not greeted favorably. And while the future direction of urban politics was uncertain, one fact was relatively certain: Whatever course they took would be guided, in large measure, by generation hip hop.

• • •

Soon after defeating Hill in the November mayoral election, Kilpatrick was touted as America's hip-hop mayor. It is a tag he wears cleverly and cautiously. The day after the voters had made their choice the new mayor-elect appeared at a press conference sporting a diamond earring. During the campaign he chose not to wear the earring, concerned that it might convey the wrong message to older voters. In a relatively short period of time, Kilpatrick rose to become a widely respected figure in Detroit. As longtime city resident and *Detroit News* city hall reporter Darren Nichols notes, "He makes everyone feel comfortable around him. If you go out into the streets of Detroit and ask about the mayor they are talking about 'Kwame' rather than 'Mayor Kilpatrick.' The tone around the previous city leader was 'Mayor Archer' it was never 'Dennis.'" In Detroit Kilpatrick also makes regular appearances on a local urban hip-hop radio station for a segment titled "Ask the Mayor." The radio appearances provide young Detroiters access to the mayor and likewise, the mayor access to a constituency he represents in more ways than one.

Kilpatrick was also aware that the "hip-hop mayor," tag produced some problems. He believed that some used the tag to challenge his ability to live up to the expectations of the mayoral position. He told the *Detroit News* that the reason for this was "the hip-hop generation, still, is a generation to mainstream America that is lost, that are not organized, that are not thinking people."

The "hip-hop mayor" marker, in reality, was more than a matter of stylish politics, hip symbolism, or negative stereotyping. Most significantly, it represented the dawn of a new era in urban politics. "I think it says something on the surface that's humorous, but there's really a lot of substance in that statement," says Kilpatrick, referring to the moniker. "Finally, someone from the Run DMC generation from the '80's generation, has made it into some of the political circles that we don't look like we belong in." According to Nichols, "[Kilpatrick] does not hide from the fact that he is from the hip hop generation. But he also doesn't hide from the fact that he is very smart and an astute politician."

Kilpatrick braced himself for the challenges that lay ahead by taking a crash course in the art of big city mayoring. Just a few weeks after winning the election, he visited a couple of major urban metropolitan areas and consulted with people from the worlds of business, politics, and education. He even attended Mayor's School at Harvard University, a program designed to provide newly elected officials valuable insight about the challenges that come with big city leadership. One of the things he learned, Kilpatrick noted in his January 4, 2002, inauguration address, was the prudence in establishing two priorities for his first year in office. As he opened up to a city that had opened up to him, he announced that cold day in January, "Today, I'm here to tell you what the two priorities of the Kilpatrick administration will be."

His first priority was the city's much maligned police department. As late as 1972 the Detroit Police Department was overwhelmingly white in a city that saw blacks emerging as the majority. Like many major urban areas around the country, the relationship between Detroit's black community and police department was volatile and charges of police harassment and brutality fanned the flames of racial hostility. After his election in 1973, Coleman Young used his political machine to radically alter the racial makeup of the city's police department. By the time he left office in 1994 more than half of the city's police force was African American. But the racial composition of the department did not eliminate the problems that tore at the force's fabric and sullied its reputation. By the time Kilpatrick stepped in as mayor, the city police were widely criticized for being inefficient, ineffective, and corrupt.

Kilpatrick's second priority was a program he called Mayor's Time. The mayor explained in his inauguration address that "the program will work with young people in developing cognitive skills, employability skills—and not just throwing a baseball and basketball around to keep them occupied." Kilpatrick made a plea to parents, senior citizens, and others to get involved in Mayor's Time. He also made a special plea to the city's business community. "Yes, we want your financial resources," he told them, "but we also want your human resources. We're going to ask you to get involved with our young people in the city of Detroit." Speaking about the need to re-think the partnership between the city of Detroit and business, Kilpatrick declared, "Communities that are not involved with business and business that is not involved with communities don't work any-more." He envisioned an environment in which this new partnership would "engage our young people in new technology, innovations and creativity in business." He concluded, "Everyone is allowed to partic-ipate in the progress and prosperity of this city."

After discovering research that suggested that young people were particularly vulnerable to the perils of idleness from the hours of 3 p.m. to 8 p.m., Kilpatrick and his advisors developed Mayor's Time. The premise is that if you provide young people with proper re-sources, spaces, and adult instruction, they will not only stay out of trouble but actually thrive. The program was motivated by research from the U.S. Department of Education; the YMCA; Fight Crime, In-vest in Kids; and the Robert Johnson Foundation, which suggests that successful after-school programs build successful cities by culti-vating healthy adolescents.

Many experts believe that because kids who live in working-class and poor households often lack the resources and outlets to provide them with additional instruction, activities, and stimulation outside of school, their environment can become especially unhealthy, even hazardous. A key principle of Mayor's Time is that by investing in youth on the front end, you reduce the likelihood of having to make costlier investments on the back end. The latter investments typically involve dealing with crime, substance abuse, teen pregnancy, and academic underachievement.

The implicit message in Kilpatrick's two priorities was that his administration would make the citizens of Detroit and its youth the centerpiece of his agenda. This was a not-so-subtle response to the concerns expressed by some Detroiters that the outgoing mayor, Dennis Archer, spent too much time focusing on business and not enough time on the city's neighborhoods and residents. Archer is widely credited with revitalizing Detroit's once moribund downtown district. His major accomplishments included convincing General Motors and the software giant CompuAmerica to establish their world headquarters in downtown Detroit. Archer also brokered deals that brought Ford Field, casinos, and CoMerica Park, a new state-of-the-art baseball facility, downtown. These and other efforts did a great job in selling downtown Detroit as a center of global enterprise and first-class entertainment. And though such accoutrements helped to refurbish the city's battered image, many of Archer's detractors complained that it came at the expense of the city's deteriorating infrastructure, neighborhoods, and quality of life beyond downtown.

At least for some Detroiters, rescuing its youth was just as important as rescuing the city from its notoriously gloomy image and the dilapidated and abandoned buildings that dotted its urban landscape. Proponents of a more community-based political agenda dreamed of a world in which the city's most vulnerable population—children and teens—could be inspired to reach for some of the higher goals and things life has to offer. It was a vision that the hip-hop movement had desperately needed to see realized for more than two decades.

•••

"In choosing Kilpatrick over the 70-year-old Hill," it was reported in the *Detroit News* the day after the city's election, "voters recognized the future rests with a new generation of young, energetic and determined Detroiters who have lived their entire lives in a city on the decline." It was true. Detroit-area youths had come face to face with many of the problems—unemployment, poverty, segregation, and decaying public schools—that have disproportionately affected the hip-hop nation and urban America. Perhaps it is only fitting that a figure touted as America's first hip-hop mayor was charged with the responsibility of leading the nation's tenth largest city, and its youthful population, out of what could only be described as a financial, municipal, and political morass that had been growing for more than three decades.

Between 1950 and 1980 America's major cities underwent a dramatic population shift known as "white flight." The changes that remapped Detroit during that period were stunning. In 1945, at the end of World War II, one and a half million Detroiters were white. In 1990 the city's population was nearly 80 percent black while its suburban ring was only 5 percent black. By 2000, only 200,000 whites called Detroit home.

As white flight kicked into high gear in the early 1970s, Detroit, well on the way to becoming a predominantly black city, elected its first black mayor, Coleman A. Young. Buoyed by the black awakening of the sixties, the election of Young signaled the arrival of a more openly defiant demeanor in black politics and a new era in the making and unmaking of America's big cities. As he delivered his inauguration speech in 1974, Young made a bold pledge to fight crime: "I issue an open warning to all dope pushers, to all rip-off artists, to all muggers. It is time to leave Detroit." The newly elected mayor continued, "Hit Eight Mile Road. And I don't give a damn if they are black or white, if they wear Superfly suits or blue uniforms with silver badges. Hit the road."

Eight Mile Road, made famous by Eminem's film debut, *8 Mile*, is a stretch of highway that divides black Detroit from its mostly white suburbs. Many whites, as well as the local Detroit press, believed Young was issuing a license to the city's presumably black criminal class to terrorize the predominantly white suburbs. They interpreted Young's remarks as nothing less than a call for racial Armageddon. Young's speech, in many ways, represented the opening salvo in what would be an ongoing and often hostile relationship between a mayor who embodied the hopes and aspirations of black Detroit and the surrounding white suburbs that saw those aspirations as a threat to their own well-being and sense of security.

For twenty years, Young dominated Detroit politics like no one before or since. His road to political power was paved by a period of extraordinary racial and political struggle. In the years immediately following the civil rights struggle, many blacks used their newly found political power and voting rights to propel a number of blacks into elected office. The efforts of black voters produced the first generation of big-city black mayors in places like Gary (Indiana), Cleveland, Los Angeles, Atlanta, Newark, and Detroit. But as African Americans' political fortunes were improving, the economic situation in many cities with substantial black populations was also worsening. It is one of the great ironies that the rise of black elected officials came at a time when many of the nation's major urban areas were undergoing severe social and economic decline. Detroit's fall from grace was one of the most dramatic.

In the aftermath of World War II, Detroit, like most of America, enjoyed a boom. Powered by what many recognized as the automobile manufacturing capital of the world, Detroit experienced a growth and prosperousness that made it an industrial titan. But as the very structure of America's industrial economy underwent massive change in the 1970s so did the cities whose economic fate was built, in large part, on the old-style manufacturing economy. Hardest hit in this scenario were America's major urban areas that began to experience rapid transformation as both jobs and middle-class income earners started abandoning them in droves. And as the global automobile industry became more competitive, Detroit's major source of economic strength and civic pride was hurt.

No one understood the problems that besieged Detroit better than Young. In his typically combative style, the longtime Motor City mayor wrote in his 1994 autobiography, "I don't dispute the gravity of Detroit's problems. They are basically the same problems that beset every American city, except that they are magnified by the fact that modern Detroit was built around the auto industry, which has been losing blood for two decades, and the accompanying reality that white flight, industrial and social, has left Detroit with the damnedest demographics in America."

The problems that undermined Detroit—the erosion of substantive industry and income-earning opportunities for poor and working-class families—were bigger than the city. These issues were intricately connected to the transformation and globalization of capitalism. Like virtually every other major urban metro area in the U.S., in the 1970s, Detroit experienced the high costs of racial re-segregation. Despite the legal defeat of segregation in the 1960s, the out-migration of white and affluent families left many black schools and neighborhoods in the condition most of black America was in before the civil rights movement: separate and unequal.

Thus many of the problems Kilpatrick inherited in his attempt to revitalize Detroit—high crime rates, middle-class flight, unemployment, and the failure of public schools—were, in reality, several decades old. In some instances, like education, the problems were intractable, formidable, and, seemingly inevitable. By the third year of Kilpatrick's first term, the city's public schools were beyond the crisis stage.

In 2000, black students represented 90 percent of the Detroit public school system's student population. Whites made up 3 percent of the city's student body. In the surrounding suburbs the pattern was reverse. In Dearborn, for instance, whites made up 93 percent versus just 3 percent black. More than forty years after the Supreme Court ruled against racial segregation in public accommodations and institutions, Detroit schools were more segregated than ever before.

According to Harvard's Civil Rights Project, a 2002 study, Detroit's public schools, not surprisingly, mirrored the patterns of racial segregation that defined the city's demographics for several decades. The study reported that "in Detroit public schools, white student enrollment declined from forty-seven percent in 1967 to just below four percent in 2002."

The problem was not simply a matter of segregation but rather the drastic inequities in the resources available in suburban and urban school districts. Whereas Bloomfield Hills, an affluent suburb, spent about $11,455 per pupil in 2000, Detroit spent $6,584. Predictably, the achievement gap between urban and suburban schools, in essence, black and white schools, was alarmingly wide leaving cities like Detroit imperiled with the social costs of low educational attainment—poverty, broken families, crime, and an overall high misery index. According to Kids Count 2004, a national and state-by-state project that tracks the status of children in the U.S., a third of young people, eighteen to twenty-four, living in Detroit in 2000 were school dropouts. In consultation with education experts and access to more than three thousand pieces of data from eighty-eight school districts, the *Detroit News* concluded that in Bloomfield Hills, only 2 percent of its students failed to graduate high school.

From the start of his administration Kilpatrick had to rethink his political goals and reorganize his vision for rebuilding Detroit. In the first year of his term, Kilpatrick's ideas for a new Detroit had to contend with a $169 million budget deficit. As Nichols, of the *Detroit News*, explains, when facing a budget crisis, "you have to decide what are going to be the essential city services that you have to provide versus things like Mayor's Time." In a city where many residents complained about water, malfunctioning street lights, poor emergency unit response time, and a city bureaucracy that made even the most mundane matters seem unfixable, Kilpatrick was forced from the very beginning to face the harsh realities that challenged even further his desire to elevate the quality of life of the city's young population.

• • •

Similar to his young counterparts seeking office and political responsibility around the country, Kilpatrick finds himself in a high profile but highly unenviable position. Though hip-hop-identified elected officials bring a new swagger to the tough job of rebuilding America's cities, they are also confronted by decades-old problems. In many instances their vision of stronger schools, improved city services, and safer communities demands economic, intellectual, and political resources that have been elusive.

The problems Kilpatrick faces developed profound dimensions a few months before he was even elected. On the morning of Detroit's primary elections, Kilpatrick and the city woke up ready to make history. If he did well at the polls that day, he would be one step closer to becoming that city's youngest mayor ever. History was certainly made that Tuesday morning, the eleventh day of September 2001. But not even Detroit is likely to remember that Kilpatrick won 51 percent of the mayoral vote, making him the front-runner in the upcoming November general election. The aftershocks of September 11 produced a political and economic climate that left America's big cities all but abandoned in national political discourse.

But America's abandonment of urban America has been building for at least four decades. In the sixties and seventies it was marked by the massive out-migration of white and middle-class families as well as meaningful employment. In the 1980s it came in the form of the war on drugs. America's inner cities were hit hard again in the nineties by the prison industrial complex. The passage of what was billed as "welfare reform" in 1996 was the culmination of a political retreat from the weighty problems that plague the urban poor and working classes. Back then the nation appeared to at least notice the challenges troubling urban America. The problems that leaders like Kilpatrick must address will have to be tackled in a political world that demonstrates little, if any, concern for America's longstanding urban crisis and the young people who stand to suffer most.

Meanwhile, public schools continue to deteriorate. The health status of the racially and economically marginal, a notably urban-based population, grows more precarious. And the gulf between America's suburbs and cities widens. Soaring state and federal deficits mean that big-city leaders will receive little, if any, help from government coffers to rebuild key aspects of the city. In the post-9/11 world the issues confronting urban America are no longer on the nation's radar. Simply put, they do not matter.

This is the political moment that Kilpatrick and the hip-hop movement inherit. A moment in which the uphill struggle to revive America's cities grows steeper. Through it all Kilpatrick strives to maintain his commitment to a city whose future rests in the hands of the youth it struggles to nourish. The effort to translate hip hop's pop capital into political capital is well under way. But the challenges facing the movement are real and persistent.

Despite the fresh faces, buoyant voices, and exuberant hopes accompanying the arrival of urban America's next wave of leadership there are no guarantees, no certain outcomes even though the hopes, expectations, and stakes are high. Still, Kilpatrick's 2001 campaign theme is right. The future is now and the time has come for the hip-hop generation to step up and take on the issues that define so much of its experience in America.

# CHAPTER EIGHT

# "We Love Hip Hop, But Does Hip Hop Love Us?"

*The house of hip hop was built*
*on the backs of black women.*
—TA-NEHISI COATES

On May 13, 2004, another hip-hop magazine, *Fish 'N' Grits,* hit newsstands, opening in markets like New York, Los Angeles, Detroit, and Atlanta with an initial launch of 50,000. Like so many other would-be hip-hop moguls the magazine's publishers, Sharif Profit, Camille Burgos, and Joe Fatal, were confident they could translate hip hop's pop currency into a hot consumer lifestyle brand. *Fish 'N' Grits* certainly had a hook that distinguished it from all other hip-hop magazines. According to its publishers, hip hop's latest magazine was "where music meets porn."

"Upscale and urban," is how Burgos described hip hop's latest publication. "Magazines for men generate top sales in today's marketplace. But no one is able to offer what we offer. Either they don't showcase women of color on a regular basis, or they tease you with partial nudity," she noted. "*Fish 'N' Grits* is able to bring it to you full and up front and no holds barred. We combine the no-compromise attitude of both cultures and explode with it. Music and sex have always been kissing cousins and *Fish 'N' Grits* expounds upon that truth!"

Burgos had made her mark in hip hop as a music industry executive working mainly in Artist & Repertoire (A&R), scouting and signing acts for labels like Arista and Jive. She also spent time at MCA Records as director of marketing. As the aftershocks of the various mergers, downsizings, and other cost-cutting moves made employment in the music business unstable, she was intrigued when Fatal, a music producer, approached her about his idea for a new book.

They maneuvered to exploit one of the newest niches produced by the multifaceted industry hip hop spawned, sexually explicit entertainment. There had been earlier flirtation between hip hop and porn, but the plunge into hard core was in a league of its own. The rise of hip-hop porn was stimulated by Snoop Dogg (Calvin Broadus), one of hip hop's most popular and enduring personalities. From his commercial recording debut in 1992 with Dr. Dre to his series of commercial sex videos with Larry Flynt's *Hustler* in 2001 and 2003, Snoop got maximum mileage out of his "pimpsta"—part gangsta, part pimp —persona. His *Snoop Dogg's Doggystyle* was a blockbuster in the world of sexually explicit videos. Though he did not perform any sexual acts in the video, his presence and commentary along with the hip beats gave it a ghetto savoir faire that played well with young consumers of adult entertainment. Rather than diminish his mainstream appeal, Snoop's affiliation with porn bolstered his credibility as a "real pimp" and enhanced his attractiveness to Hollywood, advertisers, and the decision makers at MTV who awarded him his own show.

Hip hop's foray into porn was not exceptional. In fact, it highlighted the degree to which the business of sex romped into a fullfledged, multibillion-dollar enterprise. For much of its history, the stigma attached to the sex industry restricted it to America's hidden economy. But over the years the VCR, the Internet, a more permissive culture, and some of America's most reputable companies helped commercial sex to flourish like never before. The line that once divided pop culture from porn culture continues to be blurred. On one side of the line are the makers of sexually explicit materials who fashion their operations, marketing practices, and star system after Hollywood. On the other side porn chic has become increasingly visible in mainstream television, film, music, and advertising. The shoe company Pony broke new ground in a 2002 ad campaign that highlighted just how intertwined the two worlds—pop and porn—had become. The creators of the ad campaign decided to use adult film stars in their print and billboard ads. Acknowledging the pervasiveness of porn, the shoe company's vice president, Come Chantrel, explained, "When I grew up in the 80's in Paris, models were the ultimate feminine ideal. For the 20-year-old kid, porn stars have kind of replaced what models used to represent."

The hip hop and porn merger was emblematic of the societal changes that characterized what one cultural critic called "the rise of the amazing pornosphere." Hip- hop porn reflected the spread of sexual themes and imagery in American pop and youth culture. Discussing her own corporate experience in the selling of rap music, Burgos asserted, "I've been selling sex forever from a label's perspective. In America we sell sex to buy clothes, for cigarette packaging, just for everything. So now as Fatal says, we're kind of flipping it and using sex to kind of sell music with all the entrenchment and the acceptance."

*Fish 'N' Grits* co-publishers contend that the magazine services America's insatiable appetite for sexually explicit entertainment. By most accounts commercial sex is a thriving business in the U.S. In his discussion of the commercial sex industry, Eric Schlosser writes, "Americans now spend as much as $8 billion to $10 billion on 'adult entertainment'—on hard-core videos and DVD's, Internet porn, cable and satellite porn, peep shows, phone sex, live sex acts, sexual toys, and sex magazines." Porn is not only big business; it is also legitimate business. As Schlosser notes, some of America's most reputable corporations—AT&T, AOL Time Warner, Hilton Enterprises—have joined the commercial sex economy.

Hip hop's eagerness to indulge its libidinous desires is not unprecedented. In the 1950s the "blue" recordings of comics like Redd Foxx found an audience. Two decades later, the bawdy toasts of Rudy Ray Moore garnered a cultlike following. But such sexual fare was usually off-limits to teens and circulated in a more confined commercial milieu. Richard Pryor's comic genius while sometimes graphic was rarely, if ever, pornographic. More mature ears primarily enjoyed his recordings though that did not stop younger listeners from sneaking into a parent's record collection. In the late 1980s hip-hop personalities like Luther Campbell and Too Short made their early mark producing what the latter tagged "freaky tales." Though the appetite for sex in the African American cultural underground had been long and sturdy, the pursuit of hard core turned more nakedly open. As the *New York Times* reported in March 2004, "Rap has never shied away from gleefully smutty lyrics. But now, some stars are moving beyond raunchy rhetoric into actual pornographic matter, with graphic videos, explicit cable TV shows and hip-hop-themed girlie magazines."

Because the movement's constituency is so overwhelming young, the selling of hip-hop porn is troubling. The producers of hip-hop-inspired sexual entertainment assert that they are targeting the culture's older segments. In reality the widening sexual offerings are also being consumed by some of the movement's youngest and most vulnerable segments. Teens are being introduced to sexual themes at an earlier age through various mediums—video, pay-per-view television, the Internet, and network and cable television.

Equally disturbing is the occasional assertion that the move toward the sexually explicit is a way to bolster hip hop's claims of racial authenticity, or in other words, its fidelity to the movement's ghetto origins. When the vice president in the urban division of TVT Records told the *New York Times* that Lil Jon, a successful music producer, got into porn to keep his image from becoming too pop, he revealed the real calamity in hip hop's grab for authenticity. The proliferation of pimps, "playas," and hustlers in commercial hip hop implied a connection to the real and gritty world of black street culture, by now a cliché maneuver in the never-ending bid for street cred. But there was nothing racially authentic or dutiful about the portrayal of blacks as sex craved. If anything, playing up hip hop's most lurid sexual fantasies played into some of the most enduring and pernicious themes in America's racial and cultural history: black sexuality as deviant, different, and dangerous.

The most tragic aspect of hip hop's lust for the libido was the elaboration of an imagination that viewed women as cheap, consumable, and disposable. The woman-hating inclinations in corporate hip hop have become so common, they appear ordinary. Before hip hop's hardcore economy burst on the scene, however, the movement's pornographic imagination made its most pronounced impression in its most dominant visual art form, music video.

• • •

The soaring popularity of rap music in the 1990s increased the need to promote the music. Accordingly, the demand for rap music videos and the artists who could visually capture the music's energy grew. It was one of the many examples of how in addition to producing whole new industries, hip hop also produced a new and far-ranging creative class. One of the most influential figures in that new creative class was Hype Williams.

Born Harold Williams in 1968, Hype grew up in Queens. Among others, Queens produced Run-D.M.C., LL Cool J, and Team FUBU. Williams was tagged with his famous nickname because he was so hyperactive as a kid. The moniker would be a fitting description of his music clips, especially how they "hyped" up hip hop's aura and appeal. At an early age he was attracted to the visual arts. Enamored of the art of Jean Michel Basquiat, he dreamed of being a painter. He loved movies and maintained a steady diet that consisted of *The Godfather, Scarface* (a hip-hop favorite), Italian gangster films, and *Star Wars*. Hype also appreciated the cinematic brilliance of Akira Kurosawa, Japan's most widely known and influential filmmaker. What he loved most about film was the medium's ability to tell stories visually.

In the late 1980s he entered Adelphi University and majored in graphic arts. Though he owned an intriguing mind, he was an artist at heart and decided to leave college after two years. Rap music was just getting off the ground commercially, so he began hanging around music video sets working various low-paid odd jobs. "Biz Markie's 'Just a Friend,' Big Daddy Kane's 'Smooth Operator,' Public Enemy's 'Night of the Living Baseheads'—I was at all those shoots, fetching juice and shit," Hype says recalling his days as a video-set gopher. Though he was drawn to the music-video industry, he was disappointed by what he thought was a lack of imagination from the directors and financial commitment from the labels. "I wasn't seeing what I wanted to see in videos. There was no color, no originality. Record companies assumed that the people who bought rap records didn't need to see quality, so nobody was putting in the effort or the money," says Hype in a 1998 interview with the *New York Times*. It was another sign of how rap music still lacked the level of respect from the industry that was commensurate with its rising commercial status.

Sensing a challenge, and a window of opportunity, Hype set out to reinvent rap music videos. In 1998 Hype told *The Source:* "Rap and R&B were almost the joke of the industry, I just wanted to show that our videos could be beautiful, they could be as dramatic and energetic and thoughtful and intellectual as alternative and rock music videos. So I set a goal for myself to take rap and R&B music videos and make them not just equal, but superior to those genres." By the time he semi-retired from directing music videos in 2001, he had accomplished that and more.

The history of rap music videos can be divided into two eras, before-Hype and after-Hype. Instead of relying on the grainy everyday portraits and skits that characterized the pre-Hype era of rap music videos, he brought an auteur-like vision and bravado that enlarged the concept of what an urban music clip could be. He always believed that rap was as big as any other pop genre. The music was incredibly vital and occupied a prominent presence in the pop world but its visual counterpart—music clips—was small by comparison and lacked the wattage that powered the music. Hype gave rap music videos a boost by making rap performers bigger than life.

From the vast body of music clips he has directed, Hype's favorite is the one he shot in 1995 for the Wu-Tang Clan, "Can It All Be So Simple." On that shoot he found his directorial voice and established an aesthetic vocabulary, sense of style, and cinematic touch that anchored his creative vision. That effort, Hype asserts, "affected the tone of videos, the things I did and how people responded to it." The Wu-Tang song was gritty and hardcore but also delicately crafted and narratively ambitious. Hype captured all of those qualities visually, creating a perfect marriage between song, story, and clip.

To make rappers look larger than life, he often filmed them from a low camera angle. The move enlarged their aura and, as a result, the power of their celebrity. Most significantly, he used the power of his artistic imagination by drawing from an eclectic field of Hollywood and European cinema, comic books, anime, video games, and advertising. The one word that best describes the Hype Williams video is BIG. In the fantasy-scapes he created everything—the sets, locations, colors, ideas, images, style, and most notably, the budget—was big.

By adopting a serious approach to rap music, Hype also displayed a subtle appreciation for the diverse artistry in hip hop. He understood that rappers had their own unique style, voice, and place within the robust world of hip hop. Whether it was Tupac, Busta Rhymes, Jay-Z, or TLC, Hype created larger-than-life characters. One of his signature achievements was the work he did with Missy Elliott.

Hype loved her music and thought her video image should be just as spectacular. But Missy was not a typical pop diva. Her rotund body did not fit the conventional standards of pop beauty considered crucial in the marketing of female performers. As he thought about the best way to capture her dazzling sense of style and music visually, Hype derived inspiration from, of all things, French filmmakers and Grace Jones, a black woman who projected a style and image that was off-beat (albeit exotic) and effective. So Hype decided he wanted her look to be "something very new and very different and very European." The videos he directed for Missy Elliott gave her a distinct presence and made her an unlikely music-video icon. "When we did her wide-angle stuff," Hype recalls, "we nailed a specific look for her, and that was really her launchpad. We made those videos look exactly how we felt about the performances in the songs." It was an incredible accomplishment and showed how the power of imagination, along with talent, could defy the rigid gender rules in pop culture.

Hype's arrival came at a crucial moment in the history of the music video. As competition to get music clips on the major video channels, especially MTV, intensified, production budgets grew higher and so did the stakes. In the corporate-driven pop industry, creating stars was the name of the game. In this commercial climate, eye-catching music clips became one way to manufacture stardom. If a music label was going to spend half a million to a million dollars to shoot a four-minute video, it needed a proportionate buzz and payoff. Hype delivered like no one else. He was part of the sea change that remade American pop in the nineties.

Hype's quest to enlarge hip hop's status was enhanced by the rise of influential hip-hop imprint labels like Death Row and Bad Boy Records. The key players behind those labels—Suge Knight, Dr. Dre, and Sean "Puff Daddy" Combs—had both the moxie and the money to persuade their distributors to help bankroll big-budget music videos. Along with Hype they formed an elite pop-culture vanguard that defined hip hop's ghetto fabulous aura and lifestyle.

In the cluttered world of pop music culture, Hype made rap music videos matter. He believed his greatest impact on the music and the movement was the sense of size and scope he brought to the genre. "Rap artists were talented," he stated, "but I made them look much more talented than they actually were. The mastering and manipulation of technical qualities like sound, camera angles and lighting have a way of creating presence, and that impacts the consumer." Because Hype's videos impacted how hip hop was consumed, they also influenced how the movement was experienced.

But not all was fabulous in the world Hype helped create. His taste for big style relied on a misogynist gaze that produced some painful effects in the worldview crafted in rap-music videos. Hype did not introduce misogyny to the world of music videos. The mistreatment and misrepresentation of women had been a staple motif throughout the genre's history. Taking its cues from television, film, and advertising, the music video industry developed a system and a style that stymied the role women occupied. The construction of the female body/image in music videos has been an ongoing source of cultural debate and controversy. Some of the earliest critiques of MTV focused on the sexist iconography in music video.

By making the look and tone of rap-music videos more cinematic, Hype reinvented the genre. But unlike in the cinema characters in music videos seldom speak. Thus what they do, or more precisely, what their bodies do is all the more important. In the larger-than-life videos Hype created, rappers lived like kings. Mixed along with the ocean-view villas, poolside mansions, luxury cars, Cuban cigars, yachts, and bottles of fine spirits were the women, often scantily clad. They were essentially ornaments, eye-candy, part of the luscious scenery and background that catered to the adolescent fantasies of male viewers. Hype's hip-hop world was a monument to hypercapitalism and consumerism, and women were merely another object to be owned and disposed of.

Hype's stylized videos helped introduce a new and disturbing entry to our nation's pop-culture lexicon—the "video ho." This archetype has become a stock figure in rap-music videos, variously portrayed as a groupie, exotic dancer, servant, or seductress. Most important she oozes sexuality while posing meticulously for the male protagonist and male viewer's gaze. The image of the high-rolling, cash-money, pimped-out figure is so common in rap it has become a target of parody in music videos, comedy skits, reality television, film, and adult-themed parties. Even the chameleon-colored Madonna, along with hip-hop comic Ali G, "big pimped" her way through the popular music video "Music," featuring strippers and porn stars.

Using music video as his canvas, Hype's portrait of women developed sharp contradictions. Throughout his vast videography women are portrayed as sensuous and hypersexual, lovely and licentious. There is a fine line between adoring and annihilating the female body and no one straddled it quite like Hype. His directorial vision was decisive and produced some of the most exquisite images in hip hop. But that same vision also framed the female body, the legs and backside especially, in ways that were stunningly reductive.

Though Hype pushed the envelope his videos were seldom, if ever, lewd. Nevertheless, his success paved the way for the next wave of rap-music video directors whose work, lacking Hype's verve and vision, was often deliberately lewd. In the post-Hype world of rap-music videos, the female body became a mere prop used mainly to create the players and pimps that populated the music clips, which, for better or worse, stood out as hip hop's grandest and most accessible visual art form.

• • •

If imitation is the sincerest form of flattery, no hip-hop artist has been flattered more than Hype Williams. But whereas Hype combined style and spectacle the directors who have tried to emulate his achievements have often settled for spectacle. One of the worst offenses came in 2003 when the music clip for Nelly's pimp anthem, "Tip Drill" made its bow. Too racy for prime time, it aired late nights and on the Internet. It was a hit on BET's late-night video program *Uncut,* a show that earned its name and reputation by featuring some of music's most rascally clips.

*Uncut* had come under fire prior to airing "Tip Drill" from black sororities and fraternities who charged that the naughty nocturnal clips played on some of the more pernicious myths about black sexuality. But BET, owned by the media conglomerate Viacom, defended its right to air the program. "*Uncut* has developed an almost cult-like following because of the freedom of artists to express themselves," spokesperson Michael Lewellen said. "It is specifically for adults. These are music videos whose content is too strong for our *day parts*. We exercise more scrutiny than is required." *Uncut* was scheduled right before the religious program *Success N Life* with Robert Tilton. Many familiar with the late-night lineup joked that after being immersed in *Uncut's* sex-soaked videos, viewers needed a little religion.

Filled with images of women simulating sex with each other, dancing in the nude, and pictured in one degrading pose after another, the "Tip Drill" clip was quintessential soft-core porn. Just when it seemed as though the song's hook, which proclaimed a preference for the female's ass rather than her face, said it all, the video managed to say much more. When one of the male characters in the video swipes his credit card down the backside of one of the dancers, many viewers became incensed. "Tip Drill" was not the first video to celebrate the hedonism popularized in the more "thugged out" expressions of hip-hop masculinity. Still, its pornographic sensibilities touched a nerve.

In the Spring of 2004 the proverbial shit hit the fan when students at Spelman College, a historically black college in Atlanta, mounted a massive protest against "Tip Drill" specifically and the rampant misogyny in hip hop more generally. In a scenario only fate could create, it just so happened that Nelly's 4Sho4Kids Foundation was scheduled to hold a bone marrow drive on campus later that spring. After learning that his sister suffered from leukemia, Nelly launched the service organization to encourage more African Americans to register as bone marrow donors. Many of the women on campus faced a dilemma—should they remain quiet about their disgust and hold the drive or speak out and thus run the risk of a cancellation of the event.

"Nelly wants us to help his sister," Sasha Jennings, president of the Student Government Association said, "but he's degrading hundreds of us." In the days and weeks leading up to the bone marrow drive, Spelman became the site of vigorous debate. One student organization posted lyrics from the song around campus and pushed for a massive protest. According to Spelman students, when Nelly's foundation found out about the trouble brewing on campus, it threatened to cancel the event unless assurances were made that students would not confront the rap star. The outrage at Spelman made national news as the Associated Press, MTV News, the *Washington Post*, and *USA Today* covered the story. Convinced that the issue had grown beyond their control, the rap star's foundation decided not to hold the drive.

The drama that surfaced at Spelman reveals a much deeper strain in hip hop. Around the country many young women are voicing their anger with the movement. While the gender tensions in hip hop rarely make the corporate-driven, celebrity-hungry headlines that cover the pop world, they remain a topic of growing debate within the movement. For years, young women and even some men have voiced concern about the movement's women-hating inclinations. Many young women who consider themselves a part of hip hop find themselves in an awkward position. As much as they love the energy and spirit in hip hop, they are growing increasingly alienated from the movement. Among the many protest slogans to emerge from Spelman perhaps none is more telling than the simply phrased but equally compelling question, "We love hip hop, but does hip hop love us?" It is a question that many young women around the country are posing with great frequency.

The women at Spelman are smart. They understood that Nelly's "Tip Drill" was only the tip of the iceberg. Jennings told the Associated Press, "It's not so much about Nelly. It's about this culture we've kept intact by buying the music." Her remarks were astute and pointed to another problem that was never addressed in the press coverage of the uproar. Despite the vigorous protest Nelly, Universal Records (his label), BET, and Viacom essentially shrugged it off as a minor inconvenience. Their lack of a response delivered a chilling message that few dared to consider. As long as images of lewd black sexuality continued to power hip hop's mainstream appeal and platinum status, why should they care what black students had to say.

Still, the women at Spelman had taken a stand. Their move was significant because it could not be dismissed as the disgruntled views of an out-of-touch constituency. This was not Bob Dole or Joe Lieberman trying to score political points with social conservatives. Neither was it C. DeLores Tucker or the Reverend Calvin O. Butts III hoping to preserve the notions of black bourgeois respectability by putting irreverent young blacks back in their place. The outrage sparked by the "Tip Drill" clip emanated from hip hop's very own, the community the movement presumed to represent. Spelman's courageous efforts, however, did not come risk-free. Some critics agreed that while the video was contemptible the cause bringing Nelly to campus was more important. Those same critics dismissed the protest as self-centered and even simple-minded for placing media images above the health of African Americans.

But rather than cast the Spelman protest as silly the criticism revealed why the young women's voices were so desperately needed. Hip hop's raging misogyny undermines the movement's progressive claims by glamorizing a culture and sustaining a climate that routinely demeans women at virtually no cost. Significantly, the critics failed to recognize that big media's distribution of such images *is* a serious health problem, particularly for hip hop's most invisible and, arguably, most vulnerable group, black girls. All but ignored by the critics was the perilous culture that young black girls wake up to every day: a culture that offers few empowering images of black womanhood. That reality, and its implications for their health and well-being, apparently, did not matter.

• • •

Black teenage girls occupy an unseen world. For all that the public sees and hears about urban youth culture, we know very little about the cultural experiences of black girls. Even as hip hop projects images of black youth onto a glitzy global media stage, certain images emerge as more popular, pervasive, and probable than others. A look at the films that hip hop has inspired reveals a strong bias toward the plight of young black males. Likewise, corporate rap is dominated by the stories that young male MCs create. And despite the proliferation of hip-hop magazines there are virtually no empowering images of black women. The degree to which hip hop fails to speak to and understand the world that girls in the hood inhabit is striking. Amazingly, at a time in which teens are a constant and primary target of corporate media, few films, television programs, music genres, or magazines aggressively target black girls. In essence, they remain remarkably indiscernible and underserved in a youth-obsessed media culture. Despite all of this, black girls are deeply immersed in pop culture; they consume, adore, and live it.

When she was twelve years old Kenya Jordana James, like millions of young girls, was an avid reader of teen magazines. But none of the magazines reflected the images, interests, and stories of black girls like her. After conducting research and studying other magazines, she devised a plan—as well as an editorial vision—to launch her own book, *Blackgirl*. The mission of the magazine was simple. "I want *Blackgirl* to be the voice for black girls everywhere," says James. "It's a magazine that reflects the multidimensional African-American teen. My goal is to enlighten, inspire and entertain teens while encouraging them to excel and be leaders." James used $1,200 that she earned from selling homemade cakes and other baked goods to produce the first issue. In preparation for launch she did it all—design, writing, and editing. Several record companies dismissed her requests for interviews, but persistence earned her a feature with hip hop's dynamic duo, Outkast. That interview gave her confidence and the feeling that the magazine was legit. When all 3,000 of the premier 20-page issue sold out, she knew she was on to something.

Her next big coup came for the second issue of the bimonthly publication, when she scored an interview with Lauryn Hill. At the time Hill was not granting interviews. After failing to get access through Hill's record label, James says, "I sort of found her number out of the blue." After about six months of trying she finally snagged the interview of her dreams. In *Blackgirl.com* Hill talks about motherhood, family, spiritual health, and the pressures of celebrity. Discussing her next album, Hill noted that she simply wanted to be "free from the responsibility of being somebody in the world. Just free to express who I am at this moment in time."

Documentary filmmaker and activist Rachel Raimist also relied on her own instincts and concerns about the image of black women in pop culture to produce a film, *Nobody Knows My Name*, which was immensely personal and political. The film skillfully captures the struggle for recognition and respect by young women in hip hop. Raimist grew up immersed in hip hop. She bought the CDs, watched the videos, and began attending hip-hop parties at the age of thirteen. As she got older and began looking for more compelling images of women in hip hop, she realized there were not very many. "There was nothing that dealt with the inner-lives or real stories of women in hip hop." Young and eager to take on the world, she produced a fifteen-minute student short for a documentary class, which turned into a labor of love and a full-length documentary that screened at national and international film festivals.

As she toured the nation to talk about her film, Raimist was amazed to learn how many women were touched by her work. When young women—black, Latina, Asian, and white—began to thank her for having the courage to tell their stories, she knew she had touched a nerve. The film intuitively understands the dilemma many young women face in hip hop: How can they reconcile their appreciation for hip hop with the alienation they feel about the movement's misogynistic ways?

What James and Raimist's instincts told them about pop culture and its lack of respect for girls was actually a topic of great interest among social researchers. Throughout the 1990s a host of behavioral and social scientists began producing a voluminous body of research focusing on the mental and physical health of young girls. The bulk of this research maintained that compared to their male counterparts teenage girls suffer from lower self-esteem and higher levels of depression. The adolescent journey, so the theories assert, is an especially treacherous period for young girls. Much of this research documents how issues like body image dissatisfaction, eating disorders, depression, and suicidal thoughts had become a cruel rite of passage for many young girls on their way to young female adulthood. Mary Pipher, a clinical psychologist, argues that girls are immersed in a poisonous media and social world that force them to fit into narrowly defined roles in order to feel accepted by society and their peers.

As illuminating as much of this research has been, it speaks most directly to the experiences of girls from white and middle-class households. Implicit in much of this research is the idea that black girls were either wholly resistant to or only mildly affected by the "beauty myths" that cause so many girls to feel "unpretty," undesirable, and unappreciated. While black girls may avoid some of the health problems that affect white girls—anorexia, diet pill addiction, for example—they remain vulnerable in other areas, most notably, their sexual health.

• • •

The sexual world of teens has changed dramatically over the last fifteen years. Current research shows that most young people have their first sexual encounter between ninth and twelfth grade. During this period young people begin to explore and develop their sexual selves. The teen sexual experience is often a topsy-turvy one marked by exhilarating highs—excitement, a sense of independence, and pleasure—and debilitating lows—insecurity, uncertainty, and relentless peer pressure. According to the Centers for Disease Control and Prevention (CDC), "Compared with adults, adolescents are at a higher risk for acquiring sexually transmitted diseases; they are more likely to have multiple partners and short-term relationships; to engage in unprotected sexual intercourse, and to have partners who are themselves at high risk for sexually transmitted diseases."

Though all youth share an increasingly sexualized media culture and society, their sexual lives are not created equal. In fact, the sexual experiences of young people vary considerably by a host of factors: race and ethnicity, educational attainment of parents, and household income just to name a few. A 2004 report from the CDC provides a sense of just how perilous the sexual world of many young black females is.

Analyzing data from twenty-nine states for 1999 to 2002 the CDC reported that 35 percent of all new HIV cases were acquired through heterosexual encounters; 64 percent of those cases occurred in females and, amazingly, 74 percent of those cases occurred in non-Hispanic blacks. The CDC report found that "the proportion of infected females was highest among persons aged 13–19 years, consistent with a previous finding" and that "females in this age group engage in behaviors that place them at increased risk for acquiring HIV infections."

The susceptibility of black girls and young women to HIV/AIDS is particularly haunting and cause for great alarm. Though blacks and Hispanics represented 21 percent of the total population included in the twenty-nine states evaluated in the study, they accounted for 84 percent of the heterosexually acquired HIV infections. An overwhelming percentage of the black cases, 64 percent, were among young women aged thirteen to nineteen. The study illustrates how the story, face, and politics of HIV/AIDS have changed dramatically in America. Once considered a white, gay, male disease, it has evolved to become the disease of the racially and ethnically marginal, poor, young, and female.

In recent years young black women have found themselves on the frontlines of the battle against HIV/AIDS as their sexual world and experiences put them at a disproportionately high risk for infection. Black girls are more likely than their white or Hispanic counterparts to have multiple partners (four or more), more likely to engage in vaginal intercourse without a condom, and more likely to have sex with an infected partner. Because black girls are also more likely to begin having sexual intercourse at an earlier age, the duration of their potential exposure to HIV is also longer.

The hazardous conditions that define the sexual worlds of black girls cannot be simply dismissed by the assertion that they are more sexually active or promiscuous than their peers. A majority of teens across the racial and ethnic spectrum report being sexually active by the time they reach twelfth grade. Still, the environment out of which black girls make choices about sex is both distinct and compelling.

Gina Wingood, a professor in the Rollins School of Public Health at Emory University, has been researching the sexual lives of black teenage girls for more than thirteen years. During that time she has seen a lot and learned even more about the complex sexual lives and health of black girls. She began her research in San Francisco in 1991. At that time San Francisco stood out as one of the epicenters of HIV/AIDS because of its large and politically robust gay community. Though the disease was largely associated with white gay men, Wingood suspected that because it is sexually transmitted it would eventually hit women, too. When she began her work "most researchers focused on the psychological factors that increased people's risk for HIV infection." Instead, she chose to focus on the "social, cultural, and gender factors that increased women's risk for HIV." Her particular emphasis would soon be a crucial area of research as the AIDS health crises spread to affect many different populations.

A number of factors—attitudinal, personal, parental, environmental, and cultural—influence young people's sexual choices and behaviors. Black girls, Wingood maintains, face a number of risks when they choose to become sexually active. "Some of it's very environmental," she asserts. "Their partners are often riskier, meaning they may have had multiple sex partners. Their partners may be more likely to be HIV-infected themselves." Most experts who study sexual behavior and outcomes believe these are public health issues. Thus, the sexual health of black girls is a political rather than moral matter largely because of the relationship between race and health in America that continues to belie claims of progress or equality. On virtually any health measure of note—infant mortality, life expectancy, HIV/AIDS, access to care—black and Latinos fare far worse than their white counterparts. But the health outcomes of black and Latina girls generate very little public attention, advocacy, or outcry.

Wingood maintains that black girls, rural and urban, are an important population for HIV prevention programs. The Emory University professor is not surprised by the upsurge in HIV among young black girls. "It indicates that prevention messages and educational programs are not being disseminated, or are not being understood, or are not effective," she says. The failure in delivering that message to the communities that need it the most further explains why the media and pop-culture worlds of black girls are so important. It also underscores why the hypersexual depictions of young black females in hip hop *matter*.

Wingood has also studied black girls' consumption of rap-music videos and pornography. Not surprisingly, she contends that hip hop's distorted images of black femininity produce adverse outcomes for black girls. Despite decades of research, the extent to which media affects the attitudes and behaviors of young people remains a hot topic of debate. Wingood believes there is an important connection between the images of black femininity black girls consume and their own self-esteem and degree of satisfaction with their bodies and their lives. Like their white and Latina female counterparts, black girls are immersed in a pop-culture world that is bombarded with sexual themes and imagery. Many teens report that as they strive for greater independence from their parents they often turn to their peers and the media for knowledge and information about the issues most central in their lives. Around this time young people not only begin to devote greater attention to their media environment; they also devote more time to their bodies and their desire for intimacy.

Given the sexual travails of black girls, their media environment becomes an especially crucial front in the struggle to enhance their sexual knowledge and health. This is why hip hop is such an important discourse in the lives of black girls and why the movement's failure to speak to and for them is so profoundly tragic. Once thought to be nearly immune to the unhealthy images and beauty myths popularized in pop culture, black girls are increasingly confronted by images of black femininity that are just as pernicious as the images white girls often fall victim to. In the face of such an onslaught, the view that black girls can remain resilient is certainly optimistic but not necessarily realistic.

• • •

Perhaps no case describes how disturbingly real these issues have become than the child molestation charges that were brought against and later dropped involving the R&B hit maker R. Kelly. Rumors about the man *The Source* called the "Teflon Don" and his sexual appetite for young girls have been swirling since the middle 1990s. In 2001 those rumors took on a whole new dimension when news broke of a sex tape allegedly involving R. Kelly and a minor. News of the tape spread like wildfire and soon it was available for view on the Internet and bootleg videotapes. A few stations, most notably, WBBM-FM (B-96) in the singer-producer's hometown of Chicago, pulled his music off the air for a short period of time. Soon, however, a backlash against the initial backlash ensued. Within a year, R. Kelly, the self-professed "pied piper of R&B," was back on B-96's playlists. Todd Cavanah, the station's program director explained, "Right now, he's innocent until proven guilty, and there are stations in town playing this record, and listeners requesting that we play it, and to stay competitive I have to play it too."

As the allegations made their way through the entertainment news circuit, many blacks began to rally around R. Kelly. Concerns about his career, his image, and whether he would be able to continue making platinum hits became magnified. Strangely enough, R. Kelly became the "victim" in the unfolding saga. Next, came the push to embrace R. Kelly and his music. That all of this was expressed under the banner of racial solidarity is troubling, but, sadly enough, also predictable. Even R. Kelly began to thank his "real fans" for standing by him.

Lost in the furor over R. Kelly was the young black girl and others like her who fall prey every day to the sexual exploits of older men and a sex-obsessed culture. No one stood up for them. The fact that the public, and the hip-hop public, in particular, cared more about R. Kelly than the girl was more than a cautionary tale. Tragically, it confirms that the misogyny that runs rampant in hip hop is a deeply rooted part of the movement's aura and "ghetto realness" façade.

CHAPTER NINE

# *Artificial Intelligence?*

*We are hip-hop, we preserve it, we protect it and*
*we are the ones who are doing it, and we are not*
*criminals. In fact, we are scholars, we are philosophers,*
*we are priests, we are ministers, we are activists.*

—KRS-ONE

Located in the heart of Boston's Back Bay neighborhood, the Berklee College of Music is known for its innovative approach to music education and training. Berklee proudly boasts that its 3,800 students and 460 faculty members make it the world's largest independent music college and the leading institution for the study of contemporary music. Decades ago Berklee broke away from the more conservative approaches that have long defined most music conservatories, particularly the emphasis on European classical music. Along the way, the music school made its mark by incorporating musical forms that existed outside the classical music canon. In the 1940s Berklee incorporated improvisational jazz into its curriculum at a time when few were willing to accept it as a music form that was worthy of serious academic study and training. Again, in the 1960s the school began offering courses on the electronic guitar, a technology that revolutionized the aesthetics of rock and pop music.

Despite its history as a visionary institution, school administrators, faculty, alumni, and students were caught off guard when Stephen Webber, a professor of music production and engineering, proposed teaching a course in turntablism. The course was a reference to the wizardlike skills and techniques of hip hop DJs, the original creative force in rap music. In essence, Webber wanted to include a musical form many believe lacks the rigor, structure, and prestige that define the musical styles typically taught by the more staid music schools. Its popularity and commercial appeal notwithstanding, rap music is widely viewed as unsophisticated street music at best and thievery (a reference to the musical sampling) at worst. But Webber was convinced that DJs are musicians and the unorthodox beats, grooves, and compositions they craft are a crucial part of contemporary music.

The idea came to him after watching a videotape of a professional competition. The level of craftsmanship stunned him. What DJs were doing with turntables, specifically, how they were using them as percussive instruments, blew him away and opened his eyes to a new musical frontier. In his words he was "astonished by their ability to rock a party, to read a crowd and do many of the things that musicians aspire to." He immediately purchased two turntables and a mixer and began practicing hours a day, immersing himself in the serious study of the art and science of the hip-hop DJ. He viewed it as a paradigm shift, another groundbreaking chapter in the history of contemporary music.

After authoring a book that identified a set of terms and techniques that gave the work of the hip-hop DJ more structure and formality, he proposed teaching a turntablism course. Berklee officials denied his request. He tried two more times only to be denied again on both occasions. At that point he requested a meeting with top officials to make the case that what hip-hop DJs were doing with turntables—making music—placed it on the cutting edge of the contemporary music scene. He saw turntablism and hip hop as a crucial part of where the culture is going. "If we plan to be relevant in academia," Webber explains, "we have to address it [hip hop] and learn about it ourselves."

He realized the assertion that you could "play" the turntable ran up against conventional wisdom. He also knew that calling turntablism a serious art form and mode of instrumentation was no less bizarre in the eyes of many. But then again, everything about hip hop—its rise, popularity, and influence—was out of the ordinary and nearly impossible to fully explain. His uphill battle to persuade administrators to adopt the course was made steeper by the stubbornly persistent image that hip-hop music was not "real music."

It was not only stodgy school officials who felt that way about rap. Over the years even a few outspoken popular musicians and other critics openly questioned the value of hip-hop music, suggesting that the very fact that you make music by beginning with someone else's music belies the assertion that something genuinely creative is happening. But the producers of hip-hop music have long insisted that by cutting, fragmenting, and reconstructing previously recorded material they are, in fact, building a new aesthetic and a new way of experiencing music. Webber likens it to what artists from Matisse to Mozart have done in other fields, asking, "How many times has the basic premise of Romeo and Juliet been retreaded to be more contemporary?"

Berklee officials were not convinced that the proposed course fit the school's educational mission or rigorous standards. The idea that turntablism was a legitimate form of instrumentation was an offbeat concept and one that tested the liberal norms and culture of the institution like never before. But officials also knew there was growing interest among students in hip-hop music and that it was part of their contemporary experience. So, rather than dismiss the idea completely, they conducted a year-long study to determine the merits of such a class.

Webber's most immediate challenge, in the eyes of school officials, was developing a formal instructional language that encompassed the various methods in turntablism while adhering to the school's rigorous standards. They considered whether techniques like scratching, beat matching, cutting, and cueing might be comparable to the techniques taught in other courses. Webber noted that all of the things you need to know before approaching an instrument, "your scales, your cadences, and hand positions" also applied to the turntable. There were aesthetic considerations, too: Students would be required in their original compositions not only to master technique but to strive for originality, a distinct voice, and emotional impact.

At stake for Berklee, of course, was its reputation as one of the premier music schools in the world. There was always the chance that such a course would be a disaster, both in terms of the potential public-relations hit the school might take and any subsequent erosion of its image as a serious music school. Nevertheless, when these same questions about tradition and the risks associated with breaking new ground had faced them in the past, Berklee had refused to capitulate—choosing instead to expand rather than preserve the status quo in American music education.

That is why Webber thought turntablism was a natural fit. Since the arrival of hip hop, he thought, what other musical form had altered the landscape of contemporary music more than rap? Hip hop reinvented the image and the status of the DJ by pioneering a whole new musical vocabulary and array of techniques that also reinvented the turntable. Rather than simply play previously recorded music, hip hop DJs used the turntable to make new music. Part of Webber's responsibility would be to try to capture, document, and formalize that language. In other words, render it comprehensible so that it could be incorporated into the curriculum and, ultimately, made more teachable and intelligible.

There were certain risks associated with that. Some defenders of the movement might view this work as yet another example of outside forces and figures co-opting and redefining hip hop in ways that had little to do with the movement and those who peopled it. The idea that a professor and a music college with little connection to hip hop would now play a role in codifying what had always been perceived as improvisational, street-oriented, and club-based represented a potential threat to the image and culture of turntablism. But many turntablists saw the move as a sign of long overdue respect.

After all of these years, and despite the critics, the art they created was worthy of serious study and recognition.

Though some Berklee officials were reluctant to do so, they agreed to adopt the course. In the end, they felt that because the constituency that mattered most, their students, wanted the class they should have the option to experience it. Here was yet another reminder of how hip hop and those who came of age in the movement were changing American culture. Turntablism, it turns out, was also at the heart of Berklee's musical mission. "What Berklee is all about is pushing the envelope, being innovative, exposing our students to the important musical movements of our time—and hip-hop is certainly that," says Webber.

Webber likened Berklee's embrace of hip-hop music to the school's history of thinking outside the box. "People take it for granted today that jazz is serious music worthy of the same disciplined study as classical music," he says. "But when Berklee began teaching jazz improvisation in the 1940s and rock guitar in the 1960s, most other music schools perceived those musical forms as a threat to 'serious' music. It's the same situation with hip hop and turntablism today."

Three years before Berklee's adoption of hip-hop music, Harvard, located just a few miles from the music college, established the Hiphop Archive. According to the director, Marcyliena Morgan, the archive is designed to facilitate and encourage the pursuit of knowledge, art, culture, and responsible leadership through hip hop. Before moving to Stanford the archive was affiliated with Harvard's African American Studies department. Henry Louis Gates, Jr., the architect of the highly regarded department, is a proud and notable product of the civil rights struggle. By his own admission, Gates is not a connoisseur of hip hop. Like Berklee officials, however, he realized that hip hop was the real deal, a genuine cultural and economic force that could not be ignored by a department many regard as a tower in African American studies. "While I'm not especially a fan of hip-hop—perhaps I'm too old—there can be no doubt that it is one

of the most important cultural phenomenons in the second half of
the 20th century," he told the *New York Times* in 2003. "We would be
remiss if we did not treat it accordingly," he added. Before the creation of the archive, his most notable contribution to the movement
came when he testified on behalf of rap's free speech rights in the 1989
Florida obscenity trial against 2 Live Crew, a Miami-based rap crew.

Berklee and Harvard are two prominent examples of a development that has been years in the making. Hip hop's spreading sphere
of influence knows no boundaries. As the voice of a new generation,
hip hop's presence is raising hell in arenas that do not necessarily
understand or appreciate it. Like it or not, even the nation's premier
places of higher learning are moving to the sway of the movement.
Hip hop's impact in America, like the vivid cultural imagination it
has spawned, simply put, cannot be denied.

• • •

Over the course of its career, hip hop has produced an impressive
array of thinkers—writers, performance artists, poets, and scholars
—who have come to embody its complex ideological makeup.
Though the hip-hop intelligentsia is one of the rarely discussed aspects of the movement it is, without question, one of its greatest
achievements. The growing array of hip-hop intellectuals is a spectacular indication of the movement's multifaceted demeanor and
ceaseless energy. Trying to define or describe the hip-hop intelligentsia is a risky enterprise in part because it is such a diverse group
and one that refuses to parrot a uniform, or even predictable ideology.

Naturally, many of hip hop's "best and brightest" belie the traditional definitions of intellectuals. Within this emergent strata a premium is placed on the ability to identify with and articulate the
gritty experiences and irreverent sensibilities that anchor hip hop's
inner soul. What has emerged is a body of thinkers who articulate a
wide range of ideas that, in their unique way, map out the contradictory currents, ideas, and worldviews that percolate throughout the

phenomenal world of hip hop. From spoken-word artists to academic scholars hip-hop intellectuals are translating the movement into a vast mix of critical commentary and artistic expression. The results both energize and expand the image and imagination of the hip-hop intelligentsia.

Nowhere is this more evident than in the rise of hip-hop fiction. Variously referred to as street, ghetto, and urban fiction, the rise of hip-hop lit is a fascinating story. Much like rap music, hip-hop lit defies any effort to define it under one genre label or aesthetic. Still, though the novels published up to this point cut across a wide range of literary genres—romance, thriller, crime—this growing community of writers is attempting to expand hip hop's presence in American contemporary fiction.

Most book publishers and booksellers agree that Sista Souljah's *The Coldest Winter Ever* put the genre on the map, selling more than 400,000 copies and far exceeding anyone's expectations. The book follows the life of Santiaga Winter, a young black American princess, who grows up in the lap of luxury provided by her father, a drug kingpin. Her life is turned upside down when her mother becomes the victim of a revenge murder. Her father's assets are seized, and he is imprisoned. On her own for the first time in her life, Santiaga faces a cold and brutal world. Driven to save herself, her father, and family, she relies on her instincts, feminine wiles, and a cold heart to manage a rough-and-tumble underworld. The book establishes a tone—raw and uncompromising in its prose, action packed, and populated by a cast of characters fighting for survival, respect, and upward mobility in the underserved and underhanded ways of the ghetto underworld—that has become the trademark of hip-hop lit. Lloyd Hart, a longtime black bookseller in Boston, says *The Coldest Winter Ever* "made Sista Souljah the Terry McMillan of the urban genre."

Malaika Adero, senior editor at Simon and Schuster's Atria Books, notes that *The Coldest Winter Ever* "was the tip of the iceberg in terms of the number of people from this generation who were expressing themselves in literature." Sista Souljah was a recognizable figure who decided to expand her artistic expression to another field. "What comes behind her," Adero explains, "is a stream of people who not only use literature as an artistic expression but as a means of economic survival.... It is an entrepreneurial movement as well as an artistic movement."

Like the creators of hip-hop music, the creators of hip-hop lit believed in the genre when no one else did. When the writers could not gain attention or recognition from the publishing industry, they relied on sheer hustle and innovation to get their product in the hands of readers. They self-published their books and then sold them from their cars targeting barbershops, beauty salons, street corners, and night clubs and anywhere else they could find readers. The parallels of hip-hop lit to the rise of rap music are striking and certainly not accidental. Hip-hop fiction writers were fully aware of rap's past, aware that in the beginning few seemed to care about or even think rap music had much of a future. Like the early pioneers in the production of rap music, those who helped to launch street lit sensed that their stories could resonate with hip hop's urban core.

This is what inspired one of hip-hop lit's best-selling writers, Vickie Stringer. By 2004 her publishing company, Triple Crown Publishing, was one of the fastest growing outfits in the industry, drawing attention from top editors and publishers interested in getting in on the emergent urban-lit market. Stringer's path to becoming one of hip-hop lit's signature personalities was not typical of a hot-selling American author. Her personal tribulations were no stranger to generation hip hop. Before self-publishing her debut title in 2001, Stringer served seven years in prison for her involvement in the drug trade. While in prison, her writing became both a creative and therapeutic outlet. She mined the depths of her soul to pen a contemporary novel, *Let That Be the Reason*. The book's main character is based loosely on her life.

After her release, Stringer found herself working in the fast food industry and shopping her novel. Reportedly she received twenty-six rejection letters and then decided to self-publish the book. She ended up selling more than 30,000 copies. Soon Stringer found herself publishing other people's books. She assembled a roster of authors of urban fiction titles, and by 2004, combined sales totals exceeded 300,000 copies. Those results produced a palpable buzz, and soon Stringer and a few of her authors were being courted by some of the major publishing houses.

Stringer was part of an onrushing wave of writers who were driving a genre that had stumbled across an untapped market for books. It was assumed that hip-hop America did not read. But the rapid sales of street fiction proved that theory wrong. Many retailers and publishers pointed out that hip-hop fiction is consumed mainly by young black readers, ages eighteen to thirty-five. Just when it seemed as though small, independently owned black bookstores could no longer survive in a book world dominated by giant retailers, such as Barnes & Noble and Borders, street lit breathed life into them. Most book retailers and editors note that fiction is a genre consumed primarily by women. According to insiders like Adero though, hip-hop lit "seems to be consumed more by males than any other category of contemporary fiction." She believes that what diminishes hip-hop lit's literary value to some—the profanity, street vernacular, and rough-edged stories—attracts young black male readers. Hip-hop lit, she explains, "captures their voice, their experience, and their concerns. It is something that they can relate to. This is not your mother's ordinary romance novel."

Boston bookseller Hart believes people as young as thirteen have been drawn to hip-hop fiction. "Though I'm not necessarily crazy about many of these books, I'm an advocate of book reading," says Hart. "So any genre that attracts young black readers is a move in the right direction."

In the midst of reports that book sales are continuing to slump, hip-hop lit has become a surprising cash cow, which explains the growth in titles and the recent big push by established publishers who once looked down on the genre. In spring 2004 Hyperion Books, a division of the Miramax media company, launched an unprecedented campaign to promote Erica Kennedy's hip-hop novel, *Bling*. Falling somewhere between a dishy Jackie Collins novel and a satire of the excesses in the rap-music industry, the book stood apart from street lit both in tone and the promotional muscle behind it. Still, *Bling* reflected just how far hip-hop-oriented fiction had come. Adero maintains that when it is all said and done, the readers of hip-hop lit "may end up being our salvation in this industry."

Yet not everyone is thrilled about the hip-hop lit craze. The genre's detractors charge that like the cultural inventions it draws its imagination from—the profanity-laced, street-themed narratives made popular by Iceberg Slim and Donald Boines, as well as blaxploitation and ghetto action flicks—hip-hop lit glorifies the sordid side of street life in Ghetto USA. Many of the novels thrive on the illegal drug economy, murder, mayhem, sex, and a ghetto patois that some find indecipherable and unfit for contemporary fiction. James Fugate, owner of Esowon Books, the largest black-owned bookstore in Los Angeles, believes the books are potentially damaging to the young audience drawn to them. He says, "The books are usually self-published and suffer from poor writing, grammatical and spelling errors, and lack any redeeming values."

Stringer though, vehemently defends her work: "I don't release titles that perpetuate stereotypes, I release novels that tell harsh realities." She believes her tumultuous experience in the drug trade and subsequent incarceration positioned her "to communicate to the youth of black communities, in a language they can understand, to help them comprehend the reality of life in the streets and the consequences of their decisions." Adero, who signed Stringer to Atria Books, agrees. "The books I publish are cautionary tales. They do not glamorize this [criminal] world," she explains. "Yes they are gritty and in-your-face, but it isn't Superfly."

Hip-hop lit, no matter its artistic and intellectual merits or lack thereof, reflects the spreading influence of hip hop into spheres that ten years ago would have seemed unimaginable. If nothing else, hip-hop lit boldly confirms the arrival of a vivid cultural imagination that embodies the movement's irrepressible soul. Like other aspects of hip hop's steadily evolving world, contemporary street fiction exemplifies the warring sensibilities, mood shifts, and worldviews that makes hip hop a lively phenomenon. The arrival of hip-hop lit, like the music two decades ago, came from nowhere to make its mark.

In the end, the street novels that hip hop inspire add another chapter to the compelling story of the movement and its very own class of street philosophers, poets, and pundits. A close connection to urban America endows their particular expertise—street knowledge —with an edge and authority that has become, in some instances, a beacon of light for a generation all too familiar with darkness and the unfulfilled promises of a brighter day.

• • •

The new wave of urban griots in hip-hop lit is part of a longer tradition within the movement: the creation of a street-based intelligentsia that drew much of its vitality and credibility from its close proximity to and connection with hip hop's ghetto trenches. There was something notable and noble about the making of this loose band of creative artists and thinkers. They did not propose to simply speak for the dispossessed in hip hop; they were a part of the dispossessed. One of the most arresting street philosophers to emerge from hip hop is KRS-One. His personal biography and rise in hip hop came straight out of the fictional wells of hip-hop lit.

The pressures of growing up in a poor, single-parent household drove him to the streets, literally, where he became homeless at the tender age of thirteen. Over the next few years he bounced around shelters, street corners, subways and public libraries, virtually anywhere he could find a roof over his head. He met Scott Sterling, a young social worker, while staying in a men's shelter. Scott, it turns out, was also a club DJ on weekends, named Scott La Rock. The two hit it off and ended up developing a mutual affinity for hip hop. Together they formed the group Boogie Down Productions and went on to release one of hip hop's most influential albums, *Criminal Minded,* in 1987. The album featured many of the hallmark traits that established rap music's pop aura and appeal—sparse beats, clever samples of soul and reggae music, a facility with street vernacular that gave it an air of ghetto authenticity, and a gangsta ethos that formed the outline for hard core hip hop's big commercial push.

Just as they were climbing their way atop a hip-hop world that was on the verge of "blowing up," Scott La Rock was murdered. The death of his friend, mentor, and musical partner left a lasting impression on KRS-One. The tragedy forced him to take stock of his own mortality as well as his artistic, professional, and spiritual well-being.

Even though *Criminal Minded* inspired the rise of gangsta, KRS-One pursued a different creative path. His next slate of albums, titles like *By All Means Necessary, Ghetto Music: The Blueprint of Hip Hop,* and *Sex and Violence* propelled him forward as a major voice in hip hop. Along with hip-hop messengers like Chuck D, Sista Souljah, and Paris, an Oakland-based message rapper, KRS-One began to put socially conscious rap on the map. Their lyrics took on some of the major issues of the period—poverty, violence, racism, the ravages of drugs, corrupt law enforcement, the shake-down ways of the music industry, and the commercial takeover of hip hop. This crew of hip-hop intellectuals recognized the movement's larger potential, the idea that popular media gave them and their communities precious air time. In the midst of their historic contributions to rap, they reconfirmed the idea that the genre could express a political point of view in the world of pop. As hip hop's voice of New School consciousness, they embraced the notion that they were real life intellectuals and made the pursuit of knowledge, at least temporarily, a popular aspect of rap music. Whereas venerable organizations like the NAACP and the Urban League failed to fashion a political personality that excited young people, the bombastic style and rhymes cultivated by socially conscious rappers spoke to them with conviction, if not a program to realize their vision.

Years before the Hip Hop Summit Action Network—or any other

effort to realize hip hop's potential for social change—KRS-One played an instrumental role in the creation of the "Stop the Violence Movement." That late 1980s project was hip hop's answer to Willie Nelson's Farm Aid or Quincy Jones's USA for Africa effort. The campaign represented one of the first attempts to channel hip hop's celebrity toward a social change agenda. The orchestration of the campaign convinced KRS-One that hip hop could be a powerful educational force rather than merely an entertainment vehicle. His claim that "hip hop is beyond entertainment—it's a behavior, a consciousness, a way to view the world" became a personal mantra.

Rap music, in the worldview he created, was a vehicle to counter the educational curricula that structured the more formal classroom experiences of ghetto youths. That system, he believed, left many black students apathetic, unenlightened, and suffering from low self-esteem. In a 1989 op-ed piece for the *New York Times,* he spelled out why he thought education was the major problem facing troubled black youth. "While no single cause accounts for the problems of inner-city kids, much of what black youth is missing—self-esteem, creative opportunity, outlook, goals—can be traced to what we're not learning in schools," he said. That was why he crafted an image of himself as a teacher, a scholar, someone committed to elevating the minds of the hip-hop masses.

He was one of the first pop figures to use the term "edutainment" asserting that even as hip hop stayed true to its origins of "moving the crowd," it could move minds, too. With that philosophy serving as a guiding light, he appointed himself hip hop's education czar, determined to salvage and celebrate what he believed was true, divine, and revolutionary about the movement. His new role, and belief that knowledge is power, was personified in the new acronym he made for his stage name KRS-One, Knowledge Reigns Supreme Over Nearly Everyone.

As his career and vision for hip hop evolved, KRS-One grew to become one of the more intriguing minds in the movement. In 1996 he created the Temple of Hip Hop. It was a provocative idea and one that endeavored to institutionalize his own vision of hip hop as a unified culture, organized movement, and source of spiritual uplift. According to the organization, its purpose is "to promote, preserve, and protect Hiphop as a strategy toward Health, Love, Awareness and Wealth for all who declare 'Hiphop' their lifestyle." The Temple's spelling of Hiphop as one word signifies the effort to bring the movement together. "We're talking about unifying hip-hop," KRS-One says, referring to the Temple. "This is an affirmation of society; this is a group of hip-hoppers saying, 'We are hip-hop, we preserve it, we protect it and we are the ones who are doing it, and we are not criminals. In fact, we are scholars, we are philosophers, we are priests, we are ministers, we are activists.'"

Though the concept for the Temple continues to evolve, it appears to be a vehicle for documenting hip hop's history and promoting the spiritual values that KRS-One believes can make the movement a true moral, intellectual, and political force. KRS-One's philosophies about life, the human condition, and hip hop developed an intense religious and theological tone. The idea that hip hop can be taught through religious thought and doctrine is a radical approach and one that adds another interesting dimension in the struggle for hip hop. His album *Spiritual Minded* was a sharp and deliberate contrast to his breakout debut, *Criminal Minded*. If the latter emphasized hip hop's fervor for all things street, the former emphasized KRS-One's longing for all things spiritual. It symbolized his hip-hop journey and unique hope that the movement could find a higher state of consciousness. In many ways, the trajectory of his career personifies the changing state of hip hop and the ensuing struggle for its soul—a struggle also reflected in KRS-One's religious and spiritual beliefs.

Even during his run as a successful recording artist, KRS-One expressed concerns about hip hop's dalliance with corporate America. His fear that hip hop would become a vehicle of profiteering and corporate engineering was realized. As his commercial appeal faded, he began to profess that hip hop was more than something you performed onstage or with turntables. It was also more than the ability to consume the seemingly endless lists of hip-hop-inspired lifestyle products. He emphasized the totality of hip hop—the expressive, entrepreneurial, and evangelical. His philosophy that hip hop was a way of life to be cultivated, and not a lifestyle brand to be consumed, was a clear rejection of the corporate takeover of hip hop. His religious zealotry for hip hop's spiritual side countered the movement's idolatry of money, celebrity, and the thug-life ethos he and other hip-hop heads believed eroded hip hop's soul. He had always had strong opinions about who and what was hip hop. Now, armed with both street knowledge and religious doctrine, he carved out a unique piece of turf in hip hop. Like everyone else that ever mattered in the movement, KRS-One was making a particular claim for hip hop. While his claims took on the armor of righteousness, they did not constitute gospel for everyone.

No matter what one thought about his attempts to "save" hip hop from itself KRS-One's voice has always struck an urgent chord. His sense of hip hop's place in history has always been finely tuned. "If hip-hop was to end today—no more records, videos—there would be still a thirty-year history about a specific group of people that called themselves hip-hoppers," says KRS-One. He adds: "That's already part of world history, no matter what we do. Now, what image do we want to project of ourselves in world history? It may not mean anything to anyone else, but to me it's my life. We are dealing with a very unique and magnificent opportunity." The opportunity he refers to—the chance to make hip hop matter beyond the world of pop culture—is the main challenge in the escalating bid for hip hop's soul.

Over the years hip hop's street philosophers have worked to rewrite hip hop's history and expand its creative terrain. Meanwhile, a largely unrecognized part of the hip hop intelligentsia has been waging its own struggle for the movement and doing its best to keep hip hop real.

• • •

The decisions by Berklee and Harvard to incorporate hip hop into their highly regarded curricula were, in truth, merely the latest in a flurry of developments that underscored how the struggle for hip hop was unfolding in America's premier colleges and universities. It was an unlikely development and one that no one could have predicted.

Like the changes it wrought in the music industry, youth culture, and the world of politics, hip hop is also making its mark in America's colleges and universities. Though few outside of academe realize it, this particular struggle for hip hop has been long and arduous. The first dissertation with hip hop or rap music in its title appeared in 1989. That was right around the same time that MTV, consumer brands like Nike, and pop culture, in general, began to take notice of the burgeoning world of hip hop. Since then more than eighty such dissertations have been published in the U.S. and Canada.

For more than half of hip hop's career, scholars have viewed it as one of the more arresting aspects of contemporary culture. Hip hop intersects with many different aspects of contemporary life—technology, pop culture, linguistics, globalization, geography, race, and electoral politics just to name a few. This explains why a cross-section of scholars has turned a critical gaze toward the movement. Over the years, the number of scholars incorporating aspects of the movement into their research and teaching has grown, suggesting that the presence of hip hop in academe, like the movement itself, is real and here to stay.

But just as with the arenas of pop music and politics, resistance to the coming of hip hop has been intense in America's Ivory Towers. Questions about its academic value and rigor have constantly dogged efforts to establish hip-hop studies as a viable area of scholarly inquiry. The early resistance was fueled by the belief that hip hop and the music it produced, rap, were just a fad. The battle for hip hop in America's colleges and universities was part of a larger sphere of conflict, what in the 1990s became known as the culture wars. Few places became more embattled than the university along this front. As one of America's most cherished and vital institutions, the university has long helped define what the nation values and how it understands the pursuit of knowledge, enlightenment, and freedom.

With the exception of the debate about affirmative action, many of the contested issues in higher education have developed far from public view. Just as contentious as the questions "Who gets admitted?" or "Who gets hired as faculty?" is the question "What subjects, philosophical ideas, and texts define classical liberal arts education?" Over the last twenty-five years, a new crop of professors, intellectuals, and cultural critics have been storming the gates of the Ivory Tower. Slowly, more women, blacks, Latinos, and Asians have moved into American higher education as tenured and tenured-track scholars. Their arrival embodies the sea shifts in perspective, pedagogy, and purpose that began to alter the character and curriculum in higher education after the contentious decades of the sixties and seventies.

Rather than see academic life as a distant and elite domain (it still is in many ways), key segments among the post–civil rights generation of academic professionals have fought to make their institutions' connections to the real world, to real people, and to real communities more viable. Accompanying that approach has been a bold attempt to redesign the curricula in higher education, placing a greater emphasis on non-Eurocentric courses, ideas, and ways of thinking about the world. That has led to a call to add new thinkers, theories, and texts to the established canons that shape the basic architecture of the liberal arts. In this context the idea that the cultures, histories, and voices of historically marginalized populations should —and must—be added to a more open and diverse curriculum has stirred passionate debate about the state of the American mind.

The call to break down the traditional hierarchies in academe led to the bold idea that popular culture, not just the classics or high arts, was an important site of intellectual inquiry. That meant that what had long been derisively labeled "mass culture," or the culture of the working classes, was not only a viable but a critical area of study. The idea that you can analyze hip-hop music with the same intellectual dexterity used to probe the works of William Shakespeare, treat hip-hop beats as seriously as the music of Mozart, or critique the music clips of Hype Williams with the same textual rigor you would the films of Martin Scorsese is an intriguing discovery for many students. The struggle for hip-hop studies comes on the heels of this larger movement within academe to challenge the established norms, gate-keepers, and bodies of thought that reign supreme in academe.

• • •

Hip-hop scholars also struggle for recognition beyond the erudite confines of higher education. If the focus on hip hop strikes some as not scholarly enough in the Ivory Tower than the reverse holds true beyond the walls of university life. By virtue of their position in academe, hip-hop academics are perceived as too scholarly and, therefore, largely irrelevant to the movement. Key sectors of hip hop have been reluctant to embrace the scholars the movement has produced. There is a perception, that because of their academic standing, hip-hop scholars are disconnected from hip hop. At least part of the reservation can be attributed to the perception that scholars, tucked away in their academic cocoons, adopt a "know-it-all" demeanor that is both off-putting and demeaning to those close to hip hop's cultural trenches. Part of the resistance can be attributed to an uncertainty about scholars that runs through the American public. Additionally, the unease between scholars and hip hop is influenced by the incessant pressure in the movement to valorize all things street—street culture, street philosophers, and street credibility.

One of the more telling moments was when Suge Knight, co-founder of Death Row Records, openly challenged Michael Eric Dyson, a widely respected author and scholar, and his license to write a critical biography of Tupac Shakur. In essence Knight argued that despite his hefty intellect, Dyson's assessment of Tupac and the les-

sons the movement might learn from his tragic legacy was invalid because he did not know Tupac or have any intimate connection to the
thug-life exploits associated with the slain rapper. The criticism reflected the general tension that continues to strain the relationship
between hip-hop scholars and the movement: the belief that to be
down with hip hop (i.e., supportive of the movement) you must
be immersed in street culture. Thus, a major challenge scholars interested in hip hop face is how to develop a critical vocabulary and
assessment of hip hop that earns them respect in two seemingly op-
posed worlds: academe and pop culture. The potential risk is falling
prey to the temptation to produce scholarship that lacks the subtlety
and thoroughness that, ultimately, will mark this community as a
valuable feature in and beyond the academic world. Even as scholars
of hip hop struggle to "keep it real," they must also fight to "get
it right."

• • •

The role of any intelligentsia varies according to the currents of history and culture. The hip-hop intelligentsia is flourishing for a variety of reasons—the movement's commercial appeal, technology like
the Internet, which creates a space for seemingly limitless commentary about the movement, and the inevitable need to explore and expand the rich reservoirs of hip hop. The movement as a whole is only
beginning to come to terms with the vast body of thinkers and artists
it has produced. Part of the hip-hop intelligentsia's mission is to make
sense of the movement and its purpose in the world. In its effort to
realize its unique role in the struggle for hip hop, the intelligentsia
must help pose the tough questions and offer the critical, though not
always favorable, insight that captures the passion, predilections, and
perils that define the movement.

Whereas the goal of hip hop's intelligentsia back in the day may
have been to defend the movement in the face of a barrage of criticism that neither understood nor respected the movement, its calling

has moved well beyond that limited role. One can only hope that as hip hop's intellectual class grows, both in size and perspective, it will develop a finer understanding of its true calling, and thus not only stand up and be heard but also stand up and engage hip hop's triumphs and tragedies, perceptiveness and perversities, in a manner that is as unconquerable as the movement itself.

# *Bigger Than Hip Hop*

*Vote or Die!*

—SEAN "P. DIDDY" COMBS

November 2, 2004 was hip hop's first day of real political reckoning. For more than a year efforts to energize the "hip-hop vote" had been in full swing. Russell Simmons's Hip Hop Summit Action Network (HSAN) had called on some of the movement's biggest stars to attract huge crowds to rallies with the intention of registering young voters. In June of 2004 the National Hip-Hop Political Convention gathered in New Jersey. Organizers, aware that hip hop lacks a formal political agenda, tried unsuccessfully to craft a party platform. That same summer Sean "P. Diddy" Combs's Citizen Change, a hip-hop inspired initiative, tossed its hat in the national political arena. Combs even attended the Democratic and Republican political conventions, drumming up support for his initiative and the quest to make young people's voices heard on election day.

Two weeks before election Tuesday, Combs took his act to Ohio, Michigan, and Florida, three crucial battleground states. Citizen Change, like the HSAN, relied on a number of well-known faces, including Leonardo DiCaprio, Ben Affleck, and Mary J. Blige, to capture young people's attention. The T-shirt sporting Combs's political slogan, "Vote or Die!," was a huge hit. In Detroit he told an enthusiastic crowd of about six thousand that, "This year we're not going to sit on the sidelines and complain, we're going to decide the next president of the United States." It was a bold claim and an even bolder goal for a segment of the voting population—urban youth—that had shown little interest in electoral politics. Uninspired by a political process they believe is irrelevant and unresponsive, black and Latino youth are less likely to vote than their white counterparts.

Hip hop was not alone in the effort to energize young voters. MTV launched its "Choose or Lose" project and produced a number of specials focusing on the candidates, the issues, and the importance of young people exercising their right to vote. Filmmaker Michael Moore, fresh off the success of *Fahrenheit 9/11*, a punishing critique of the Bush administration's policy of preemptive war, took his Slacker's Tour to more than sixty cities, determined to heighten young people's interest in the election. College Republicans, too, made a pitch to rally young supporters to their cause.

Amid all of the pre-election hype young voters and their potential impact on the election became a constant source of speculation. Election officials around the country reported that efforts to increase voter registration had led to an impressive increase in young and first-time voters registering. Bitterly contested issues like the war in Iraq, terrorism, and gay marriage were driving a deeper wedge between an already heavily polarized electorate. In this climate, many political gurus argued that a record turnout was not only possible but likely. In the weeks leading up to the election political pundits and reporters found very little to agree on. They did agree, however, that young voters were an unknown factor. If they turned out in record numbers, their votes could be crucial in what was a long and bruising campaign that remained too close to call.

The image of young and first-time voters swinging the election made for an intriguing storyline. In 2000 only 34 percent of voters age eighteen to twenty-nine voted. Over the course of the last two national elections the youth vote declined steadily. But in a world made uncertain by terrorism, a soaring deficit, the future of Social Security, and growing prospects for a military draft, young people understood that the stakes were unusually high.

...

Two days after the election, the data profiling who voted and why began slowly to emerge. According to Peter Levine, the deputy director of the Center for Information and Research on Civic Learning and Engagement (CIRCLE), the election was a watershed moment in terms of the youth vote. In 2000 young adult voters made up 16.4 percent of the vote. Despite a much more aggressive effort to increase the youth vote, the 2004 data indicates that youth made up 18.4 percent of the vote. But those numbers are misleading. In reality 4.6 million more young people voted in 2004 than in 2000. For the first time since 1972—the year eighteen-year-olds were first allowed to vote—a majority 51 percent of young people voted. In 2000, 42.3 percent of people that age voted. The early data indicates that this age group was the only one that Massachusetts senator John Kerry won, 54 to 44 percent. Some news editorials and commentators noted that the youth vote in states like Michigan and Pennsylvania helped provide Kerry his margin of victory.

It is difficult to determine from the early data what, if any, discernible impact the intense political churn and electioneering in hip hop had on young voter turnout. Still, there are many lessons for hip hop to learn from an election that produced a few surprises at the end.

Shortly after the election, the hip-hop movement, like other interested factions, began to assess its political future and ponder its next move. Something had been tapped in the hip-hop movement and there was widespread recognition that the momentum needed to be sustained. "I think it's obvious that the youth voter turnout increased," said Combs. "You gotta understand, this community was going backward; it wasn't going forward. This was a community that was going the other way, getting disinterested. We were effective enough to turn them around." To his credit Combs acknowledged that the efforts of groups like Citizen Change were merely the beginning of an uphill struggle to make hip hop matter in the world of electoral politics. Combs told reporters, "We just finished step one—getting people engaged. Step two is to build an infrastructure around the people we've engaged that will help us continue in our mission to educate people about the power they have."

If the hip-hop movement learns anything from the 2004 election it should be that the business of politics is serious. Whereas most of the political activity in hip hop was devoted to rallies, celebrity appearances, and voter registration drives, the two major parties invested enormous resources into what political professionals call the "ground game." Both parties understood that despite the millions of dollars spent on TV ads the difference between winning and losing hinged on the ability to enlist an army of paid and unpaid activists to do the real work of politics, identifying and then connecting with real people. Using tactics ranging from knocking on doors to making phone calls to specific voters the ground game is based on the science and principles of market research. The goal is precision—identifying a base of voters and then targeting them relentlessly with a message tailored just for them.

According to Republican party consultant Frank Lutz, winning and losing in electoral politics is driven by emotion, the idea that knowing how voters *feel* is more important than knowing how they *think*. Lutz believes, "How you feel is something deeper and stronger, and it's something that's inside you." It is this kind if thinking, many believe, that has enabled Republicans to surge past their Democratic opponents. Republicans, simply put, do a better job than Democrats of exploiting voters' emotions—particularly anger and fear. Targeting evangelical Christians with a precise message and vision of America was a major element in Karl Rove's strategy for getting George W. Bush reelected. By making cultural issues like gay rights (gay marriage) and stem cell research (abortion) crucial in the election Republicans managed to tap into a bed of anger and fear that motivated the evangelical community to vote in large numbers, thus providing a crucial bloc of voters in a tightly contested race.

Before the hip-hop movement can have any real impact in electoral politics it will have to develop a more sophisticated appreciation of the high stakes gamesmanship in political electioneering. That includes understanding the importance of a finely orchestrated ground game and the power of emotions in motivating a bloc of constituents to actually vote.

The challenges facing hip hop's entry into politics are immense. First and foremost, the movement will have to define and identify its constituency—who it proposes to speak for. Doing so leads to the second and equally important challenge, defining its political mission and vision. That is, what will hip hop stand up for? If politics are driven by the science of marketing (identifying voters) and the power of emotions (knowing what they feel) hip hop has some serious catching up to do.

The challenges facing hip hop are easy to identify but there is nothing simple about resolving them. Hip hop has always been a community of different voices, experiences, and perspectives. In a hip hop world divided by race and region, pop culture and political aspirations, age and perspective, the challenges are deep. Reconciling these tensions, however, is crucial, especially now that a number of different initiatives are struggling to control hip hop's political destiny.

Despite all of the challenges it faces hip hop is poised to seize the political moment. It has access to the financial, political, and intellectual capital necessary to make a difference in electoral politics. No one understands the art and science of marketing better than hip hop's entrepreneurial elite. Hip hop has a grassroots constituency that is passionate about the movement and what it potentially represents. And yet applying these resources and skills to the world of politics, especially on a national level, demands a level of focus, intensity, and organization that has not been forthcoming.

But even as hip hop develops a finer appreciation of its political future and possibilities it will also have to develop a more astute understanding of a steadily changing world. The key issue that has always permeated hip hop—providing young people real life chances and choices—is and always has been bigger than hip hop.

...

Like so many others my relationship with hip hop as well as my thoughts about the movement continue to evolve. Before writing this book I was aware of hip hop's impact in America and beyond. I also knew that I wanted to talk with a wide range of people who have experienced and defined the many different dimensions of hip hop. Still, after writing this book I came away amazed to see just how far hip hop's influence reaches. No matter whether it is the sexual and mental health of young people, the shifting theater of racial and urban politics, the global spread and influence of America's media and pop culture economy, or the untapped power of digital media, hip hop is in the mix.

As I reflect on these pages and the various people and ideas that figure into my account of the struggle for hip hop, I mined my own experiences with the movement and discovered a rich and revealing place in which to ponder. Like many thirty-somethings, I have watched and participated in hip hop as it grew into a full-fledged industry, cultural force, and global phenomenon. The passage of time offers perspective. Though I can recall a world without hip hop, I find it impossible to imagine the world without it today. I was fortunate enough to be among the earliest waves of Ph.D.-trained scholars who grew up with hip hop as part of their cultural experience. Many of us sensed early on in our graduate studies that hip hop was writing a new chapter in America's racial and cultural history. We knew that hip hop had to be reckoned with. We also understood that hip hop was more than a fad and that, like it or not, it embodied some of the period-defining changes of its era. Hip hop produces it own distinct sensibilities and ways of seeing the world that have implications far beyond pop culture.

As a result of my own professional interests regarding issues related to race, youth, politics, media, and pop culture I have had the opportunity to meet, consult, and work with public school teachers and administrators, parole officers, media planners and producers, community activists, state officials, scholars, and students. That such a varied community makes up the sprawling world of hip hop is testament to the movement's resonance in American life. Not surprisingly, each of those communities develops a unique and, for some observers, curious interest in hip hop. It is easy, for example, to dismiss advertising agencies interested in hip hop as simply maneuvering to exploit the culture's appeal with young consumers. Likewise, it would be easy to dismiss a state-run campaign designed to motivate young people to enroll in post-secondary education as a misguided and ill-informed attempt to rob hip hop of some of its charm with young people. But my own experience with these and other efforts tells me that something else is occurring.

Namely, there is considerable and even widespread recognition that hip hop has changed the very nature and disposition of the world we all inhabit. The widespread interest underscores hip hop's undeniable influence in the lives of the young people who live and breathe the culture. But more than young people recognize that hip hop matters.

For the educators I work with it is the recognition that hip hop's influence cuts like a double-edged sword. On one hand, they hear hip hop's impact in the language young people use. They also see it in the dress and behavior of young students. But while those aspects of hip hop may cause some teachers and administrators to panic, they also comprehend hip hop's poetic presence and vivid imagination. They realize that at its best, hip hop can spark the creative mind and the will to learn. For the media professionals I work with it is acknowledgment, after years of denial, of hip hop's power to cultivate new identities, markets, cultures, and lifestyles. No matter whether they are selling soft drinks or messages of empowerment, makers of media messages understand that hip hop forges a path into the hearts, minds, and habits of many young people.

Hip hop's true significance for the community activists and leaders I have worked with resides in its ability to encourage young people to believe that they have the power to make a difference in their lives and communities. Even in the midst of all of the temptations—the money, celebrity, and pop prestige—hip hop continues to inspire young people to believe they matter and can change the world.

My most revealing experiences have come from my encounters with hip hop's youngest constituency, students in middle and high school. It is uplifting to see young hip-hop heads reading voraciously and thinking quite seriously about the movement they claim as their own. Despite concerns that hip hop's youth are materialistic, apolitical, and self-indulgent, many are socially conscious, engaged in politics, and concerned about the plight of others. Occasionally, the emails that I receive from students include questions that reflect a maturity and vitality that are light-years beyond their actual age. Many young students are making a distinction between what is oftentimes marketed as hip hop and what defines a more optimistic vision for hip hop. Young people, in their own way, understand and even animate the struggle for hip hop.

The purists in the movement believe that in the midst of a commercial explosion hip hop has lost its edge, its spirit of innovation, and its capacity for inspiration. But this view assumes that hip hop has only one destiny, only one true historic course. As the voices, people, and places that define hip hop grow more diverse, the movement continues to develop many different identities and interests. Despite a fascinating history and undeniable influence in America's pop cultural, political, and intellectual life, the struggle for hip hop, amazingly, has only just begun.

Peace.

# Acknowledgments

Writing *Hip Hop Matters* has been an incredible experience, much more than I expected and I expected a lot when I committed to this project. Along the way I have met so many people that it has become impossible to mention them all.

Three people played a pivotal role in the launch and completion of this book. From the beginning Gayatri Patnaik, senior editor at Beacon Press, has been nothing but a true believer in me and this project. She has not only guided this project from proposal to completion but demonstrated enormous patience as I worked to bring so many different resources and ideas together, oftentimes past deadline. Robin D. G. Kelley offered the kind of steady advice and extreme generosity that has made him one of academe's most influential figures. I also owe a great debt to John Wright, an extraordinary literary agent who has worked to push me and my writing to another level.

The staff at Beacon Press has embraced this book with both excitement and their usual exquisite touch. Thank you Jennifer Yoon, Tom Hallock, Lisa Sacks, and Kathy Daneman for your fortitude and support. Patricia Duque Campos went the extra mile to create the idea and the image that produced the book's cover. Thank you to Gail Cohen for copyediting the manuscript.

There were a number of people who went out of their way to help make parts of this book possible. Rachel Raimist was gracious with her time and work. Margot Edwards at the Berklee College of Music helped me line up interviews and get access to University materials. Gina Schulman, publicist for the Hip Hop Summit Action Network, tried hard to hook me up with Dr. Benjamin Chavis Muhammad but we ran out of time. Al White helped me with key contacts in the city of Detroit. So many busy individuals took time to talk with me on the record. A list of the people I formally interviewed for this book appears near the Notes and Bibliography sections of the book.

I have a number of friends at the University of Texas who have been consistent in their encouragement. I want to thank my fellow colleagues in the department of Radio-Television-Film. In particular Thomas Schatz, Laura Stein, Cauleen Smith, Ellen Spiro, Karin Wilkins, and Charles Ramirez-Berg either offered ideas, readings, or encouraging words that enlarged my perspective. Former colleagues John Downing and Horace Newcomb have also been voices of experience and expertise. Many colleagues in Sociology including Christine Williams and Johnny Butler are always there to supply a keen eye or friendly ear. I also want to thank Ted Gordon and Joni Jones for their hard work and commitment to the Center for African and American Studies at UT-Austin. Thanks also to Dean Richard Lariviere, Liberal Arts, and former Dean of the College of Communication, Ellen Wartella for their support.

One of the most incredible things about academe is the opportunity to meet so many provocative thinkers around the U.S. and the world. Whether it is an occasional or ongoing conversation, the access to such insight and imagination about the world is uniquely thrilling. Big props and big thanks to my boy Mark Anthony Neal. The late night sessions about work and family have been a constant source of sustenance. I always feel enriched after spending time with people like Herman Gray, Rosa Linda Fregoso, Howard Winant, Debbie Rogow, Nicole Fleetwood, Eithne Quinn, Murray Forman, Jon Jackson, E. Patrick Johnson, LaTonya Rease Miles, Richard Iton, and Doug Mitchell. I also want to thank George Lipsitz, Darnell Hunt, Karolyn Tyson, Karla Slocum, Ronald Greene, Ed Guerrero, Harry Elam, Kristal Brent-Zook, Patricia Hill Collins, Michael Awkward, Jannette Dates, Dipa Basu, Aldon Morris, Alford Young, Jr., and Donald Deskin for reaching out to build community and/or providing crucial support. Michael Eric Dyson, thanks for not only trying to "keep it real" but also to "get it right."

Major props to the Chase Crew—John Beal, Joe Elston, Kelly Faykus, and Jason Vickers—who keep me grounded and thirsty for life, humor, and good times. And no matter if he is in L.A. or London, Thailand or Texas shooting a film or simply vibing with hip hop's global grooves, Jerry Henry is never more than a phone call, email, or text message away. Long-time friends/brothers Randy Bowman, John McCormick, Bernard Shaw, and James Wilson are greatly appreciated.

My family continues to keep me going. Sherry Watkins, Jeffrey Watkins, Karen Munson, Larry Munson, Dodge, Myrtle Robinson, Dorothy Robertson, Carolyn Castaldi, Jeff Currin, Gloria Hall, Ray Nelson, Kenneth J. Hall and Kenneth R. Hall, and Bedester Peoples.

The biggest thanks of all goes to the three closest people in my life, my beautiful wife, Angela Hall Watkins, our incredible daughter, Cameron Grace, and my mother, Jeweline Watkins. With any endeavor that takes so much time, energy, and commitment you need motivation and inspiration. Despite a career on the fast track and numerous commitments to several boards, my wife was my most reliable pillar of support. Thank you for making this book happen. Cameron, thank you for the permanent smile in my heart. In just three years you have shown me the true meaning of life and love. Finally, to my mom and to the memory of my father. I'm forever in your debt.

# NOTES

*A Note on the Reference Materials*

I used a diverse range and number of sources to inform my account of the hip-hop movement. In addition to reading a variety of scholarly, trade, and journalistic publications I also conducted interviews with performers, media executives, community activists, scholars, elected officials, journalists, and hip-hop aficionados. A number of books aided the development of this book, including titles that focused on hip hop, the changing state of the media and cultural industries, American cultural history, politics, and the sociology of race. Likewise government data and reports from the U.S. Census, the Centers for Disease Control and Prevention, the State of California, the House of Representatives, Senate, and the U.S. Justice Department were immensely helpful.

Another crucial source for this book was a number of newspapers that provided detailed information that informed both my description and analysis of the key figures and events considered in the pages above. Newspapers that became a constant read for me included the *New York Times, Washington Post, Los Angeles Times, San Francisco Chronicle, Houston Chronicle, Chicago Tribune, New York Daily News, Detroit Free Press, Atlanta Journal-Constitution, USA Today, Wall Street Journal,* and *Austin-American Statesman.*

Transcripts from sources like *ABC News, CBS News,* and National Public Radio also work their way into the manuscript. Several trade publications provided sales data, information on industry trends and economics and reliable reporting on the shifts that influence the business of pop culture. Corporate and conglomerate media and the surrounding culture have played a pivotal role in the history of the hip-hop movement. *Billboard* was a key source for Part I of the book and my portrait of the rise of rap music and the reinvention of the pop music industry in the nineties. Other trade industry sources such as *Advertising Age, Brandweek, Broadcasting and Cable,* and *Inside Radio* were quite useful. A number of magazines—*Atlantic Monthly, GQ, Time, Newsweek, U.S. News & World Report, Village Voice,* Salon.com, and *Rolling Stone*—added useful details and context. Of course the rise of the hip-hop press has provided very useful references. *The Source, XXL, Vibe,* and *Fish 'N' Grits* are all interesting examples of hip hop's growth and spread into other spheres of American pop culture.

And then there is the virtually endless stream of Web sites— Davey D's Hip Hop Corner, AllHiphop.com, Chuck D's rapstation .com just to name a few that provide around-the-clock coverage of the business, activist, and celebrity culture hip hop has spawned.

The Notes identify if the quotes used in the book come from secondary sources or interviews I conducted. Finally, the Bibliography is a listing of the books, essays, articles, and reports that I found useful.

### *Prologue: Hip Hop Matters*

1   "Stakes Is High": 1996. De La Soul, *Stakes Is High.* Tommy Boy Records.
4   "They [the hip hop audience] want you to stay 'hood": Ja Rule—*Blood in My Eye,* interview, October 29, 2003, with Minister Louis Farrakhan. http://www.rapindustry.com/jarule_farrakhan.htm.
4   "see, if you let the public dictate and you": Ibid.
4   "When Malcolm [X] went down": Ibid.
5   "God has given you a gift, the opportunity to": Ibid.
5   "may God bless hip-hop to rise to its": Ibid.

### *Introduction: Back in the Day*

9   "Let's keep it underground": Chuck Miller, "Grandmaster Cuts Faster: The Story of Grandmaster Flash and the Furious Five," *Goldmine,* 1997.
11  "I'm making pizza and Joey and his mother": Fricke and Ahearn, *Yes Yes Y'all: The Experience Music Project Oral History of Hip-Hop's First Decade.* Da Capo Press, 2002, p. 182.
11  "was the manager of the store, but he left": Noam S. Cohen, "An Entertainment

Industry That Started Out in an Englewood Pizzeria," *New York Times,* June 15, 1997, Section 13NJ; p. 4.

11   "I did my thing, not thinking of the": Fricke and Ahearn, p. 184.

11   "I can rap, too": Ibid., p. 184.

12   The $750 figure comes from Joey Robinson and is reported in Lee Hildebrand, "Sweet Hip-Hop Originals," August 29, 2004, http://sfgate.com/cgi-bin/article .cgi?file=/chronicle/a/2004/08/29/.

13   "According to Love Bug Starski": Fricke and Ahearn, p. 181.

14   "those tapes would then become circulated": Ogg and Upshal (2001), p. 41.

14   "it was all about tapes back then": Ibid., p. 42.

14   "people would go tape these shows": Ibid., p. 42.

16   "at first it was challenging for us to market": J. R. Reynolds, "Rhino Tells Sugar Hill's 'Story,' " *Billboard,* November 23, 1996.

16   "That night, a local distributor phoned in": Ibid.

16   "Everybody wanted to know immediately": Jean Williams, "Quick Nat'l Reaction to Sugarhillers," *Billboard,* October 13, 1979.

17   "he [Crocker] wouldn't play the record because": Ibid.

17   "is the biggest selling 12-inch single": Ibid.

17   "This record is something": Ibid.

20   "That sounds funny": Robert Palmer, "The Pop Life," *New York Times,* July 4, 1987, section C; p. 14, col. 1.

20   "I had come up with—'It's like a jungle,' " Ogg and Upshal, p. 67.

21   "This record ain't gonna sell": Ibid., p. 67.

21   " '[m]an, I got a verse that seems like": Ibid., p. 67.

21   " 'well, what is it?' ": Ibid., p. 67.

23   "you [also] had people who were": Fricke and Ahearn, p. 45.

23   "we went from a negative thing to": Fricke and Ahearn, p. 45.

23   "Just to see how these black people": Fricke and Ahearn, p. 44.

24   "It was my decision they had": Adam Nossiter, "Hip-Hop Club (Gang?) Is Banned in the Bronx; Cultural Questions About Zulu Nation," *New York Times,* October 4, 1995, section B; p. 1; col. 2.

24   "In the five months since": Ibid.

25   "actionary rather than reactionary": Carol Becker and Romi Crawford, "An Interview with Paul D. A.K.A. DJ Spooky—That Subliminal Kid," *Art Journal,* Spring 2002, p. 88.

25   "he gave the notion of channeling the anger": Ibid.

27   "[Herc] might play something": Rashaun Hall, "Grandmaster Flash: Rap Pioneer," *Billboard,* August 9, 2003.

27   "disarray unison factor": Ibid.

28   "that's when I had to come up with": Ibid.

28   " 'clock theory' to describe": Ibid. Flash also displayed and discussed this and other techniques on a three-part series, ABC News *Nightline,* September 6/September 8, 2000.

28  " 'Today,' Flash says, 'you can buy turntables' ": Ibid.
29  "I heard this record on the radio almost every ten": Eric Berman, "The Godfathers of Rap," *Rolling Stone*, December 23, 1993/January 6, 1994.

## Chapter One: Remixing American Pop

33  "As Shalett listened to the various ideas": Andrew Ross Sorkin, "SoundScan Makes Business of Counting Hits," *New York Times*, section D; p. 5; col. 1, April 11, 1997.
35  "In 1991, the 'two Mikes,' as music industry insiders": Ibid.
38  "There was definitely some reservation": Ibid.
38  "this is a week of historic change for": Howard Lander, "Billboard Debuts Piece Counts On Two Music Sales Charts," *Billboard*, May 25, 1991, p. 1.
38  "It's full-speed ahead into the future for": Ibid.
39  "cause some drastic movement of titles up and down": Ibid.
40  "See what they [the major record labels] can't see": Chris Rubin, *Billboard*, "Successful Specialists," February 25, 1995, p. 100.
40  "SoundScan's weekly reports show that": Moira McCormick, "SoundScan: Boon or Bane for Indies," *Billboard*, March 21, 1992, p. 14. In this week's issue *Billboard* published a series of notable articles profiling the state of independent music labels.
40  "SoundScan is a great thing for indies": Ibid.
41  "I can't explain how I got": Errol Nazareth, *Toronto Star*, "Rap Still a Priority for Bryan Turner," March 5, 1999.
41  "I got lucky in terms": Ibid.
41  "had those sales numbers before but never": McCormick, "SoundScan," *Billboard*.
42  "I don't think there could be a better": Wendy Blatt, "Spirit of Independents Burns On," *Billboard*, March 21, 1992, p. 13.
42  "Rap has been around for a while": Ibid.
43  "Music is going to change": David Wild, "Inside the Hit Factory," *Rolling Stone*, April 3, 1997.
43  "We were looking at a long shot.... It was a guy": Ibid.
44  "Jimmy has become a real thorn": Shelly Branch, "Goodbye, Gangsta," *Fortune*, July 7, 1997.
45  "Man, everybody in the hood is": Mark Tran, "Taking the Rap," *The Guardian* (London), December 13, 1993, p. 4.
47  "shaping street culture for consumption": Lynn Hirschberg, "Does a Sugar Bear Bite?" *New York Times Magazine*, January 14, 1996, 24–31, 39–40, 50, 57.
48  "Nobody wanted to be in business with": David Wild, "Inside the Hit Factory."
49  "there aren't three people like him": Jonathan Gold, "Day of the Dre," *Rolling Stone*, September 30, 1993.
50  "there were always people who wanted": Havelock Nelson, "Radio Acceptance Eases for Hard Rap," *Billboard*, August 28, 1993, p. 10.

50  "When we test records": Ibid.

51  " 'the majors,' he warned in 1992": McCormick, "SoundScan."

53  "We [Tommy Boy records] were hip hop": Shaheem Reid, "Hip-Hop Is History: Tommy Boy Records Unloads Rap Acts," http://www.mtv.com/news/articles/1452827/03082002/digital_underground.jhtml, March 11, 2002.

53  "I'm still interested in hip hop": Ibid.

## Chapter Two: A Great Year in Hip Hop

55  "The streets have spoken" appears in a 1998 Def Jam ad published in *Billboard*.

55  "hip-hop made me respect black people": Evelyn McDonnell, "The Source Shoots from the Hip-Hop," October 16, 2003.

56  "We don't think of ourselves": James Surowiecki, "Hip-Hopped Up," *New York Magazine*, April 5, 1999.

56  "is to be as important as": Ibid.

56  "I would like to see some straight": Michel Marriot, "Hip-Hop's Hostile Takeover," *New York Times*, September 20, 1992, section 9; p. 1; col. 1.

57  "given the culture we cover": Alan Light, "A Renegade-to-Riches Story at Vibe," *Quality & Participation*, Jan/Feb 98.

59  "not only do we want you": Interview with Sheena Lester.

60  "This is beautiful," proclaimed Flash. Elena Oumano, "Stars Come Out for Hip-Hop's Big Picture," *Billboard*, October 31, 1998, p. 24.

61  "I've been doing this for six years": Ogbonna Hagins, "A Great Day in Hip Hop," *Philadelphia City Paper*, October 15–22, 1998.

61  "This is definitely historical and memorable": Elena Oumano, "Stars Come Out," *Billboard*.

61  "[hip hop] has endured so many": Ibid.

62  "rap was the biggest story": 1998 Yearend Marketing Report on US Recording Shipments. http://www.riaa.com/news%5Cmarketingdata%5C1998_us_yearend.asp

62  " 'the Real King of Pop' had spent more": Bruce Feiler, "Gone Country: The Voice of Suburban America," *New Republic*, February 5, 1996, pp. 19–23. Feiler's reporting on the early nineties' boom in country music also appears in the *New York Times* and in Feiler (1998).

64  "not only are these artists": Melinda Newman, "Consolidation, 'Titanic,' Garth Brooks, Teen Groups Make for a Peculiar '98." *Billboard*, December 26, 1998, p. 22.

65  "I looked at the way these guys": Rhonda Baraka, "Q & A with 'P,' " *Billboard*, March 16, 2002.

65  "we took no equity": Rhonda Baraka, "What They Say: Business Associates Recall P's Dedication to His Dream," *Billboard*, March 16, 2002.

65  "unlike other artists, who earn only": Roy Johnson, Jr., "Diamond in the Rough," *Fortune*, September 27, 1999, p. 166.

66 "a closer look at these numbers": Geoff Mayfield, "Rap It Up," *Billboard,* June 20, 1998, p. 100.

66 "the streets have spoken": appears in a 1998 Def Jam ad published in *Billboard.*

67 "as hip-hop roars as a social force": *Advertising Age,* "21 Brands to Watch in the 21st Century," September 20, 1999, p. C30.

67 "for $20, I could make 20 of these a day": *People Weekly,* "Gift of Garb," March 17, 1997, p 62.

67 "I would get up at 8": Ibid.

68 "wanted to come up with an acronym": Kevin Chappell, "Young Businessmen Score with 'For Us By Us' Clothing Line," *Ebony,* October 1999, p. 108.

69 "the consumer making for the consumer": http://www1.fubu.com

69 "At first, we [blacks] were just used as": Jeffrey McKinney, "Rags to Riches," *Black Enterprise,* September 2002, p. 98.

71 "were few and far between, like treats": Datu Faison, "Rhythm Section," *Billboard,* August 8, 1998, p. 28.

73 "a 'world gone mad' ": Geoff Mayfield, "World Gone Mad," *Billboard,* November 7, 1998, p. 116.

74 " 'Back then,' Jay-Z remembers, 'I would say it was like' ": CBS News Transcripts, *60 Minutes II,* August 13, 2003.

75 "[I]n the chorus they're not singin' ": Toure, "Jay-Z," *Rolling Stone,* October 29, 1998.

77 "People always say [my music] is": Rashaun Hall, "Jay-Z Crafts Similar 'Blueprint' on Roc-A-Fella/Def Jam CD," *Billboard,* November 2, 2002.

78 "R&B—and music in general—have been": George, *The Death of Rhythm and Blues.* Pantheon, 1988, p. x.

79 "sales representatives were instructed": Terry Pristin, "Radio Ad Marketer Apologizes for Memo Offending Minorities," *New York Times,* May 16, 1998, section B; p. 3; col. 3.

80 " 'everybody I knew—all the PDs—called me' ": Sean Ross, "New Regs, Fewer Jobs and the Whole Damn Thing," *Billboard,* May 23, 1992, p. 62.

80 "these stations forced everyone else to come": Interview with Sean Ross.

81 "In 2004, according to *Inside Radio* an industry": Tom Taylor, "Format Statistics," *Inside Radio,* March 12, 2004.

81 "in the top twenty to twenty-five markets": Interview with Dana Hall.

81 "[rap] has certainly become the dominant": Ross, interview.

81 "in the middle of the 1990s": Ross, interview.

82 "In the past the major labels gave away refrigerators": Charlie G. Woletz, "Technology Gives the Charts a Fresh Spin," *New York Times,* January 26, 1992, Section 2; Page 26; Column 1.

82 "I have to hire a guy": Ibid.

82 "N.W.A. was #1 on the pop chart": Moira McCormick, "SoundScan: Boon or Bane for Indies," *Billboard,* March 21, 1992, p. 14.

## *Chapter Three: Fear of a White Planet*

85 "Rap fortified whatever claim": David Samuels, "The Rap on Rap," *New Republic,* November 11, 1991, p. 24.

86 "bringing this tape to the public": Randy Lewis, "Eminem: Tape Was 'Foolishness,'" *Los Angeles Times,* November 20, 2003, p. E5.

86 "a primitive drum machine": Big Dee Irwin, "Eminem Says Tape Was Made as a Frustrated Teen," *AllHipHop News,* November 19, 2003, http://www.allhiphop.com/ hiphopnews/?ID=2574

86 "the tape contains what is clearly identifiable": Sarah Rodman, "MUSIC; Teen Eminem's racist track may fuel latest rap beef," *Boston Herald,* November 19, 2003, p. 056.

87 "The tape they played today was something": Lola Ogunnaike, "Rivals Call Eminem Racist Over Lyrics from the Past," *New York Times,* November 19, 2003, section B; p. 3.

87 "That word is not even in my vocabulary": Anthony Bozza, "Eminem Responds," *Rolling Stone,* August 3, 2000, p. 18.

88 "According to the Record Industry Association of America's": The Record Industry Association of America's 2002 Year-end Statistics, Washington, D.C.

88 "It is estimated that more than": Hilary Rosen, "Oversight Hearing on Piracy on Peer-to-Peer Networks," Subcommittee on Courts, the Internet and Intellectual Property Committee, U.S. House of Representatives, September 26, 2002.

88 "taking music on the Internet": Ibid.

89 "had gone from white trash": Anthony Bozza, "Eminem Blows Up," *Rolling Stone,* April 29, 1999.

94 "N.W.A.'s solid but unspectacular track record": Paul Grein, N.W.A. Album Charges onto Chart at No. 2; Abdul Is Tops in Pop; AIDS Benefit Set Bows, *Billboard,* June 15, 1991, p. 6.

94 "We're speechless. The euphoria of": Deborah Russell, "N.W.A. Displays a Winning Attitude; Stickered Album Is Nation's Top Seller," *Billboard,* June 22, 1991, p. 7.

94 "We thought it was gonna be": Alan Light, "Beating Up the Charts," *Rolling Stone,* August 8, 1991.

94 "I thought it was gonna be": Ibid.

94 "We're just thanking that new system": Ibid.

94 "We got fucked around on": Ibid.

95 "T.B.W.A.S. [teenage boys with attitude], that's": Jay Cocks, "A Nasty Jolt for the Top Pops," *Time,* July 1, 1991, p. 78.

95 the "monster" reference comes from Deborah Russell, "N.W.A. Displays A Winning Attitude; Stickered Album Is Nation's Top Seller," *Billboard.*

95 "they're selling boxloads of records": David Browne, "Recording's View; For Adults Only: Love and Sorrow...Lust and Hate," *New York Times,* June 23, 1991, Section 2; Page 25; Column 4.

95   "a situation thick with irony, but N.W.A.": David Browne, "Recording's View," *New York Times.*

96   "*Efi14zaggin* is an entire open season for negative": Jay Cocks, "A Nasty Jolt for the Top Pops," *Time.*

96   "I guess it's because rap is": Deborah Russell, "N.W.A. Displays a Winning Attitude; Stickered Album Is Nation's Top Seller," *Billboard.*

98   "It was an honor to hear the words out of Dre's": http://www.eminem-planet.com/ biography.html.

99   "I remember if I lost a battle": http://www.8-mile.com.

100  "Infinite was me trying to figure out": http://www.eminem-planet.com/ biography.html

101  "I thought the tape was incredible": Bozza (2003), p. 23.

101  "I'm ready to bounce": Ronin Ro, "Escape from Death Row," *Vibe*, October 1996, p. 76.

104  "Now I'ma be able to do whatever": Ibid.

104  "I'm gonna make a lot of superstars": Ibid.

104  "For the last couple of years": Jon Pareles, "The street talk, he says, is a Bum Rap," *New York Times*, November 14, 1999, section 2; p. 18; col. 3.

105  "It had been quite a while since": Chris Morris, "Future Divined in New 'Trendsetters Study,'" *Billboard*, September 26, 1998.

105  "are yearning for an emotional connection": Ibid.

105  "[m]ore of an interest in lyrics": Ibid.

105  "feel as if music today": Ibid.

105  "want music and musicians they can": Ibid.

106  "not fake, phony, and superficial": Ibid.

107  "Eminem is an extremist by inclination": Kelefa Sanneh, "The Voice of America," *Rolling Stone*, July 24, 2003, p. 64.

108  " 'In the suburbs,' Eminem told *Rolling Stone*": Anthony Bozza, "Eminem," *Rolling Stone*, July 4, 2002, p. 70.

109  "in the race to imbue Eminem with some": William Jelani Cobb, "White Negro, Please!," *The Progressive*, January 2003, pp. 32–33.

110  "I think corporate radio—I call it white-owned": Marty Hughley, "Public Enemy: Bring the Noise, Bring the Net," *The Oregonian*, October 22, 1999, p. 43.

## *Chapter Four: The Digital Underground*

111  "Technology will beat technology each and every time": *The Charlie Rose Show*, Transcript #2681, May 12, 2000.

112  "had to be eradicated for everybody to participate": Chuck D testimony from the Committee on Small Business, House of Representatives. "Online Music: Will Small Music Labels and Entrepreneurs Prosper in the Internet Age?," Serial No. 106–59, May 24, 2000.

112  "a business model will come up out of this new": Ibid.

112 "The Internet, he noted, was like a shower of meteors": Kristin Thomson, Report from The Hill: Government Hearings on Effect of Internet on Small Labels, http://www.futureofmusic.org/articles/smallbizhearing.cfm

113 "It really is about this whole perception about if it's intellectual": Lars Ulrich comment from *The Charlie Rose Show,* Transcript #2681, May 12, 2000.

114 See "Declaration of Chuck D. in Support of Defendant Napster's Opposition to Plaintiff's Motion for Preliminary Injunction" from A&M Records, Inc. et al. Plaintiffs V. Napster, Inc. July 26, 2000.

115 " 'Rappers,' he wrote in 1997, 'only rap about what they know' ": Chuck D (1997), p. 59.

117 "The sound has a look to me, and Public Enemy": Kembrew McLeod, "How Copyright Law Changed Hip Hop," Stay Free! Magazine, http://www.stayfreemagazine .org/archives/20/public_enemy.html.

117 "We didn't want to use anything we considered traditional R&B stuff": Ibid.

117 "If you separated the sounds, they wouldn't have been anything": Ibid.

118 "Offensive remarks by Professor Griff are not in line with": Jon Pareles, "Rap Group Disbands Under Fire," *New York Times,* Section C; Page 19, Column 3, June 29, 1989.

118 "we apologize to anyone who might have been": Ibid.

118 "we're back in action," Jon Pareles, "Public Enemy Rap Group Reorganizes After Anti-Semitic Comments," *New York Times,* section C, p. 3, col. 2, August 11, 1989.

120 "[all] that talk about us being family was just bullshit": This quote comes from an interview with Chuck D conducted by Jason Gross, at http://www.furious.com/ perfect/chuckd.html.

121 "It seems like the weasels have stepped into": Matt Richtel, "Public Enemy Fights the Music Industry With Online Releases," *New York Times,* December 4, 1998.

121 "murder his contract with Def Jam": Throughout the ordeal with Def Jam this became a frequent Chuck D quote in interviews. See the Chuck D interview conducted by Jason Gross, at http://www.furious.com/perfect/chuckd.html.

122 "He's a great promotion man. The reason our": David Wild, "Life After DEF: The Post-Rap, Post-Metal World of Rick Rubin," *Rolling Stone,* October 15, 1995.

122 "the black punk": Ibid.

123 "I don't know why you're wasting your time with this": M. Seliger, "Kings of Rap," *Rolling Stone,* November 15, 1990.

123 "has largely been about promoting the anger, style, aggression, attitude, and aspirations": Simmons (2001), p. xiii.

124 "I felt like rap had left me more than I had left rap." M. Seliger," Kings of Rap," *Rolling Stone,* November 15, 1990.

124 "When I started, nobody had really made any money doing it, so that": David Wild, "Life After DEF: The Post-Rap, Post-Metal World of Rick Rubin," *Rolling Stone,* October 15, 1995.

124 "became a way to make money": Ibid.

124 "a serial acquirer": Daren Fonda, "French Fiasco: Following Messier's Fall at

Vivendi, Investors Ask, Are Big Media Companies Better Off Broken Up?"
*Time,* July 15, 2002: p. 36.

127   "[I]n the first ten to twelve years of rap recordings": Chuck D interview (by A to
the L), April 11, 2003 at http://www.altrap.com/features/interviews/pe/pe.html.

128   "the industry's No. 1 priority as a whole is to emerge from the new": Al Teller,
"MCA: Poised for Int'l Growth with 6 New Euro Companies," *Billboard,* May 14,
1994, p. 52.

128   "Change is inevitable, and everything is about": Neil Strauss, "Rap Revolutionaries
Plan an Internet Release," *New York Times,* section E, p. 5; col. 5, April 16, 1999.

129   "utopia for an artist": Eileen Fitzpatrick, "Online Retailers, Artists Team for Exclu-
sive Deals," *Billboard,* p. 1, April 24, 1999.

129   " 'At its core,' Teller noted": Ibid.

131   "There's a lot of misconception out there that the rap": Brett Atwood, "Chuck D:
The Billboard Interview," *Billboard,* July 17, 1999, p. 82.

132   "I made up my mind in 1999 that I was": Davey D, "An Interview w/ Chuck D:
Part I—Revolverlution—The Album," September 5, 2002, http://www.daveyd.com/
Chuckdrevinterviewpt1.html.

133   "My thing was just looking at the community and being": Kembrew McLeod,
"How Copyright Law Changed Hip Hop," Stay Free! Magazine, http://www
.stayfreemagazine.org/archives/20/public_enemy.html.

134   "It was a great experience. That's when we": Chuck D (1997), p. 94.

134   "The thing that got me into the MP3 technology was necessity": http://www
.horizonmag.com/1/chuck-d.asp.

134   "Chuck, it is going to cost you about $750,000": Chuck D testimony from the
Committee on Small Business, House of Representatives. "Online Music: Will
Small Music Labels and Entrepreneurs Prosper in the Internet Age," Serial No.
106–59, May 24, 2000.

135   "virtually all the songs played on a typical commercial radio station": Eric
Boehlert, Salon.com, "In the Wild World of Urban Radio, Money Buys Hits,"
March 14, 2001, http://archive.salon.com/ent/feature/2001/03/14/payola/print.html.

136   "This law is truly revolutionary legislation that will bring": Mike Mills, Ushering
in a New Age in Communications, *Washington Post,* February 9, 1996, p. C01.

136   "It will provide for more information": Ibid.

137   "deprives citizens the opportunity": "Radio Deregulation: Has It Served Citizens
and Musicians? Executive Summary," http://www.futureofmusic.org/research/
radiostudyexecsum.cfm

137   "called Clear Channel the 'big bully' of radio": Eric Boehlert, "Radio's Big Bully,"
http://archive.salon.com/ent/feature/2001/04/30/clear_channel/. April 30, 2001.
Also, see Lynnley Browning, "Making Waves on Air: Big Radio's Bad Boy," *New
York Times,* section C, col. 5, p.1, June 19, 2002.

138   "People should have choices": Russ Feingold, U.S. Senator Russ Feingold on the
Competition in Radio and Concert Industries Act. http://www.senate.gov/
~feingold/speeches/03/01/2003012802.html, January 28, 2003.

## Chapter Five: Move the Crowd

143 "The most important thing we gotta do": Ta-Nehisi Coates, "Compa$$ionate Capitali$m," *Village Voice*, January 7–13, 2004.

144 New York State Department of Correctional Services, http://www.docs.state.ny.us/docs.html.

145 "I also want to see": Al Baker, "Movement Seen for Change on Rockefeller Drug Laws. *New York Times*, June 4, 2003.

145 "Repeal or reform, I think, are semantics": Al Baker and Thomas J. Lueck, "Pataki and Hip-Hop Mogul Discuss Revising Drug Laws," *New York Times*, June 3, 2003.

145 "I negotiate deals everyday": Lynda Richardson, "Turning Hip-Hop Rhyme Against Long Jail Time," *New York Times*, June 17, 2003.

145 "in this session, there will not be a full": Ibid.

146 "the President of hip-hop": Ta-Nehisi Coates, "Compa$$ionate Capitali$m," *Village Voice*, January 7–13, 2004.

147 "It is the clearest example of the wealthy": Tome Precious, "Celebrity Access Breeds Albany Discontent," *Buffalo News*, June 20, 2003.

147 "we have to close this": James C. McKinley Jr. with Lynette Holloway, *New York Times*, June 25, 2003.

147 "I'm out of here": Johnnie L. Roberts, "Beyond Definition," *Newsweek*, p. 40, July 28, 2003.

147 "I feel it is disservice to the people": Al Baker, "Albany Leaders Say They Fell Just Short on Drug-Law Deal," *New York Times*, Section B; p. 6; Column 5; June 20, 2003.

148 "I have never targeted": R. Thomas Umstead, "Keeping a Fabulous Outlook," *Multi-channel News*, Jan. 27, 2003, p. 1.

148 "helping provide a voice": Austin Fenner, "A Hip-Hopping Mad Rally Over '70s Drug Laws," *New York Daily News*, June 4, 2003, p. 31.

152 "is a non-profit, non-partisan national": see the section About Hip-Hop Summit Action Network at http://www.hsan.org/.

153 "I'm not a stranger in the hood," Neil A. Lewis, "Veteran of Rights Movement to Lead N.A.A.C.P.," *New York Times*, section 1, p. 6, col. 3, April 9, 1993.

153 "He's not judgmental": April McClellan-Copeland, "Ben Bounces Back," p. 11, *Cleveland Plain Dealer*, June 8, 2003.

155 "According to the U.S. Census Bureau": "Voting and Registration in the Election of November 2000," U.S. Department of Commerce, Economics and Statistics Administration, U.S. Census Bureau, February 2002.

155 "Apparently, if you're 23, you're against": Brain McCollum, "Detroit Hip-Hop Summit Storms In, Slips Away," *Detroit Free Press*, May 24, 2004.

155 "Simmons and his summit": Ibid.

156 "I'm hoping that we get to see": Robert Stanton, "Hip-hop Fans Promote Activism in Community,"; p. 01, *The Houston Chronicle*, January 29, 2004.

156 "Many of them left the event": Interview with Ada Edwards.

156 "You don't use episodic rallies": Edwards, interview
156 "I wish that we would stop": Edwards, interview
156 "I have no [political office] aspirations": Miles Marshall Lewis, "Russell Simmons's Rap," *The Nation*, 276(2), January 13, 2003.
157 "business is politics and politics is business, so": Ta-Nehisi Coates, "Compa$$ionate Capitali$m," *The Village Voice*, January 7–13, 2004.
157 "The hip-hop community takes pride in": Susan Berfield, "The CEO of Hip Hop," *Business Week*, October 27, 2003.
157 "The most important thing we gotta do": Ta-Nehisi Coates, "Compa$$ionate Capitali$m," *Village Voice*, January 7–13, 2004.
157 "Dear Russell: YOU ARE NOT": Rosa Clemente, "You Are Not Hip Hop," *Village Voice*, May 2, 2001.
157 "Many of us have this conversation": Ibid.
158 "How many fundraisers have you": Ibid.
160 "is now emerging as potentially the most credible": Johnnie L. Roberts, "Beyond Definition," *Newsweek*, p. 40, July 28, 2003.
161 "civil rights progress has desimplified": Mark Bowden, "Pompadour with a Monkey Wrench," *The Atlantic Monthly*, pp. 88–106, July/August 2004.
162 "You don't get people back by just": Pam Lambert, "An Uncivil War," *People Weekly*, pp. 44–45, September 5, 1994.

## Chapter Six: Young Voices in the Hood

163 "Ain't no power like the power": David Hill, "Hip-Hop vs. Lock-Up," The Annie E. Casey Foundation, http://www.cya.ca.gov/research/charfa_59-01.pdf.
164 " 'In the Bay Area' ": Interview with Andreana Clay.
167 "seems a solution in search of a problem": Joan Ryan, "Proposition 21 Locks Out Common Sense," *San Francisco Chronicle*, March 7, 2000, p. A23.
167 "In 1959, the state made 4,059": The 1959 and 2001 figures come from, "Characteristics of First Admissions to the California Youth Authority, 1959–2001," http://www.cya.ca.gov/research/charfa_59-01.pdf.
167 "Today's juvenile justice system was designed in the": Pete Wilson, "California Needs Juvenile Justice Reform," *San Diego Union-Tribune*, February 23, 2000.
168 "It has the potential to be overwhelming": Rene Sanchez, "California Toughens Juvenile Crime Laws; Rules to Treat Young Offenders More Like Adults," *Washington Post*, May 13, 2000, A Section; p. A03.
169 "like the military-industrial complex that": Donziger, p. 85.
169 "The Report of the National Criminal Justice": Ibid, p. 36.
170 "the legacy of an infrastructure of punishment": Rupert Cornwell, "American Jail Population Hits Two Million," *The Independent (UK)*, April 8, 2003, p. 13.
170 "Blacks and Latinos combined made up": According to The Sentencing Project, 45 percent of U.S. prison inmates in 2002 were black and 18 percent were Hispanic.

The Sentencing Project, "Facts About Prisons and Prisoners," Washington, D.C., May 2004.

170 "Bureau of Justice Statistics reported that more than": Ibid.

170 "By the time the prison boom had run its": Ibid.

172 Statistics from California's twelve largest counties come from the Center for Juvenile & Criminal Justice, http://www.cjcj.org/jjic/race_jj.php.

172 "In 1980, in America, 12, 331 women were": U.S. Department of Justice, Bureau of Justice Statistics. 1994. *Sourcebook of Criminal Justice Statistics*—1993. Washington, D.C.: U.S. Government Printing Office: 600.

172 "Fifteen years later the number of": U.S. Department of Justice, Bureau of Justice Statistics. August 27, 1995. "The Nation's Prison Population Grew Almost Nine Percent Last Year." Washington, D.C.: U.S. Government Printing Office: 4.

172 "from 1988 to 1998, the male": State of California, Office of the Attorney General Bureau of Criminal Information and Analysis, "Report on Juvenile Felony Arrests in California," 1998. March 2000. p. 5.

172 "We were simply losing young women": Interview, Rachel Bolden-Kramer.

173 "grim, unfair, and continued to be": Ann Lehman, "Out of Sight/Out of Mind Task Force on Girls and the Juvenile Justice System," Commission on the Status of Women, City and County of San Francisco, Final Report.

173 The arrest rates for boys and girls are reported by the California Department of Justice Statistics on Juvenile Felony Arrest.

175 "when they put me in YA": Tchris, "Survivor of California Youth Authority Tells His Story," *TalkLeft*, March 20, 2004, http://talkleft.com/new_archives/005731.html.

176 "Before he was incarcerated": Laura Talkington, "CYA Incarceration Amounts to Abuse," *San Francisco Chronicle*, May 23, 2004.

176 "I have seen him lose confidence": Ibid.

176 "California fulfills its obligation to": Ibid.

177 " 'They killed my son,' " Mark Martin, "Inside Youth Justice System; Violence and Gangs Shape Life in Juvenile Facility," *San Francisco Chronicle*, February 11, 2004, p. A1.

177 "Located forty miles southeast of Sacramento": http://www.cya.ca.gov/about/locations/preston.html.

177 "You're going to get tested when you get here": Mark Martin, "Inside Youth Justice System," *San Francisco Chronicle*, February 11, 2004, p. A1.

177 "When I came to California in the early": Conditions at a Correctional Facility in the California Youth Authority, *All Things Considered* (National Public Radio), February 19, 2004.

177 "how did we (the state of California": Ibid.

179 "a factory of misery and child abuse": http://ellabakercenter.org.

180 "Politics of liberation in the new century that": David Thigpen, "Criminal Justice," February 9, 2003, http://www.usaweekend.com/03_issues/030209/030209BHM-criminal.html.

180 "The people we see on a daily basis": Ibid.

180 "It's a very different fight": Ibid.

180 "All of our staff, my co-workers and co-organizers, we all": Interview with David Kahn.

181 " 'For us,' Kahn maintains, " 'hip hop is not some exotic thing' ": Kahn, interview

181 "Young people are amazing because they can take hip hop": Interview with Andreana Clay.

182 "represent all of the stereotypes of people of": Alexandra Marks, "Ex-Delinquents Seek Rethink of Jail," *The Christian Science Monitor,* January 9, 2002.

182 "Young people have a lot of energy": David Hill, "Hip-Hop vs. Lock-Up," The Annie E. Casey Foundation, Spring 2003, pp. 39-45.

182 "They're smart, funny, charismatic": Ibid.

183 "These youth came out of nowhere, won at the state": Chuck Armsbury, "Oakland Youth Rally to Oppose Jail," The November Coalition, http://www.november.org/ razorwire/rzold/25/page10.html.

184 "Ain't no power like the power": David Hill, "Hip-Hop Vs. Lock-Up."

## Chapter Seven: "Our Future...Right Here, Right Now!"

187 "Our day is coming. It's inevitable": Paul Russell, "KRS-One Praises Eminem, Gives His Views on the State of Hip-Hop." http://www.rapnewsdirect.com/ StaticArchive/256096/, May 22, 2003.

188 "What about Detroit? What about": Christina Fuoco," Live Review: Eminem at Ford Field, Detroit," July 14, 2003, http://www.livedaily.com/news/5210.html.

188 "For you and the city": Ibid.

188 "Three years before Eminem had actually run": Brian McCollum, "Eminem's the All-Time Best: Ford Field Performances Flawless, Confident," *Detroit Free Press,* July 14, 2003.

189 "remediation for children with low MEAP scores": Naseem Stecker, "A Kilpatrick Administration for Detroit," http://www.michbar.org/journal/article.cfm? articleID=400&volumeID=30.

190 " 'That day,' Kilpatrick told reporters throughout the campaign": Lisa M. Collins, "Kwame Kilpatrick: Making of a Parable," *Detroit Metro Times,* Oct. 10, 2001.

191 "you want an experienced driver behind the wheel": Charlie Cain, "Is Hill Too Old, Kilpatrick Too Young to Be Mayor?" *Detroit News,* October 15, 2001.

192 "I'm your grandson. I'm your great nephew": Darren A. Nichols, "Kilpatrick Makes Bid for Mayor," *Detroit News,* May 18, 2001.

192 "what is new and particularly troublesome is the sheer hostility": Dyson (2001), p. 120.

192 "for perhaps the first time in our history, blacks over thirty": Ibid.

195 "The question embedded in Booker's candidacy,": Dale Russakoff, "In Newark Race, Black Political Visions Collide," *Washington Post,* p. A01, May 14, 2002.

196 "he makes everyone feel comfortable around him": Darren Nichols, interview.

196 "Because the hip-hop generation, still": Brian McCollum, "Q&A with Mayor Kilpatrick on Detroit's Music Legacy," *Detroit Free Press*, May 21, 2004.

196 "I think it says something on the surface": Alexandra Marks, "Hip Hop Mayor Aims to Rev Motor City Engine," *Christian Science Monitor*, August 7, 2002.

196 "[Kilpatrick] does not hide from the fact": Nichols, interview.

197 " 'Today,' he told the citywide television": Kwame Kilpatrick Inauguration Speech, http://www.ci.detroit.mi.us/mayor/speeches_inaug.htm, January 4, 2002.

197 "the program will work with young people": Ibid.

198 "Yes, we want your financial resources": Ibid.

198 "Communities that are not involved with": Ibid.

198 "engage our young people in new technology": Ibid.

198 "everyone is allowed to participate in the programs": Ibid.

199 "In choosing Kilpatrick over the 70-year-old Hill": editorial: "Challenges for Detroit's Next Mayor," *Detroit News*, November 7, 2001.

200 "I issue an open warning to all dope pushers": "Coleman A. Young, 79, Mayor of Detroit and Political Symbol for Blacks, Is Dead," *New York Times*, November 30, 1997.

200 "Hit Eight Mile Road. And I don't": Ibid.

201 "I don't dispute the gravity of Detroit's": Young (1994).

202 "In 2000, black students represented ninety percent of the Detroit public school system's student population": Ron French, Brad Heath, and Christine MacDonald, "Metro Classrooms Remain Separate, Often Unequal." *Detroit News*, May 16, 2004.

## Chapter Eight: "We Love Hip Hop, But Does Hip Hop Love Us?"

207 "The house of hip hop": Ta-Nehisi Coates, "Caught on Tape," *The Village Voice*, November 21, 2003.

207 "Upscale and urban," is how Burgos described": "Redman Gets Funky on Cover of an Adult Entertainment Magazine," June 8, 2004, http://www.hiphop-elements .com/article/read/4/6261/1/.

207 "Fish 'N' Grits is able to bring it to you": Ibid.

208 "The rise of hip hop porn was stimulated by": Martin Edlund, "Hip-Hop's Crossover to the Adult Aisle," *New York Times*, March 7, 2004, Section 2; Column 1; Arts and Leisure Desk; p. 1.

209 "When I grew up in the 80's in Paris": Stuart Elliot, "Stars of Pornographic Films Are Modeling in a Campaign for Pony, the Shoe Company," *New York Times*, February 24, 2003, Section C; Column 1; Business/Financial Desk;p. 9.

209 "the rise of the amazing pornosphere," McNair, p. 37.

209 "I've been selling sex forever from a label's": Carl Chery, "Player Watch 2004: Camille Burgos Redefines the 'Nasty Girl' w/Fish & Grits," *Daily Hip-Hop News*, http://www.sohh.com/thewire/read.php?contentID=5905, June 2, 2004.

209  "Americans now spend as much as $8 billion": Schlosser (2003), p. 113.
210  "rap has never shied away from gleefully smutty": Edlund, "Hip-Hop's Crossover to the Adult Aisle," *New York Times*, March 7, 2004.
210  "When the vice president in the urban division": Ibid.
212  "Biz Markie's 'Just a Friend,' Big Daddy Kane's": Chris Norris, "Believe the Hype," *Spin*, October 1996, p. 28.
212  "I wasn't seeing what I wanted to see": Lola Ogunnaike, "A Visual High Style for Hip-Hop Voices," *New York Times*, December 20, 1998, pp. AR35, AR46.
212  "Rap and R&B were almost the joke": Hawa Macalou, "Too Hype," *The Source*, December 1998, pp. 97–100.
213  "affected the tone of videos, the things I did": Charisse Nikole, "Believe the Hype," *Blaze*, December 1999/January 2000.
214  "When we did her wide-angle stuff, we nailed a": Hype Williams, "Through a Lens, Widely: A Master of the Hip-Hop Video Explains the Fish-Eye Look," *GQ*, September 2000, p. 184.
214  "Rap artists were talented, he stated": Nikole, "Believe the Hype."
217  "Uncut has developed an almost cult-like following": Associated Press, "Whoa, Nelly—They Call Your Videos Trash," *Ottawa Citizen*, May 8, 2004,p. 111.
217  "Nelly wants us to help his sister": Gracie Bonds Staples and Vikki Conwell, "Spelman Women Dis Sex-Laden Rap Videos," *The Atlanta Journal-Constitution*, April 21, 2004, p. 1A.
218  "it's not so much about Nelly": "Spellman Students Draw the Line," *Atlanta Journal-Constitution*, April 19, 2004, Editorial, p. 10A.
220  "I want Blackgirl to be the voice for black girls": www.blackgirlmagazine.com.
221  "I sort of found her number in the blue": *The Oprah Winfrey Show*, August 8, 2003.
221  "free from the responsibility of being somebody": Interview with Lauryn Hill, http://www.blackgirlmagazine.com/laurynhill.htm.
221  "There was nothing that dealt with the innerlives or": Interview with Rachel Raimist.
222  "Current research shows that most young people": National Center for Health Statistics, "Health, United States, 2000, with Adolescent Health Chartbook. Hyattsville, MA, 2000.
222  "compared with adults, adolescents are": Centers for Disease Control and Prevention. "Sexually Transmitted Disease Surveillance, 2000." Atlanta, GA: U.S. Department of Health and Human Services, Centers for Disease Control and Prevention, September 2001.
223  "The proportion of infected females was highest": Centers for Disease Control and Prevention, Morbidity and Mortality Weekly Report, "Heterosexual Transmission of HIV—29 States, 1999–2002," February 20, 2002.
224  "most researchers focused on the psychological": Interview with Gina Wingood.
224  "social, cultural, and gender factors that": Ibid.
224  "Some of its very environmental": Wingood, interview.
224  "Their partners are often riskier, meaning they": Wingood, interview.

225 "indicates that prevention messages and educational programs": M. A. J. McKenna, "More HIV Infections Tied to Heterosexual Sex," *Atlanta Journal-Constitution,* February 19, 2004.

226 "right now, he's innocent until proven guilty": Greg Kot, "R. Kelly Cops to Troubles, But Sets His Tales to Uptempo Beats," *Chicago Tribune,* February 18, 2003.

## Chapter Nine: Artificial Intelligence?

229 "We are hip-hop, we preserve it, we protect it": Teri VanHorn, "KRS-One Builds 'Temple of Hip-Hop Kulture,'" http://www.vh1.com/artists/news/519607/11051999/krs_one.jhtm.l.

230 "astonished by their ability to rock a party": Interview with Stephen Webber.

230 "If we plan to be relevant in academia": Ibid.

231 "How many times has the basic premise of Romeo": Ibid.

231 "your scales, your cadences, and hand positions": Ibid.

233 "What Berklee is all about is pushing the envelope,": Don Aucoin, "Starting From Scratch," *Boston Globe,* March 7, 2004.

233 "People take it for granted today that jazz": Webber, interview.

233 "While I'm not especially a fan of hip-hop": Sara Rimer, "Harvard Scholar Rebuilds African Studies Department," *New York Times,* July 16, 2003, Section A; Column 1; National Desk;p. 16.

234 "We would be remiss if we did not treat it": Ibid.

235 "made Sista Souljah the Terri McMillan of the": Interview with Lloyd Hart.

235 "was the tip of the iceberg in terms of the number": Interview with Malaika Adero.

236 "'What comes behind her,' Adero explains": Adero, interview.

237 "trend seems to be consumed more by males": Ibid.

237 "captures their voice, their experience, and their concerns": Ibid.

237 "Though I'm not necessarily crazy about many": Hart, interview.

238 "The books are usually": James Fugate, interview.

238 "I don't release titles that perpetuate": Kevin Benoit, "Author Vickie Stringer Speaks," http://www.harlemlive.org/community/peeps/stringer%20speaks/Stringer.html.

238 "to communicate to the youth of black communities": Ibid.

238 "The books I publish are cautionary tales." Adero interview.

239 "Over the next few years he bounced around from": http://www.templeofhiphop.org/faq-3-AbouttheFounder.html.

241 "While no single cause accounts for the problems": KRS-One, "A Survival Curriculum for Inner-City Kids," *New York Times,* September 9, 1989, Section 1; Page 23, Column 1; Editorial Desk.

242 "purpose is to promote, preserve, and protect Hiphop": http://www.templeofhiphop.org/index.php.

242 "We're talking about unifying hip hop": Teri VanHorn, "KRS-One Builds 'Temple of Hip-Hop Kulture,'"

243 "If hip-hop was to end today—no more records": Roni Sarig, "Hip Hop," http://www.thebulletin.com/archives/2002/june/hiphop.htm.

244 The following dissertation is the earliest to appear in the Digital Dissertation Database. Rap music actually appears in the authors' abstract. Berry, Venise Torriana. 1989. "The Complex Relationship Between Pop Music and Low-Income Black Adolescents: A Qualitative Approach." The University of Texas at Austin.

## Epilogue

249 "This year we're not": Cecil Angel, "Vote or Die Rally, Star Come to WSU," *Detroit Free Press*, October 27, 2004.

251 "I think it's obvious": "P. Diddy's Group Will Stay Involved," Associated Press Online, November 6, 2004.

251 "You gotta understand": Ibid.

251 "We just finished step one": Ibid.

252 "How you feel is something deeper": http://www.pbs.org/wgbh/pages/frontline/shows/persuaders/interviews/luntz.html.

# BIBLIOGRAPHY

## Interviews

MALAIKA ADERO, senior editor of Atria Books (Simon and Schuster)

BAVU BLAKES, recording artist

RACHEL BOLDEN-KRAMER, San Francisco activist and performance artist

ANDREANA CLAY, assistant professor, sociology, San Francisco State University

ADA EDWARDS, member, Houston City Council

JAMES FUGATE, owner, Esowon Books

DANA HALL, urban/urban adult contemporary editor, *Radio & Records*

LLOYD HART, Hart's Black Library Booksellers

DAVID KAHN, program director, Let's Get Free

SHEENA LESTER, former editor, *XXL*

DAVE MULHOLLAND, manager, Tower Records

RACHEL RAIMIST, documentary filmmaker

DARREN NICHOLS, city hall reporter, *Detroit News*

SEAN ROSS, vice president of music and programming, Edison Media Research

TOM TAYLOR, editor-in-chief, *Inside Radio*

STEPHEN WEBBER, associate professor, Berklee College of Music

GINA WINGOOD, associate professor, Rollins School of Public Health, Emory University

JEFF GRIFFITH, communications director for Mayor's Time, City of Detroit

## Books, Essays, Articles, Reports

Baker, Houston A. 1993. *Black Studies, Rap, and the Academy.* Chicago: University of Chicago Press.

Bozza, Anthony. 2003. *Whatever You Say I Am: The Life and Times of Eminem.* New York: Crown Publishers.

Chuck D. 1997. *Fight the Power: Rap, Race, and Reality.* New York: Delacorte Press.

Cohen, Cathy J. 1999. *The Boundaries of Blackness: AIDS and the Breakdown of Black Politics.* Chicago: The University of Chicago Press.

Compaine, Benjamin M. (Ed.). 2001. *The Digital Divide: Facing a Crisis or Creating a Myth*. Cambridge, MA: MIT Press.

Donziger, Steven A., ed. 1996. *The Real War on Crime: The Report of the National Criminal Justice Commission*. New York: Harper Perennial.

Dyson, Michael Eric. 2001. *Holler If You Hear Me: Searching for Tupac Shakur*. New York: Basic Civitas Books.

Farley, Reynolds, et al. 2000. *Detroit Divided*. New York: Russell Sage Foundation.

Feiler, Bruce. 1998. *Dreaming Out Loud: Garth Brooks, Wynonna Judd, Wade Hayes, and the Changing Face of Nashville*. New York: Avon Books.

Forman, Murray. 2002. *The 'Hood Comes First: Race, Space, and Place in Rap and Hip-Hop*. Middletown, CT: Wesleyan University Press.

Forman, Murray and Mark Anthony Neal. 2004. *That's the Joint! The Hip-Hop Studies Reader*. New York: Routledge.

Fricke, Jim and Charlie Ahearn. 2002. *Yes Yes Y'all: The Experience Music Project Oral History of Hip-Hop's First Decade*. Cambridge, MA: Da Capo Press.

George, Nelson. 1998. *Hip Hop America*. New York: Viking.

George, Nelson. 1988. *The Death of Rhythm and Blues*. New York: Pantheon Books.

Hager, Steven. 1984. *Hip Hop: The Illustrated History of Break Dancing, Rap Music, and Graffiti*. New York: St. Martin's Press.

Hooks, Bell. 1994. *Outlaw Culture: Resisting Representations*. New York: Routledge.

Kelley, Robin D. G. 1994. *Race Rebels: Culture, Politics, and the Black Working Class*. New York: Free Press.

Kelley, Robin D. G. 1997. *Yo' Mama's Disfunktional!: Fighting the Culture Wars in Urban America*. Boston: Beacon Press.

Keyes, Cheryl Lynette. 2002. *Rap Music and Street Consciousness*. Urbana: University of Illinois Press.

Lipsitz, George. *The Possessive Investment in Whiteness*. Philadelphia: Temple University Press.

Massey, Douglas S. and Nancy A. Denton. 1993. *American Apartheid: Segregation and the Making of the Underclass*. Cambridge, MA: Harvard University Press.

Mauer, Marc. 1999. *Race to Incarcerate*. New York: New Press.

McChesney, Robert W. and John Nichols. "Media Democracy's Moment: Suddenly, There Are Widespread Discussions about the Dangers of Monopoly Power," *The Nation*, Feb. 24, 2003, p. 16.

McNair, Brian. 2002. *Striptease Culture: Sex, Media and the Democratization of Desire*. New York: Routledge.

Morgan, Joan. 2000. *When Chicken-Heads Come Home to Roost: A Hip-Hop Feminist Breaks It Down*. London: Touchstone.

Neal, Mark Anthony. 2002. *Soul Babies: Black Popular Culture and the Post-Soul Aesthetic*. New York: Routledge.

Ogg, Alex and David Upshal. 2001. *The Hip Hop Years: A History of Rap*. New York: Fromm International.

Perkins, William Eric, ed. 1996. *Droppin' Science: Critical Essays on Rap Music and Hip Hop Culture.* Philadelphia: Temple University Press.

Pipher, Mary Bray. 1994. *Reviving Ophelia: Saving the Selves of Adolescent Girls.* New York: Putnam.

Quinn, Eithne. 2004. *Nuthin' But a "G" Thang: The Culture and Commerce of Gangsta Rap.* New York: Columbia University Press.

Ramsey, Guthrie P. 2003. *Race Music: Black Cultures from Bebop to Hip-Hop.* Berkeley: University of California Press.

Reeves, Jimmie Lynn and Richard Campbell. 1994. *Cracked Coverage: Television News, the Anti-Cocaine Crusade, and the Reagan Legacy.* Durham, NC: Duke University Press.

Rich, Wilbur C. 1989. *Coleman Young and Detroit Politics: From Social Activist to Power Broker.* Detroit, MI: Wayne State University Press.

Rivera, Raquel Z. 2003. *New York Ricans from the Hip Hop Zone.* New York: Palgrave Macmillan.

Rose, Tricia. 1994. *Black Noise: Rap Music and Black Culture in Contemporary America.* Middletown, CT: Wesleyan University Press.

Schlosser, Eric. 2003. *Reefer Madness: Sex, Drugs, and Cheap Labor in the American Black Market.* Boston: Houghton Mifflin.

Silver, Tony (dir.). 1983. *Style Wars.* Public Arts Films, Inc. Brooklyn, NY: Plexifilm.

Simmons, Russell. 2001. *Life and Def: Sex, Drugs, Money, and God.* New York: Crown Publishers.

Sugrue, Thomas J. 1996. *The Origins of the Urban Crisis: Race and Inequality in Postwar Detroit.* Princeton, NJ: Princeton University Press.

Toop, David. 1984. *The Rap Attack: African Jive to New York Hip Hop.* Boston: South End Press.

Watkins, S. Craig. 1998. *Representing: Hip Hop Culture and the Production of Black Cinema.* Chicago: The University of Chicago Press.

Watkins, S. Craig. 2002. "Black Is Back, and It's Bound to Sell!, Nationalist Desire and the Production of Black Popular Culture." In Eddie Glaude Jr., ed. *Is It Nation Time? Contemporary Essays on Black Power and Black Nationalism.* Chicago: The University of Chicago Press.

West, Cornel. 1993. *Race Matters.* Boston: Beacon Press.

Wilson, William J. 1987. *The Truly Disadvantaged: The Inner City, the Underclass, and Public Policy.* Chicago: The University of Chicago Press.

Wilson, William J. 1996. *When Work Disappears: The World of the New Urban Poor.* New York: Knopf.

Wingood, Gina. 2001. "Exposure to X-Rated Movies and Adolescents' Sexual and Contraceptive-Related Attitudes and Behaviors." *Pediatrics,* May, 107(5):116.

Wingood, Gina, et al. 2004. "Efficacy of an HIV Prevention Intervention for African American Adolescent Girls: A Randomized Controlled Trial." *JAMA: Journal of the American Medical Association,* July 14, 2004, 292(2):171–179.

Wingood, Gina, et al. 2003. "A Prospective Study of Exposure to Rap Music Videos and African American Female Adolescents' Health." *American Journal of Public Health,* March 93(3): 437–439.

Wingood, Gina, et al. 2002. "Body Image and African American Females' Sexual Health." *Journal of Women's Health & Gender-Based Medicine,* June 11(5):433–439.

Young, Coleman A. 1994. *Hard Stuff: The Autobiography of Coleman Young.* New York: Viking.

# INDEX

Abdul, Paula, 94
Adelphi University, 114–15, 211–12
Adero, Malaika, 235–38
*Advertising Age*, 66–67
Affleck, Ben, 249
African Americans. *See* blacks
Aftermath Entertainment, 104
Aguilera, Christina, 34
AIDS/HIV, 223–25
"Ain't No Nigga," 77
Ali G, 216
Allen, Harry, 59
All-Platinum Records, 11, 12
*Annie*, 75–76
anti-Semitism, 118
AOL Time Warner, 209
*Aquemini*, 73
Archer, Dennis, 188, 190, 196, 199
Asian Americans, 150, 171, 172, 245
*The Atlantic Monthly*, 161
Atomic Pop, 128–30
Atria Books, 235, 238
AT&T, 209

Backstreet Boys, 34
*Bad*, 94
Bad Boy Records, 214
"bad man" figure, 75
Bambaataa, Afrika (Kevin Donovan),
  22–25, 26, 40, 149
Basie, Count, 59
Basquiat, Jean Michel, 211
Bass, Jeff, 99–100
Bass, Mark, 99–100
battle rap competitions, 98–99
Beastie Boys, 62, 71, 122
Benzino. *See* Scott, Raymond "Benzino"
Berklee College of Music, 229–33, 234, 244

BET, 3, 49, 70, 109, 216–19
Beyonce. *See* Knowles, Beyonce
Biggie. *See* Notorious B.I.G. (Christopher
  Wallace/Biggie)
"Big Pimpin'," 77
*Billboard* magazine: ads in, 57, 63; Chuck
  D on Internet in, 131–32; collection of
  sales data by, before SoundScan, 33;
  impact of music charts of, 36; rap
  music on charts of, 39, 41, 44, 49, 62,
  66, 71, 72, 73–74, 83–84, 93–94; on sales
  of rap music, 64; SoundScan's impact
  on, 36, 38–39, 82, 83, 93, 94–95, 96;
  Teller's editorial on music industry
  in, 128
Bin Laden, Osama, 107
"Bitches Ain't Shit," 48
Biz Markie, 212
*Black Album*, 77
*Blackgirl*, 220–21
black music establishment, 78–79, 82–83
blacks: child molestation of young black
  girls, 226–27; and criminal justice system, 170, 172, 179; cultural experiences
  of black girls, 219–22; education of,
  189–90, 202–3, 204, 241; health issues
  of, 225; in higher education, 245; and
  HIV/AIDS, 223–25; as mayors, 201; and
  police, 197; population statistics on,
  170, 171, 172; sexuality of young black
  females, 223–26; sexual stereotypes of,
  210–11, 216–19
Black Spades, 22–23, 24
Blige, Mary J., 249
*Bling* (Kennedy), 238
block parties, 21, 23, 26, 29, 58
Blondie, 60
*Blood in My Eye*, 1

*283*